MARK OF THE GRIZZLY

MARK OF THE GRIZZLY

Revised and Updated with More Stories of Recent
Bear Attacks and the Hard Lessons Learned

Second Edition

SCOTT McMILLION

LYONS PRESS
Guilford, Connecticut
An imprint of Globe Pequot Press

To Jennifer

Copyright ©1998, 2012 by Scott McMillion
Originally published by Falcon® Publishing, Inc.

Lyons Press is an imprint of Globe Pequot Press.

Project editor: David Legere
Text design: Sheryl P. Kober
Layout artist: Kirsten Livingston

Library of Congress Cataloging-in-Publication Data

McMillion, Scott, 1956-
  Mark of the grizzly : revised and updated with more stories of recent
bear attacks and the hard lessons learned / Scott McMillion. — 2nd ed.
      p. cm.
  Includes bibliographical references and index.
  ISBN 978-0-7627-7325-1
  1. Grizzly bear. 2. Bear attacks. I. Title.
  QL737.C27.M3595 2012
  599.784—dc23

                                                                    2011033008

Printed in the United States of America

10 9 8 7 6 5 4

Contents

Acknowledgments

I could not have written this book without the help of many. Researchers, scientists, doctors, veterinarians, and "bearocrats" both in the United States and Canada went out of their way to assist, to provide insight, and to correct my often faulty thinking.

They include, but are by no means limited to, Bruce McLellan, Stephen Herrero and Brian Horejsi in Canada; Kevin Frey, Steve Frye, Amy Vanderbilt, Tim Thier, Rick Schoening, Dale Becker, Keith Aune, John Murnane, Tom Roffe, Dave Moody, Dan Reinhart, Marsha Karle, Wayne Brewster, Mary Meagher, Chuck Schwartz, Chris Servheen, Tim Manley, Jamie Jonkel, Chuck Jonkel, Mike Madel, Chuck Bartlebaugh, Jim Halfpenny, and Kerry Gunther in the lower forty-eight states; Rick Sinnott, John Quinley, Dr. John Middaugh, Dr. Jim Scully, Bob Barbee, and Dick Shideler in Alaska.

My sister and brother-in-law, Laura and Randy Van Diest, who introduced me to Alaska many years ago, provided refuge when it was sorely needed. So did Jim and Mary Hasbrouck. My late mother helped immensely, and Tusco Heath gave me, without knowing it, a piece of advice I'll always remember. Steve and Jamie Potenberg helped with editorial advice and friendship. My wife, Jennifer, gave constant support and encouragement.

Newspaper reporters were almost always the first to ferret out the bear stories in this book, doing it under intense deadline pressures. I owe a special debt to Craig Medred and the late Natalie Phillips of the *Anchorage Daily News;* to Ben Long and Jim Mann of the *Daily Inter Lake* in Kalispell, Montana; Angus Thuermer of the *Jackson Hole News and Guide;* and to my good friend and colleague Joan Haines, formerly of the *Bozeman Daily Chronicle*.

But special gratitude goes to the people who shared their bear stories with me. They faced great pain and incredible fear, yet told their stories with dignity and courage, opening scabs on sore memories simply because I asked them to. For that I thank them.

Any errors, of course, are my own fault.

Introduction to the Revised Edition

Many things have changed since 1997, when I wrote the original edition of this book.

In Wyoming and in Montana, where I live, grizzly numbers keep on growing. We now have at least six hundred bears in the Yellowstone National Park area, which gives the species a much better chance at long-term survival. We have eight hundred or more bears in the Northern Continental Divide ecosystem, anchored by Glacier National Park. This is good news. It says something positive about us as a culture, and I hope those numbers can keep growing. And grizzlies have been turning up in places where they haven't been seen in decades: 165 miles into the Montana prairies, in the sagebrush flats of Wyoming, in the southern reaches of the Wind River Mountains, and at least one bear even made it over the border to the Idaho side of the Bitterroot Mountains.

The bear scientists tell us that the mountain habitats are filling up, so the bears are nosing around, trying to find new places to live. Few of them last long. In the spring of 2011, a rancher near Fairfield, Montana, out among the wheat fields and cow pastures, found two grizzlies tearing through his sheep one morning in a pen near his house. The rancher shot one of them, and the other escaped. A farmer shot another one that spring after it raided his chicken coop in Montana's Mission Valley, and a guy looking for elk antlers pulled a pistol and blew a hole in a mother bear that approached him in the Blackfoot River drainage. It's a sad and too-common fate: When bears meet civilization the bears generally lose.

That doesn't mean we have to abandon wild country, that everybody has to move to town and stay on the pavement. But in this complicated world, determining the places where grizzlies can live seems an endless piece of bickering and one that's not likely to be settled soon. Too many lawyers and advocates and politicians have skin in the game. Sometimes, it seems the fight isn't even about bears anymore.

But an increasing bear population does mean we all need to be even more careful when we enter places where the bears live. Doing so can help both humans and bears, let us capitalize on our own success.

In 2002 I interviewed a Massachusetts veterinarian named Tom Crosson. He had recently survived a grizzly attack in the Yellowstone backcountry and was still in the hospital in Jackson, Wyoming. He'd read *Mark of the Grizzly,* and he told me at the time it had helped save his life.

That's flattering, but I think what really saved him from further damage was the quick thinking and strong nerves of his friend, Nils Wygant, who doused the bear with pepper spray and sent it packing.

And the main point is that the two men had educated themselves before they entered grizzly country. They could have done so with any number of excellent books. They just happened to choose this one. And they bought some pepper spray and kept it handy. Crosson's wounds have healed, and the bear lived. The pepper spray helped make that possible.

A few critics have taken issue with my endorsement of pepper spray. Some have accused me of being antigun. Nothing could be further from the truth. I own several guns and use them every autumn. I consider my guns to be good tools for making a winter's meat. They're not so good for fending off a charging bear. Fish and game departments and a wide variety of bear biologists share that opinion, and I stand behind it. I have incorporated in this edition some recent scientific studies of the effectiveness of bear spray. That said, I have no bone to pick with people who prefer guns for protection. I just think that in most cases they're reducing their own odds of coming home safely.

Another way to reduce your safety margin in grizzly country is to move quickly and quietly, increasing the chances of surprising a bear. In recent years mountain biking and trail running have exploded in popularity, and I have included a new chapter about mountain biking and greatly expanded one about trail running.

I also have added information about the ongoing phenomenon of "dinner bell" grizzlies, bears that are attracted not necessarily by gunshots but by the knowledge that hunters leave lots of nutritious gut piles and bones behind. At least one more hunter has died in that type of situation since this book first appeared. A few others have been mauled. A larger number have had close encounters.

Two of the new chapters in this edition focus on people killed by grizzlies in the summer of 2010 near Yellowstone. One of the incidents involved a bear that attacked people sleeping in their tents. While incredibly rare, that attack caused some squirming among grizzly advocates, and I count myself among them. Infrequent predatory attacks on people are an unpleasant reality, but one we must acknowledge if we are to protect the vast majority of bears that prefer to avoid us but will tolerate us if they must. Blaming the attack on the impacts of global warming, as some media accounts have attempted, is a nonstarter in my mind.

The second fatal attack was even more rare. In fact, it was unprecedented. A seventy-year-old botanist on a hike came across a grizzly bear that had recently been drugged for research purposes, then left to recover in the field. Nothing like that had ever happened before, and I use that chapter to outline some of the controversies surrounding current grizzly research. Do we need to capture and radio-collar so many bears? It's a valid question, but the practice is unlikely to end soon.

I have retained the original chapters and written postscripts for most of them. I very much enjoyed catching up with the people I interviewed many years ago. All are still alive, and with one notable exception all are doing very well. They all seemed glad to hear from me again, and I felt good about that. It indicated I got the story right the first time.

I hope readers will enjoy the stories in this new edition. And I hope you'll be careful in the magnificent places where grizzlies live. Your safety depends on it. So do the bears.

I like what John Rogers says about traveling in grizzly country. He runs bear-viewing tours in coastal Alaska. "In bear country, you have to accept the fact that the decisions you make will determine the safety of bear encounters. Bears use their instinct, learning, and keen senses to make choices that are best for them. Our choices must be the best for them, too."

August 3, 2011

Introduction to the Original Edition

I NEVER EVEN SAW THE CUB, BUT I HEARD ITS LONG, DRAWN-OUT BAWL. It sounded like a newborn calf. I knew immediately what it was, and I didn't like it a bit. It was too close. I froze. Then the mother grizzly spelled things out. She jumped out of the brush about seventy yards away, leaping toward me twice, moving maybe fifteen yards closer. I remember the way her little round ears stood out from her big skull. I remember her tan pelt with the silvery tips and her dark underbelly, the way her fur and muscles rippled. I don't remember taking four or five backward steps. I remember being close to another hiker when I first saw the bear, and then I wasn't close any more. I remember fumbling with the big can of bear spray on my belt.

The bear stopped after the two big lunges, resting her weight on her front legs, ready to leap again.

"Wise up," she was saying. "And here's why."

I had been crossing a little knob in open ground, on the Iceberg Lake Trail in Glacier National Park in Montana, when I saw the bear. The trail led into the timber, and the bears were above the trail. I was hiking alone but trying to stay close to a man from Colorado who wore a couple of bear bells on his daypack. I was pretty dubious about the bells doing any good, but it seemed like a good idea to stick with somebody. After the mother grizzly stopped moving, I stepped closer to him. I was starting to think by then, and I knew we should stand together, should make ourselves look as big and imposing as possible. We both had our pepper spray ready by this time. The bear turned her head, a branch twitched, and she disappeared, melting into the forest. Then I saw two other people, a man and a woman down in the tiny sidehill drainage between us and the bear. They carried big backpacks and were moving slowly backward, their hands in the air, and talking to the bear. "Hey, bear," they said. "Yo, bear. We're backing up."

They were a lot closer to the bear than I was, maybe seventy-five feet from where she stopped. They were smart, doing the right thing. Not running, not panicking, and they were making noise: not screaming but not squeaking either, talking in a steady voice. Telling the bear what they were and that they wanted no trouble. Unlike me they hadn't taken the first involuntary steps toward flight. But then, they were at a different angle and couldn't see the bear through the brush. They only heard the cry of the cub, the crashing as its mother lunged. They kept talking and moving backward until they joined us, and we clustered alongside the trail, watching for movement in the brush and stopping the other hikers who came along.

We never saw the bear again.

That's my own grizzly bear story, and it's not much, as bear stories go. I wouldn't call it a charge or even aggression. It was merely a warning, an announcement that something much bigger and stronger wanted me to pay attention, to know she was there and in no mood for nonsense. But it illustrated in a personal way a lot of the things I learned while researching and writing this book.

First of all, grizzlies are incredibly fast. People had told me this many times, but now I had seen it for myself. I had watched grizzlies for hours on end, had seen them run down elk calves and skedaddle into the timber, but none had ever paid much attention to me. Mostly, I had watched them through binoculars, and their incredible speed had always been an abstraction. If this one had so chosen, she could have been on me or any of the other nearby hikers in an instant. Her appearance was so sudden, so strong. I had started backpedaling the instant I saw her, and it took a while for my brain to override my twitchy legs. If she had charged, what would I have done? I still don't know. I didn't even start thinking until after she had stopped moving.

But the bear didn't charge, and that is an even more important lesson. She probably saw dozens of people that morning on that popular trail. She had a vulnerable cub to protect both from people and from other grizzlies. The berry crop had been poor. It was fall, a time when bears feed voraciously and protect their food sources. We were too close and hadn't been making noise. At least one of us—me—took the first scrambling steps toward flight. There were thirteen grizzlies using the vast Many Glacier drainage that season, I learned later, and nobody knows how many people walking through every day, a stressful combination for any bear. There were a number of factors that, in retrospect, didn't look good.

But she did not charge. She did what most bears do in such situations, and she understood that her warning was sufficient. Like most grizzlies she was tolerant of people, a lot more tolerant than we are of bears.

Some people would treat grizzlies as manhunters, as dangerous vermin, things to be eradicated like a disease. These people are wrong and selfish. Luckily, their numbers are few, but their influence is not small.

A larger number of us appreciate grizzly bears. We spend big sums to travel to places where we can see them. As a society we pay scientists to study their habitat and their biology, to tell us what bears need. And as a society we tend to ignore what the scientists tell us. We build roads and campgrounds and ski hills in their habitat. We protect the bears, but only until it becomes difficult or expensive.

The scientists tell us that bears are incredibly intelligent, probably as smart as the great apes. They communicate with each other; they learn faster than their distant relative, the dog; and they put up with us.

Dr. Stephen Herrero, author of the definitive text *Bear Attacks: Their Causes and Avoidance,* once speculated about how people must appear when seen through a bear's eyes. "If a book titled *People Attacks* were written for bears, it could only depict our species as being typically bloodthirsty killers—aggressive, dangerous, often inflicting fatal injury to bears," he wrote.

We have almost eliminated grizzly bears from the lower forty-eight states, and there are maybe fifteen hundred now where fifty times that number once roamed, scaring the daylights out of people, making them pay attention. We have shot, poisoned, and trapped them almost to extinction. But our most effective weapons have been the incidental ones: the plow, the highway, and the recreation industry. The wild habitat grizzlies need to survive is almost gone. They live mostly in the remote areas in and around Glacier and Yellowstone parks and in a couple of pockets along the Canadian border, in isolated forests and rocky slopes, not because we have chased them there but because that is all we have left for them. In Canada and in Alaska, grizzlies still abound, but many subpopulations there are in trouble, too, cut off from other populations, becoming genetically isolated and increasingly threatened by more roads, more activity, more of us.

On the other hand, bears do injure people, and that is a topic some bear advocates try to avoid, although I'm not sure why. People too often portray the grizzly as a vicious killer or as Winnie-the-Pooh when neither case is true. Sometimes grizzlies kill people, and in exceptionally rare cases they even eat them. Those incidents are the focus of this book because that's what makes bears so interesting, such a huge part of our culture and our collective imagination. It's good for us, as a species, to know that we aren't always on top of the food chain, to know that we must share the wilderness with creatures that make us open our ears and eyes and noses, that force us to be more primal. As wildlife photographer Tom Murphy told me, being in grizzly country makes you more alive. And that's not because the bears are cuddly.

— ~ —

It's difficult not to anthropomorphize grizzly bears. They are so much like us. They eat mostly plants and grains and starches but love sugar and meat and fat. They stand upright. They wander, they are curious, they get angry. They can be jealous, possessive, and promiscuous. They spank their children. And they are so much stronger than we are. Imagine, for a moment, bears with opposable thumbs. Imagine the evolution of an animal so strong, so intelligent, and able to grasp a tool or a weapon.

You can find a small example of a bear's strength in most American homes, where the grizzly's ancient cousin, the dog, lives a sheltered and pampered life. My beloved Labrador, Mooch, lived to the age of thirteen. Her teeth were chipped and soft, her hips hurt, and she couldn't swim like she used to. Though, like a bear, she continued to practice her bluffing skills on the mailman when he surprised her, she remained a gentle animal, and the most destructive part of her was her tail, which often cleared off the coffee table when she was happy. And like any dog she sometimes had an itch she had to scratch. She'd lift her back leg and dig hard at her ear or her armpit with her toenails, doing it sometimes for quite a while. If she had scratched you or me that hard, we'd need stitches, even though she would have meant no harm.

Compare this to grizzly bears fighting each other. If you've never seen it in real life, you've probably seen it on television. They chew each other's faces and necks and ears, and they usually walk away unharmed, or at least they walk away, and the loser has just learned a lesson. Such jousting would tear the hide from you and crush your bones, maybe kill you. But in most cases a bear that attacks a person is trying to teach somebody some manners, trying to point out in the only way it knows that you have committed some breach of bear etiquette. Grizzlies can kill each other and do so periodically. If they wanted to kill you, it wouldn't take long, yet death by grizzly is infrequent. Mauling, unfortunately, is less uncommon, though your chances of injury while driving to a trailhead are greater than the odds of even seeing a grizzly that's close enough to hurt you.

Which spells out what I've tried to do in this book. Most of the people whose stories I tell here have surprised a grizzly bear, almost always accidentally. Through these stories I hope that others can learn more about bears and about how to avoid attacks. You can increase the odds of avoiding or surviving an attack with a few simple rules: Make noise on the trail, keep a clean camp, never look a bear in the eyes, and if you are attacked, don't try to fight, especially if you are alone.

I have outlined some cases where people fought an attacking grizzly and lived to talk about it. But in most of the cases I write about and in others not outlined here, the people had companions with them. I believe that fighting a bear may work better when there are two or more people, not because two people can beat up a grizzly bear, but because they might be able to confuse and distract it enough to make it go away. The flip side is that attacking a bear might make it drop your companion, but this almost always makes the bear attack you. Playing dead, I believe, is the best response once a bear is on you. Until that point it is best to stand your ground, offering the bear your profile and avoiding direct eye contact.

If a bear attacks your tent, the rules change. Then it's time to fight as hard and loud as you can, to tell the bear you are not the easy meal it seeks.

Guns, I am convinced, do more harm than good for most people, unless you are willing to start shooting as soon as you see a bear, before it even charges, and I cannot endorse that. Most encounters are surprises and come incredibly fast. Even experienced gun handlers often can't react fast enough or shoot straight enough to stop a charging grizzly, an animal that can run almost as fast as a greyhound, uphill or down, and do it over rough ground. Bears don't often go down with just one shot, even for hunters who get the drop on one, and a wounded grizzly becomes even more dangerous.

Pepper spray makes more sense to me, although it will not work in all situations. It is not brains in a can. You've got to have it ready, and you've got to know how to use it. Read the directions, and test the can before you go into the woods.

Trying to run from a grizzly is always a bad idea. And keep in mind that adult grizzlies can and do climb some trees, though they usually choose not to.

All of this is easy to say; none of it is easy to do, especially playing dead, keeping your mouth shut and twitching not a muscle, when a bear is biting you.

Many of the people I have written about have analyzed the attacks upon them, and I report what they found to be their own mistakes. I have tried not to second-guess them, with a couple of notable exceptions, and prefer to follow the example of Barrie Gilbert, one of the most powerful people I met while researching this book, a man who lost half his face to a grizzly bear yet remains a passionate advocate for their protection. He chooses not to criticize the decisions made by mauling victims.

"When you've been on the ground with a bear," he says, "then you tell me."

I was well aware of most of the advice I have just offered long before I ran into the bear in Glacier Park that day. And I walked around with a red face for a while afterward because I had reacted so slowly and so ineptly, almost running before I knew it, forgetting about the bear spray and then fumbling with the Velcro closure on the holster. I had been working on this book for several months, had been watching grizzly bears and writing about them for years before that, and I thought I knew better. I did know better. But a thirteen-mile walk the day before had been hard on me. My knees, laboring under the extra flab I make them carry, popped and ached whenever the trail dipped downhill. I had a couple of little blisters on my feet. It was hot. I knew a man had been mauled on that trail three years earlier, and I believed I was paying attention, but I was really thinking about writing this book, about driving to Calgary later in the day, about a big hamburger and a cold beer. That's when the cub bawled and Mom showed up.

For the rest of the hike, I was focused. I was scared, but I was exhilarated, too. I told every hiker I met about the bear, partly to warn them but also, I think, because I wanted to tell the story. I had never been so close to an excited grizzly and probably never will be again.

Even though the bear never really threatened me, I felt lucky. I had just seen something most people in the world will never see. I was glad to be alive.

As Tom Murphy had told me, I wasn't just alive, I was more alive.

Killing all the grizzlies, as the swinish among us call for, would be a simple thing. We've got helicopters and night-vision optics and high-powered weapons that would make fairly short work of it.

Keeping grizzlies alive, keeping them healthy and numerous and letting them act like wild bears, letting them teach us that the world can and should be bigger than our egos and our machines, that's the hard part. It takes work and sacrifice and wisdom.

It's worth it.

December 28, 1997

1

Treat It Right

Put yourself in Buck Wilde's shoes.

You're hiking alone in Glacier National Park in Montana when you find a blue hat lying in a trail. Then you spot a camera on a tripod, laid carefully down, the tripod legs neatly folded, the lens cap on. There's a small red backpack there, too, and this makes you suspicious and curious and you start to pay some serious attention. You move thirty feet or so back the way you came and there about three feet into the brush you spot the bad news: a pool of blood, a foot or more wide and still fresh.

Then you notice more blood, spots of it leading down the trail, and you see some grizzly bear tracks, claw marks scratched into the hard-packed ground. You follow them, making plenty of noise and moving downhill very slowly for about five hundred feet, until you find a bunch of scuff marks on the trail, a place where something heavy has been swept back and forth a few times. You keep going and you find more blood, then little pieces of what must be human flesh. You find some coins, you find a bootlace, you find more blood. Puddles of it, and a blood trail leading into the woods. You have spent a lot of time around bears, and you know how dangerous they can be, but you also know they rarely kill people. Somebody is hurt very badly and the blood trail is there and you have only a can of pepper spray with you and you know somebody will surely die if you don't help so you go into the brush, where you find more coins and a wristwatch and a boot, and then you find a man lying on his left side.

The man is bitten and clawed from head to toe and the bear has eaten the meat from one arm and one buttock but his body is warm and he might still be alive even though you can't find a pulse and still there is nobody here but you and this dead or dying man. Surely you can do something, so you hustle back to the red backpack only a few hundred feet and get a coat to cover him and keep him warm, and when you get back to him after maybe five minutes the man is gone.

Not just dead. Gone.

Smears of blood tell you the bear has come back, probably after watching you follow its tracks, and has taken the man away, so you follow this grisly trail for a few steps and you see that it leads into a patch of timber so thick that you can't see anything at all.

Put yourself in Buck Wilde's shoes.

What are you going to do?

—◆—

"That's when I knew I had really been more foolish than I thought I was being," Wilde recalls of that day, the third of October, 1992, a sunny Saturday in the high country. "I had the pepper spray in my hand the whole time, with the safety off. I was scared shitless. That was the point when I made the decision that I was in over my head and I had to get out. It was time to think about myself and other people, who I knew were alive."

Wilde was just off the Loop Trail, a steep and vigorous four-mile hike that leads from the Going-to-the-Sun Road to the Granite Park Chalet, a popular backcountry destination. But it was late in the season—the first days of October can be the early part of winter in some years—and as far as Wilde knew, there wasn't another person around for miles. Still, it was a pleasant Saturday, only about noon, and there was a good chance that other hikers would arrive soon and walk into an ugly situation. So Wilde backtracked to the trail, walked downhill a quarter-mile, and pinned a note to the middle of the trail with a small rock.

"A man has been attacked by a bear," the note said. "Turn around and go back to the highway. Shout and make noise every hundred feet or so. Don't run, but move fast. Send help."

Wilde left his bear spray with the note and gave instructions on how to use it. Then he moved back up trail to the chalet, closed at the time, and met some other hikers who had just arrived. He sent them back to Logan Pass, a relatively flat eight-mile hike away, but a place with lots of traffic and a visitor center, the quickest source of help. He gave them a note for park rangers.

"Help," it said. "Discovered signs of bear mauling about a quarter- to a half-mile downhill from chalet backcountry campsite. Followed another quarter mile and found body. He was in bad shape but alive. Went back to get coat to cover him and body was gone.

"Met these people at chalet. I plan to stay here for two reasons.

"1. To turn people back toward Logan Pass visitor center.

"2. To take National Park Service personnel to site I last saw victim."

He signed the note "Seriously, Buck Wilde" and asked the hikers to turn back anybody they met coming toward the chalet.

After the messengers left, Wilde left another note at a second trail intersection, then climbed to the chalet's second-story deck to settle in and wait, scanning the area with his binoculars, looking for bears and watching for any hikers who might be coming in. At one point he heard a scream somewhere down on the Loop Trail. He didn't investigate. He had already spent an hour or more too close to a grizzly bear's fresh kill. He'd already pushed his luck. Enough was enough.

Wilde is an unusual man. Forty-three years old at the time, he had given himself his name when, at the age of forty, he gave up a lucrative career as an electrical engineer and launched a new one in wildlife photography. He spends several months a year in the wild, moving between places like Yellowstone National Park and Alaska, Florida and Southeast Asia, with periodic stays in his adopted home of Sun Valley, Idaho. It's a tough way to make a living, but he's been successful, publishing ten photo books. He lives a lifestyle he readily describes as "eccentric," one that often brings him into close contact with grizzly bears. He's been charged several times but never attacked.

Wilde had walked into the Granite Park area the previous afternoon and spent the night in the backcountry campground. There were no other campers. He hoisted his food high into the air on the food pole there, then went to bed early and slept late. He walked around the area for an hour or so after he got up in the morning, then went back to the campground to fix breakfast in the designated cooking area, which is separate from the sleeping area to keep from attracting bears to the tents.

Sometime during the meal of hot cereal and tea, he caught a quick glimpse of a small grizzly bear. He heard a woof, probably from the cub's mother, and the little bear took off running toward the Loop Trail. Wilde hastily cleaned up his breakfast and raised his gear back up on the food pole.

He found fresh grizzly tracks, small ones, covering the tracks he had left less than an hour earlier, grabbed his camera, and took off in the direction he had seen the bear going. It was about half past eleven in the morning.

By then the bears probably had already attacked John Petranyi, a forty-year-old jazz buff from Madison, Wisconsin, who had hiked up the Loop Trail that morning.

"It was no more than five minutes to put the food up the pole, plus another ten to fifteen minutes to get to the point of the attack," Wilde says. "That's how quickly things unfolded there.

"In my mind, what happened was, the bears came in and saw me and smelled my food. They were looking at it but did the good bear thing and split when Mama saw one of the cubs getting too close to me and took off running down toward that trail."

Wilde knows a lot about bears, knows that grizzlies will almost always avoid an encounter with people if they have a chance. He had spent the previous summer guiding photographers to places in Alaska where they could watch, up close, as grizzlies fished for salmon. Less than a year earlier, a sow had bluff-charged him on Kodiak Island after he inadvertently came between her and one of her three cubs. She came close enough, charging from a hundred feet away, that he could feel her hot breath, and she got there fast enough that he never even had time to reach for the shotgun on the ground at his feet. That's when he decided guns weren't much good in a bear encounter, and he hasn't carried one since. He studies bear behavior, is a fanatic about keeping a clean camp, and is a self-professed "pain-in-the-ass person to go into bear country with."

"You've got to read the bear safety books. You've got to convince me you've read the books. You've got to obey the rules. And pay attention. Any time you're not, I'm giving you shit about it."

He was paying close attention as he walked toward the Loop Trail that morning, mostly because he was hoping for a good photograph. But he wasn't paying much attention to the trail itself. Rather, he was watching and listening for bears.

That's when he stumbled across Petranyi's cap, then the blood and the other grim evidence of bad trouble. That point in the trail is a narrow corridor between thickish stands of pine trees, a place where visibility reduces to twenty feet in some places. It's also where Wilde started paying even more attention.

He had walked right past the big pool of blood just off the trail, the largest amount of blood he would find, even when he finally located Petranyi. "It was pretty much his life in that pool of blood."

After that, he noticed the small spots of blood leading down the trail. Then he got to the bootlace, the coins, the place where it looked like the bear had taken the two-hundred-pound man in its mouth and shaken him, leaving the scuff marks in the trail.

Following the evidence was not something he had to force himself to do, he later said. But it wasn't easy either, and it got even harder when the blood and other sign pulled him off the trail and into the woods.

"I was spooked out of my mind, but I had every reason to believe I was alone in that situation and that this guy's life was on the line. It was a weird thing, but all my senses were heightened to the nth degree. I was hearing four times better than I normally do. And I was seeing and smelling four times better than I normally do. So I just set on the logical track and tried to do things as logically as I could. I mean I took my time.

"It wasn't like I had to force myself, it was like what had to be done. But I didn't just go whistling in there either. I mean I was scared. I looked. I observed everything. I heard everything. I continuously rotated in 360 degrees to make sure I wasn't missing something, and I made noise all the time. I expected the guy was, if not dead, then on his way to dying from the evidence I was seeing. But you don't know. I still don't know if he was actually dead when I found him."

Wilde could find no pulse, no breath. The blood around the man's wounds was turning dark when he left to get the coat.

Moving the 750 feet—rangers would later measure the distance—between the backpack and where the bear first left Petranyi's body took about fifteen minutes the first time, Wilde said, because he was moving so carefully. But he made the round-trip from Petranyi to the pack and back in about five minutes, goaded by the faint hope of trying to keep somebody alive. Moving fifteen hundred feet in five minutes is no sprint, but it's no dawdle either, especially when there's a grizzly in the area.

When he returned to the spot where the body had disappeared, there was no doubt in Wilde's mind that he was in the right place. The blood, his own tracks, and other evidence were too clear to be mistaken. Petranyi had been lying under a small tree, the only one in the area, and now he was gone.

That meant the chances that he was still clutching to life were even smaller, and Wilde knew what he had to do then: back off, warn other people, and wait for help.

— ❦ —

The help arrived at 5:02 p.m. in the form of a helicopter bearing two rangers armed with 12-gauge shotguns, loaded with heavy slugs. A pair of hikers had found Wilde's note on the Loop Trail (they were probably the source of the scream he had heard earlier) and hustled back to the trailhead to call rangers. The lead man in the helicopter was Charlie Logan, a Glacier veteran with long experience in managing grizzly bears.

But the rangers weren't the first ones on the scene. As Wilde waited at the chalet, scanning the hillsides and trying to control his tension, a group of four hikers arrived. They had walked in on the Highline Trail, ignoring the warnings from the people Wilde had sent that way with another note.

"They came in, like, 'Hey, let's go see that bear that killed that guy.'

"When they got in there, I was irate," Wilde recalls. "I lectured them like I probably shouldn't have. I was all over them, and they came right back at me. They said they were from Montana and live with this kind of thing all the time and wanted to see it."

The rangers were almost as disgusted with the people as Wilde was. The hikers no longer were having much fun either. They got to thinking about the bear they had seen on the hike to the chalet, and one of them asked for a ride out on the helicopter. They were in the air within moments.

— ❦ —

It took about thirty minutes for Logan to interview Wilde and organize gear. Then the two of them, along with ranger Curt Frain, hit the trail, hoping to find Petranyi's body before the approaching darkness fell. Stopping to inspect and photograph evidence along the way, they took twenty-four minutes to reach the body. Wilde had found Petranyi's body 175 feet from the trail. The bear had moved it another 500 feet by the time the three men found it the second time. If Wilde hadn't been there, it would have taken the rangers a lot longer to find it.

"After seeing what he had seen, it was remarkable that he offered to go back," Logan says. "It took a lot of courage."

Logan's reports described the brief trip as "challenging tracking while watching our flanks." The bear carrying Petranyi's body changed course a couple of times. Along its trail they found Petranyi's sock and bits of his shirt. Logan, a trained medic, found no evidence of life in Petranyi; the body was cold, the eyes glazed, the injuries massive.

Considering all of this and "that a real danger to us (including civilian Buck Wilde) still existed at this late hour, I decided that we quickly document and mark the scene and exit the area," Logan wrote in his reports of the incident.

Frain flagged the area and took notes while Logan stood guard, shotgun at the ready. Very fresh sign indicated the bear or bears were probably still close at hand. At this point, nobody knew for sure how many or what kind of bears were involved, but dirt had been shoved on the body, indicating the bear had claimed it as its own and was protecting it from scavengers.

The men then backtracked, continuing to photograph and document evidence, moving back to Petranyi's backpack, which they checked for food. They looked for identification, and they wanted to know if Petranyi's lunch had lured the bear. But there was no food in the pack.

That's when the bears charged.

Frain was searching the backpack "when I heard heavy, rapid pounding of feet on the trail section below us, followed by repeated woofing sounds," Logan wrote in his report. "I could not see what was running up the trail at us but guessed it was a bear so began yelling 'back bear.' Within a moment a grizzly appeared at the bend in the trail below us and stopped. I caught a glimpse of a smaller bear just behind but did not take my eyes off the larger bear, now squarely in the sights of my shotgun."

The adult bear bounced back and forth on its front paws several times, a sign of stress and agitation, looked back at its offspring, and "woofed" a few times. It was fifty feet away, measurements would show, and Logan said later that if the bear had taken one more step he would have pulled the trigger. He did not believe the bear had run upon the men by surprise, he says. It was charging.

The charge "looked like a pretty deliberate deal on the bear's part," Logan says. "But there were three of us there and we were yelling at her. I think she sized us up and decided we were too much."

Then the bears took off, but the men could still hear them, woofing and crashing in the nearby brush, tearing through the area where they had first attacked Petranyi, moving around the men in a quarter circle. By then it was getting dark fast.

Logan later would call the incident one of the biggest scares of his life, but his report is written in the deadpan style of official documents. Wilde remembers the charge a little more vividly. He says he doesn't believe that guns do much good in bear encounters, that attacks almost always happen too fast for most people to draw a weapon. But in this case Logan and Frain were ready and probably could have killed at least the sow, had they chosen to.

"We heard the bears before we saw them," Wilde says. "It was like a freight train coming up that Loop Trail, coming on full speed.

"Charlie is on the left, and [Frain] is on the right. I'm in the middle, and we're standing right on the trail. And Charlie says, 'safety off, one up in the chamber. Bead down. Start yelling.'"

So the men started yelling, "Stop bear, stop bear!" And the bears turned away.

"I don't know Charlie much outside this situation," says Wilde. "But the judgment he used right there, to not shoot those bears, I thought was very commendable. Most people would have been throwing lead. Trust me, I mean those bears were close and coming fast. But he gave them more than a fair chance, and they did enough to avoid getting shot."

Logan says he didn't shoot for a couple of reasons. First, the bear stopped when he started yelling at it. Second, he had no idea if these bears were the ones that killed Petranyi.

"I certainly didn't want to kill the wrong bear, especially one with cubs."

The men then decided, as Wilde had earlier in the day, that enough was enough. They left the pack and tripod where they lay and "cautiously retreated" to the chalet area, where Wilde broke down his camp in the increasing darkness as the rangers stood guard, shotguns at the ready.

They took Wilde to a nearby backcountry ranger station with them—he had been ready to catch what sleep he could on the second-story deck of the chalet—and spent a long, long night filling out reports, reliving the day, and trying to figure out what had happened to Petranyi. About four in the morning, they caught a couple of hours of sleep.

John Petranyi had lived a quiet life in Madison, Wisconsin, where he was a supervisor of custodians for the city government and shared a home with his father, a Hungarian immigrant. He loved jazz music, fine beers, good books, and riding his bicycle, commuting on it the six miles to his job in all kinds of weather.

But his greatest passion was getting out into wild country, according to his brother, Mark. Every year he spent his three-week vacation in the wild country of the West: climbing volcanic peaks in Oregon, exploring Alaska, mountain biking in the canyons of Utah. In 1992 he took an auto tour of the Canadian Rockies, visiting Banff, Jasper, and other national parks, camping and hiking. Glacier was the last stop on his itinerary. Had he survived the day hike to Granite Park, he would have turned toward home the next day.

"That's what he worked all year for," Mark Petranyi says. "His three-week journey into the woods."

Stocky and strong, his five foot eleven–inch frame carried almost two hundred pounds. Bicycling, jogging, and cross-country skiing kept him in good shape. He was the oldest of three sons, and his death was not the first sadness in the family: A brother had died in an accident in 1974, and his mother passed away in 1990. He was a bachelor, childless.

The evening after the day he died, a Sunday, a police chaplain came to the home of his father, also named John, and delivered the heartbreaking news. The next day, as Mark and John Senior were preparing to fly to Montana to retrieve the body, a postcard arrived at Mark's house. It was postmarked from Kalispell, just outside Glacier.

"He said he hadn't seen any bears yet but had heard they were around," Mark says. "My wife almost didn't give me the card. It was a hard one to read."

John Petranyi liked to take pictures, but he wasn't an avid wildlife photographer. Almost all of his photographs were of landscapes, Mark says, a statement backed up by the film in John's camera, developed later by rangers. The pictures were all of the jagged peaks and cliffs that make Glacier so famous. No bears were on the film.

Mark says neither he nor his father blames the bears for John's death.

"He was just in the wrong place at the wrong time," Mark says. "It's unfortunate, but he was in their home. You really can't blame the bears."

He and his father flew to Montana, where John's remains were cremated, and drove the dead man's car back to Wisconsin.

It was, as Mark recalls, a long drive.

⌁

Back in Glacier, Charlie Logan was getting ready to pull some long shifts himself.

As the bad news circulated around the park that Sunday morning, Logan, Frain, and Wilde rose in the ranger cabin to find the weather had gone to hell. Plans had called for a helicopter to arrive at first light and carry the body to park headquarters, but fog had cut the visibility to about one hundred feet when the sun rose at a little after seven. By half past eight the temperature had fallen ten degrees, the wind had picked up, and snow was coming down in big round flakes. It wasn't until half past eleven that the weather cleared enough to bring a helicopter into the alpine bowl. On the way in, rangers spotted the bears on Petranyi's body. The sow had a distinctive marking—a light-colored collar of fur around her neck and descending onto her chest.

More armed rangers came in on that flight, and Buck Wilde rode the helicopter back to park headquarters. His role was over, but the rangers' work had hardly started.

It took a couple of hours to get the six rangers and helicopter pilot Jim Kruger organized and a strategy worked out. Five rangers would walk to Petranyi's body. One would fly in the helicopter with Kruger, to observe the operation from the air. The ground crew arrived at the site at 2:15 and found Petranyi's body had been moved another seventy-five feet, where the bears had eaten more of it.

Pilot Kruger found the bear family—a sow and two cubs—still near the body. The bears didn't want to leave and kept trying to get closer, so he started hazing them with the helicopter, trying to keep them away from the body and the ground crew. "He'd get her going one way, and then she would come back another way," Logan says. All this information was traveling to the ground crew via radio, but it was still hard to pinpoint the bears' exact location. It took only twenty minutes to load the body in the airship—four men carrying and one standing guard, keeping a close eye on the bushes—but it was a long twenty minutes. Then the ground crew continued documenting all the evidence they could find, working under a constant guard. With the helicopter gone, nobody knew where the bears were. As they backtracked to the site of the backpack and camera and fanned out to search some more, the crew found Petranyi's wallet in the woods, a dozen steps from his backpack.

The wallet allowed the rangers to positively identify him and also provided a crucial piece of evidence. It had been torn by bear teeth, gouged deep enough to puncture the plastic credit cards inside it. There were a few traces of blood on the wallet and a little more blood on a nearby tree. That was enough to indicate that Petranyi had initially been attacked there and had then moved closer to the trail, where Wilde had found the pool of blood. Probably he had rested there, bleeding, and then moved down the trail the way he had come, hoping to find help.

Buck Wilde believes Petranyi met the bears in a surprise encounter, that the bears were running from the cooking area of the campground (tracks showed one bear had come within fifteen yards of Wilde while he ate breakfast), and that, when they ran into Petranyi, the mother attacked to defend her cubs.

Rangers, who had more time to investigate, came up with a handful of possible scenarios. Since the pack and camera appeared to have been laid carefully down, and because Petranyi's pants and underwear were around his ankles when he was found, they said it was possible that he had placed his things beside the trail and moved into the woods for a bowel movement or to urinate. That's where the bear hit him first. Then either she let him go or he escaped and moved back to the trail, where he stopped long enough to leave the pool of blood before moving downhill, back toward his car and the only source of help he knew about.

It's also possible that he saw the bears on the trail and set his gear down before running into the woods, where the bears caught up with him. Under this scenario they may have charged before or after he started running.

Maybe he saw the bears and put his things down, preparing to photograph them, and they attacked.

Or he could have heard a noise and moved into the woods, leaving his gear behind, to investigate.

The bowel movement theory seems likely but is not conclusive. The only evidence backing it up is that his pants were down around his ankles. But being dragged by a bear shredded his shirt and pulled a boot off his foot. It could easily have pulled his pants down, too. Besides, if he had stepped into the woods to relieve himself, why would he leave his hat in the trail? Unless, of course, he dropped the hat after being attacked, as he stumbled back to the trail. Rangers found his glasses and some other items in the woods, indicating considerable movement in a small area.

It's clear that the initial assault didn't kill him.

The blood spots that Wilde followed down the Loop Trail were round, indicating Petranyi probably walked down the trail under his own power. If the bear had dragged him down the trail, the blood would have been smeared. Also, the bear left claw marks on the trail but no pad marks, indicating the bear was up on its toes, running.

Less than six hundred feet from the pack and camera, the bear caught Petranyi again, causing the "thrashing" marks in the trail. That's probably where he died. Then it dragged him down the trail a few steps and into the woods, where Wilde would find him.

It's possible that the bear chased Petranyi down the trail, but "he probably bumped into the bear again there," Logan says.

It is those last six hundred feet of his brother's travels that bother Mark Petranyi the most.

"Apparently, he attempted to get away," Mark says. "Maybe that was the wrong thing to do. We'll never know. But that time from the first attack until she finally got him . . . it must have been sheer terror. Why didn't the bear go away? I've asked myself that question a thousand times."

Rangers asked themselves the same question. A grizzly bear had killed and eaten a man. It was an incredibly rare situation. In the ninety-year history of Glacier Park, where thousands upon thousands of people walk through grizzly country every year, Petranyi was only the ninth person to be killed by a grizzly bear. And in most of those cases, the bear left the body alone after the attack. During the same period, forty-eight people drowned in the park, twenty-three fell to their deaths from cliffs, and twenty-six died in car wrecks. Clearly, grizzly bears are only one of many perils in the park.

"In all my other cases, the bear attacks, neutralizes the threat, and leaves," Logan says.

The National Park Service met Monday morning to discuss the situation. Logan and the other rangers flew to park headquarters to participate. Chief Ranger Steve Frye called some outside bear experts for advice. After a few hours, the group of rangers and administrators decided the bears must die.

A combination of circumstances led to that decision. The initial attack on Petranyi may have been a defensive reaction by a surprised bear, and that is not normally a death sentence for a bear in Glacier National Park. But it quickly turned into a "predatory" situation when she started eating him. Add the bear's aggression on the trail, the way she had tried to buck the helicopter to get back to the corpse, and the way she had partially buried the body. Then add public and political perceptions.

"By removing that bear we perhaps saved many bears," Logan says.

That sounds like stilted logic at first, but it makes sense in the highly charged political debates over grizzly bears and their place in the modern world. If the bear had been allowed to live, "then," says Logan, "every attack after that would have been the man-killing grizzly" in the public mind.

"We're trying to have an atmosphere where people and bears can coexist," he says. But having a bear around that has earned a food reward by killing a person "is not consistent with what we want to achieve here. It was terrible to have to remove that grizzly bear, but I never had any second thoughts about it."

Logan and several other rangers packed up their weapons and flew back to the chalet at Granite Park.

The rangers searched from the air for as long as the weather held out that day but couldn't find the bears they were looking for. A family group was spotted a few miles away, but they were the wrong bears.

That night snow fell, and by the next morning—day four of the incident—a couple of inches of fresh dust coated the high country.

Kruger flew in part of a rancid deer carcass to use as bait, carrying it in a sling beneath his helicopter. Rangers on the ground had to adjust the bait, manipulating the smelly carcass and knowing there were hungry grizzlies in the area. Later that afternoon a large, chocolate-colored grizzly came in, sniffed the bait, and disappeared with the whole bundle in less than five seconds as rangers watched through binoculars. Bait would be staked to the ground in the future.

The hunt was marked with frustration. Several snares were set and baited with more deer carcasses, but they didn't do the job. The rangers caught a grizzly one day, but he was the wrong animal, a subadult male, so they let him go. Bear biologists with the Montana Department of Fish,

Wildlife and Parks flew in to help. Bear sign was everywhere. Rangers on foot patrol found tracks of the bear family in one of the places where Petranyi's body had lain, along the trail where he had been dragged, and in nearby meadows. They found places where bears had "rototilled" their previous day's footsteps as they dug up roots. Rangers spotted the bears a couple of times over the next several days, but nobody could get a shot at them.

It wasn't until October 11, day nine of the incident, that they were finally killed. Kruger had spotted them while shuttling rangers in and out of the chalet area. But there was a problem. Another family of bears was in the same area. The rangers had to make sure they were shooting the right bears, so Logan and ranger Regi Altop climbed into the helicopter and buzzed over the bears several times until Logan saw what he was looking for: that light-colored collar around the sow's neck.

Kruger dropped the two rangers off about two hundred yards from the bears, and they crept closer while the helicopter hovered overhead. The bears paid little attention to the noisy chopper and focused on digging up roots, a testament to the single-minded quest for food that grizzlies display in the fall.

When the rangers approached within one hundred yards, they took careful aim at the feeding sow with their .300 H&H Magnum rifles. Logan started counting. When he hit three, both men fired. The sow took a couple of steps and fell dead. Then they opened fire on the cubs. One dropped, and the other took off into the woods, wounded but still scampering.

More rangers arrived to help Logan and Altop search for the wounded animal, and after about an hour, Kruger spotted it from the helicopter. The four rangers spread out and went after it, walking uphill.

That's when the second bear family showed up.

Kruger had to take his eyes off the cub and haze the second family away with his helicopter, trying to keep them away from the rangers, trying to keep a bad situation from getting worse fast. It worked, but the men lost the cub.

Kruger, always sharp-eyed, spotted the cub later in the day with a spotting scope that was set up at the chalet. It had come back to the area where its mother had died, wounded and alone. Kruger flew Steve Frye and another ranger to the area. It was almost dark by then, but they walked into a thick stand of trees and finished the animal off with a final shot.

At 6:43 p.m. on the eleventh day of October, 1992, after nine bloody and grueling days, Kruger loaded the cub into his helicopter and lifted off for the last time. The whole unpleasant business was finally over.

———◆———

The three bear carcasses were shipped to the Montana Department of Fish, Wildlife and Parks diagnostic laboratory in Bozeman, Montana, where veteran biologist Keith Aune performed a necropsy, an autopsy for animals.

The National Park Service wanted to know if there was any evidence of Petranyi inside the bears, any hair or flesh or fiber. Bear scat collected near Petranyi's body contained human remains and two different types of cloth. But when Aune examined the bears, he found nothing unusual. Not that he had expected much. The bears had been passing huge amounts of food through their bodies in the days since Petranyi died. Each of them had a belly full of roots when it died.

Rangers singled these bears out for death working on the best possible evidence. They had seen these bears near the body and trying to get closer. There was no other family group in the area with cubs that size. But had they killed Petranyi? The rangers were sure, but they wanted scientific evidence, something to remove absolutely all doubt about whether they had killed the right bears. Aune couldn't give it to them. Sophisticated DNA tests, common now, weren't readily available at the time.

"There was no evidence in the stomach or gastrointestinal tract which can confirm the presence" of the bears at the scene of Petranyi's death.

A niggling doubt would remain forever, and that's the kind of thing that can bother a park ranger. People don't sign up to be rangers because they enjoy killing grizzly bears.

"It's beyond a reasonable doubt," says Glacier spokeswoman Amy Vanderbilt, whose husband, Ranger Gary Moses, helped investigate the incident. "But we'll never be able to absolutely verify it."

Aune did, however, provide some information about the bears. The sow was at least fifteen years old, in good general health, and weighed 251 pounds. She harbored a normal load of parasites, was seventy-four inches long, and carried a layer of fat an inch thick along her back, indicating she was only in moderate shape. Bears often have two to four inches of fat along their backs at that time of year. Her two cubs, both females, weighed thirty-nine pounds and fifty pounds.

The sow's left front foot had been injured recently, which could have caused an attitude problem, but the most interesting thing Aune found was in her mouth: deep cavities in her molars.

"They had to be very painful," Aune says. Also, one of her front teeth had rotted away almost entirely.

Did a constant and severe toothache make the bear more cantankerous? Aune, who has studied grizzlies for decades, thinks it probably did.

But why did she run away from Buck Wilde as he ate breakfast, then attack Petranyi twice and feed on him? Seeing Wilde was probably no surprise to her. She knew the area, knew that people were often seen in the campground and cooking area. Whether she first saw Petranyi on the trail or in the woods, it likely was a surprise encounter, which triggered an instinct to protect her cubs. The toothache probably reduced her tolerance level at least a little. That, combined with her intense focus on calories prior to denning for the winter, could have triggered some kind of switch that made her see Petranyi as food rather than as a nuisance or a threat and made her attack a second time and begin to eat him.

— ❦ —

Buck Wilde says it took him five years before he could talk about the incident with any comfort.

When the helicopter took him to park headquarters, rangers interviewed him again, then repeated Logan's earlier advice to get some psychological counseling—"to make sure from a shrink point of view that everything was sort of okay," is the way Wilde puts it.

He declined. Rather, he shouldered his backpack and slipped out the back door of the headquarters building, dodging the reporters waiting for him at the front door. Then he walked to the highway, stuck out his thumb, and caught a ride with a couple he had met two days earlier while hiking in to Granite Park. He told them the story, and the man bought him a bottle of Wild Turkey Whiskey ("It's one of my poisons, especially in high-stress situations") before dropping him at a trailhead on the east side of the park.

Wilde was seeking his own mental therapy.

"I decided I was going back into bear country."

It was an area new to him, the Triple Divide Pass, where waters run to the Atlantic, the Pacific, and Hudson Bay.

"I wasn't just scared, I was scared to death. I had been shaken, fundamentally, to the core. I wanted to handle my shakiness in a way that would be constructive, and I thought the most constructive thing to do, for my psyche, was to get back in bear country. Fear management, I guess you'd call it."

He's had other big scares since then. A couple of more charges by grizzlies and a canoe wreck that left him stranded on an island in the raging North Fork of the Flathead River for six days.

He doesn't like to talk about that one much either, for the same reason he's avoided talking much about the Petranyi incident.

"It's taken me five years to get to the point where I'm ready to do that. You get kind of weird when you spend as much time in the woods as I do. I understand firsthand what is meant by the word 'taboo.' Taboos are things that the Native Americans dealt with in special terms, by whispering or whatever."

He's still a little uncomfortable talking about it. It brings things back, he says, and he wants to treat the situation with respect for the bears and for Petranyi's family. And there is another matter. Call it practical spirituality. Long-term physical survival in the wilderness depends on having the right attitude, Wilde believes.

"I felt that if I didn't give this situation enough respect, spiritually, and with all the time I spend in bear country, the bears would get me. That sounds pretty weird, but it's really the way I look at it. One thing you should get is that I was scared shitless. It scared me enough to make it very special."

He says he doesn't expect people to understand him, but he believes what he believes. It's important to him.

The trip into Triple Divide Pass lasted five days. He saw lots of bear sign, tracks, and evidence of fresh digging. But he didn't see a bear during the whole trip, and today he's comfortable in the woods.

Put yourself in Buck Wilde's shoes.

What would you have done?

Postscript

Buck Wilde still spends a lot of time with grizzly bears. Every summer he guides tourists into the isolated coastal zone in Alaska, where controversial bear advocate Timothy Treadwell was famously mauled to death and eaten in 2003. He's good enough at this work that some people now call him a "bear whisperer." When he's not in Alaska, he's publishing books of his photography and giving what he calls "enrichment presentations." He now has twenty years of experience living with grizzlies and often finds himself within a few yards of them.

He says he makes it a point not to push his luck. Unlike Treadwell he knows the bears aren't going to fall in love with him. But if he's careful, they put up with him.

"There are some real fundamentals, and if you follow them, bears are real tolerant," he says. "You can become comfortable working with them, as a photographer."

Never approach a bear, he says. Don't try sneaking or zigzagging around. It won't work. Rather, let the bear see you, and let it approach you on its own terms and move at its own speed. Sitting down is the least threatening posture, he says.

"Just plant yourself, and be willing to pay the price that photographers pay," he says. "The bears will come check you out. Are you a threat? Are you benign?"

"Don't try to be cute," he says. "You can trip that wire, and there will be a result." If you disturb the bear, chances are it will run away. But it might charge.

If a bear does charge, stand your ground. Don't hit the ground and curl up unless a bear knocks you down. Never, never run. "That's the golden, golden rule," Wilde says.

None of his clients have been injured, and many have come home with remarkable images and footage.

Cases like Petranyi's are incredibly rare. Wilde stresses that.

"He was a victim of circumstance," Wilde said. "But I feel like I'm on a mission to show the other side of the bear. I've designed a kinship with the bear. But it will take a better psychiatrist than me to decipher it."

2

Long Day at Kitty Creek

WHEN THE BEAR TRAPPER BROKE DOWN AND CRIED, IT WAS THE NEW widow who offered comfort.

The widow's own tears had flowed earlier, when the bear trapper, Chad Dickinson, delivered his sad news: Her husband was dead, killed by a grizzly bear coming out of a drug-induced stupor.

Dickinson had arrived on horseback to tell Yolanda Evert the fate of her husband of forty-six years, Erwin Evert.

"I rode down to Mrs. Evert's cabin and she came out and asked if I had found her husband and I said yes and then she asked if he was alright and I said no, that a bear had killed her husband," Dickinson wrote three days after that cold, windy evening, part of a bleak and dreary day in Wyoming's Absaroka Mountains. "She broke down crying."

Another official arrived soon after, so Dickinson could get back to work without leaving her alone, could begin to think about the many chores that must be done when a grizzly bear kills somebody: The sheriff and coroner and biologists and wardens would all have questions, the search-and-rescue team needed a guide, the horses needed attention. The press would be along, no doubt. So many needs. So Dickinson prepped for these chores; then he returned to Yolanda Evert's cabin.

"She asked me to come in and I broke down crying and [she] gave me a hug," Dickinson wrote.

It's not the kind of thing you normally read in an investigation report. But that's what happened, and Dickinson put it down in his own hand.

It was June 17, 2010, and it was the first time a grizzly bear had killed a person in the greater Yellowstone National Park area since 1984. And never had a bear killed somebody in such a circumstance. The evening light was beginning to fade, but the day would not end for many hours.

A modern bear trapper knows many things. He knows how to find the bears' turf, lure them in and catch them, take blood and hair and maybe a tooth, attach a radio collar to the huge neck, and tattoo a bear's lip. This work is neither simple nor easy. You've got to know how to fix a horseshoe and how to fill a hypodermic with a precise amount of powerful drugs. And you've got to handle a potentially dangerous animal, one that is frightened and agitated and powerful. You sought this animal out, and now you must ease it into sleep and do your work and then release it without harm to the bear, to yourself, or to your crew. You must do all this despite fatigue, distractions, and sometimes miserable weather. Your work hitch may last for ten days in a row, and chances are you will go days and days without catching a bear. But some days you get lucky. You could catch two of them.

That's what happened on that long day at Kitty Creek. Dickinson and his partner, Seth Thompson, both field veterans, had been trying for three weeks to catch [and radio-collar] grizzly bears in the rugged drainage a few miles east of Yellowstone National Park, along the North Fork of the Shoshone River. At roughly seven thousand feet, the country still clung to winter, with wind and rain and snow flopping down. The partners set leghold snares, contraptions that use stinky bait to entice a grizzly bear to stuff its paw inside a bucket and into the loop of the snare. With the bear thus caught, the trappers approach with a CO2 pistol loaded with a powerful anesthetic cocktail called Telazol.

At their first snare location, critters sprung the snares but outwitted the trappers. That went on for a week, so the crew took some scheduled days off and returned to Kitty Creek, where they set traps in two new locations, checking them daily. There, too, bears or other animals sprung the traps. Then, after nine straight days of this, on what was scheduled to be the last day of the hitch, signaling devices at the traps told them they had two animals.

The first was a male grizzly of about 430 pounds, a sizable specimen for Yellowstone. The team put a dart in him at 9:06 a.m., and he went down in nine minutes, without event. It was breeding season, and as a mature male he bore the wounds of recent battles for sex. It took a little time to work him up—take some blood and a tooth, weigh him, and fit him with a radio collar—and since the bear was showing signs of recovery in the middle of this process, the team gave him two more small doses of Telazol.

Researchers around North America routinely use Telazol to immobilize large animals, and they report good results. It is not the "PCP," used on animals in previous decades, that can cause incredible violence when humans take it. (Doper blogs on the Internet say that some people steal Telazol from veterinary clinics and ingest it but often remember nothing of the experience.) Animals generally wake up unharmed, but full recovery can take a few hours.

By 10:48 a.m. recovery from the drugs had begun, and the team packed up their traps and bait and materials, loaded the horses, and backed off a safe distance to watch the bear. By 12:30 p.m. the bear was holding his head up and swaying it. He was lolling his tongue and beginning to push up on his front legs. When the team approached on horseback, he could focus on the riders but wasn't ambulatory yet. The team had removed the nearby warning signs, the ones that said "Danger! Bear trap in the area," and decided to move up the drainage to work the next bear, a four-year-old female. They hadn't seen a single hiker in all the time they'd labored in Kitty Creek. They'd met a group of escorted riders from a nearby dude ranch a few days earlier, but they'd been a good distance away, on an abandoned road. On top of that, bad weather was ruling the day: thick clouds, snow off and on, and bitter winds strong enough to topple trees downslope. It seemed safe to leave the bear untended.

"Due to the total lack of human activity in our area I thought this would be a safe thing to do," Dickinson wrote in his report of his decision to leave at that time. "Seth and myself both commented that due to the weather conditions (spitting snow and cold) that we would think people would not be out hiking around."

But they didn't know about Erwin Evert, a little over a mile down the trail in his cabin and itching to stretch his legs, despite the miserable weather, after spending a couple of days in a car.

"They had every rational reason to believe nobody would go up there," Chuck Neal, of nearby Cody, Wyoming, says of the trapping crew. "But on this particular day somebody did. There was this exceptional man on the trail."

～ ～

Erwin Evert was a botanist with long experience in the greater Yellowstone area. He had owned a cabin at the mouth of Kitty Creek, one of a dozen or so summer homes there, for forty years. A teacher in his native Chicago, he had recently published his 750-page life's work: *Vascular Plants of the Greater Yellowstone Area: An Annotated Catalog and Atlas*. He had logged countless backcountry miles studying plants. He found five of them that nobody had cataloged before.

At the age of seventy, he remained a remarkable physical specimen and a prodigious hiker, the kind of man who often chose the difficult route just to stretch his lungs. Breathing hard didn't scare him. And like any good scientist his curiosity compelled him.

He'd seen Dickinson and Thomas riding up the trail and wondered about their work. On the phone that morning with his daughter, and later with his wife, he said he wanted to catch up with the trapping team and see what they were up to. At about 12:45 p.m. he bundled up in a wool hat and parka and headed up the drainage.

A week or so earlier, on another hike, he'd seen signs warning of a "dangerous bear," according to his good friend Chuck Neal, a retired ecologist for the federal government and author of the book *Grizzlies in the Mist*. Like Evert, Neal is a prodigious hiker who spends many, many hours tackling the steeps in grizzly country. Neal had warned him to take the signs seriously, that they meant somebody was either trapping bears or baiting them to a "hair snag" to gather DNA samples. Either way, Neal warned, Evert needed to avoid signed areas.

But the signs were gone by the time Evert arrived at the trap site.

The bear wasn't.

The trapping crew left the male bear "probably about the time Erwin was coming up the trail," Neal says months later, a statement corroborated by the official report. And the place where he died was not the place where he had seen signs earlier. "He was not going to a trap site that he knew about."

The trap site was hundreds of feet from the main trail, but several trips with horses had left clear evidence of traffic. Evert then followed that route and walked into the bear.

"What exactly motivated him to do that is beyond me," Neal says.

"He walked nearly on top of the bear, and the bear was still groggy," says Neal, who returned to the site several times to do his own investigation. "There were no signs alerting him that he was in harm's way. He kind of poked around and then bingo. A man showed up in the bear's space, and the bear reacted."

Evert had been with Neal more than once when they encountered grizzlies. Evert stood next to him and kept his cool, while Neal, who has long experience with grizzlies, was able to deflect the charges. While not a bear specialist, Evert "knew the ground rules," Neal says. He wasn't the type to run away or panic or try to fight a bear. While he didn't carry bear spray or a weapon, those things likely wouldn't have helped anyway, not with the wind and the speed of the attack.

"He probably only had a split second," Neal says.

~

At 6:15 that evening, after Dickinson and Thompson had worked up the female bear in the second trap and were riding toward the Evert cabin, no doubt looking forward to a few days off, they met Yolanda, who told them her husband was overdue. He was up Kitty Creek somewhere. Dickinson swapped horses with Thompson, putting himself on a more manageable mount, and immediately headed up the trail, scanning for footprints.

When he came to the access route to the first trap site, the place where they had left the male bear, he made the familiar uphill turn and found disconcerting news: a human footprint. He kept riding, shouting out Evert's name. About twenty yards from the snare tree, he found his badly mangled body. The fatal wounds landed on his head, bite marks that crushed his skull. Death made itself obvious.

The bear had left. Worried for his own safety, Dickinson returned to the trailhead and delivered the grim report. Wyoming Game and Fish Department bear specialist Mark Buscino had wandered in shortly afterward. Yolanda called Neal and his wife, both close friends. There were sobs of grief and pain. A crowd gathered, and the news spread. Questions began to arise.

The Evert family reacted with "extreme grief and outrage," Neal says.

And they wanted to know: "Why are they trapping bears?"

There are two answers. First, when grizzly bears get in trouble raiding garbage, attacking livestock, or, on very rare occasions, entering buildings, officials often trap and relocate them. This means a dose of anesthesia and the attachment of a radio collar, so the bear can be located if it causes more trouble. These are known as "management" bears.

The second reason to capture a bear is for research purposes. And that's what the crew was doing in Kitty Creek that cold and windy June. They were looking to radio-collar bears, preferably breeding-age females, so they could learn where they go, what they eat, if they reproduce, when and where they die.

Widely used on a broad range of species, "radio telemetry" has revolutionized wildlife science over the past fifty years. With small creatures, such as trout, attaching a radio means minor surgery. A biologist makes a small incision, inserts a transmitter no bigger than half a pinky finger, applies a few stitches, and puts the fish back in the water. The biologist then can tell where the fish goes and when, where it spawns, the places it avoids.

With grizzly bears telemetry gets more complicated. For one thing trapping them can be difficult: In the greater Yellowstone area, crews catch on average one bear for every fourteen days a trap is in the field. And it can be dangerous: A trout can't take your head off if you make a mistake.

In areas with road access, trappers use culvert traps. In the backcountry they use snares. In both cases the trappers chum the bears with smelly bait, often roadkill enhanced with some other putrescence. In all cases the trappers need extensive training and experience.

First developed in the 1960s by twin brothers Frank and John Craighead, radio telemetry revolutionized what we know about grizzly bears and has produced a wealth of data. The Interagency Grizzly Bear Study Team (IGBST), which exists to study the great bears of Yellowstone and provide managers with the best information they can obtain, has published reams of studies on Yellowstone grizzlies.

"A lot of what we know about bears is directly dependent upon telemetry," says Chuck Schwartz, the IGBST leader. "We get survival rates, reproduction, litter size, movements, habitat use."

That information has proved valuable in a number of ways: Telemetry studies show that grizzlies avoid open roads, so hundreds of miles of little-used roads have been closed, giving the bears a bit more elbow room. Municipal dumps in the region's small towns have been sanitized. Hunters have been warned to be extra cautious because telemetry studies have proved that grizzlies are attracted by the gut piles and bones they leave behind.

Such information is particularly important in the ongoing battles over whether to remove the Yellowstone grizzly from the list of animals protected by the federal Endangered Species Act. Such decisions are not up to Schwartz, but his team provides the information that both sides—for and against delisting—cite in their arguments.

And grizzly monitoring will continue no matter what decisions courts and legislatures make about delisting, Schwarz says.

But trapping, drugging, and placing a collar on a bear is inarguably an invasive procedure.

"It certainly isn't a pleasant experience for the bear," says Barrie Gilbert, who has studied bear behavior for thirty-five years.

"The bears don't know you're doing it for their own good," says Chuck Jonkel, with more than fifty years of bear research under his belt. "If they're hurting and they see you, they're going to hurt you."

Neal maintains there is no longer as much need for extensive telemetry of grizzlies in the Yellowstone area, that the current program is overkill.

"We know what we need to have a viable bear population," he says. "We need habitat, habitat, habitat. But we don't want to give it to them."

Current guidelines call for radio monitoring of about twenty-five female bears at any given time, IGBST boss Schwartz says. But female bears are hard to target. The trapping team at Kitty Creek that year was working for Schwartz, hoping for females, but when they caught a big male, there was no option but to drug him. Trying to release him otherwise could have proved deadly for man, bear, or both. And while the bear was out cold, the trappers worked him up, adding data to what Schwartz says is already "the most studied bear population in the world, of any species." And the data set continues to grow. Most years between seventy and eighty grizzlies, both research and management bears, wear radio collars.

And sometimes bears die from trapping and drugging. In 2010 managers inside the park captured a yearling bear that was already in bad shape, missing an eye and bearing numerous infected wounds dished out by another predator. It died during a capture operation.

While the death of one bear is dwarfed by the number of bears killed by edgy hunters or even by automobiles, every animal counts in a protected grizzly population such as the one in Yellowstone, according to Sam Wasser, who holds an endowed chair in conservation biology at the University of Washington in Seattle. He has worked with large predators and ungulates across North America and Africa.

Wasser says he has a better way for scientists to recover the information they need. It involves bear turds, sophisticated lab equipment, and the enthusiasm a friendly dog shows for a tennis ball.

He calls the program Conservation Canines. In essence it uses dogs, mostly rescued from animal shelters, to find grizzly scat. He starts by selecting dogs that are obsessive about chasing a slobbery tennis ball—the more enthusiasm the better. Then his staff trains them to search out marijuana. If a dog finds the reefer, it is rewarded with a chance to drool on a tennis ball. The dogs then progress to finding samples of bear scat. The dogs that pass further tests go to the field and follow a controlled grid, taking their handlers to all the bear poop they can find. While the dog gnaws on the ball, the handler—wearing rubber gloves in concern for both the integrity of the sample and personal hygiene—then scoops the scat into a sealable plastic bag.

Back at the lab new techniques can do amazing things. The process of digestion and defecation expels enough tissue cells to identify individual bears through DNA analysis. Hormonal analysis can measure stress levels, reproduction fitness, and nutrition levels.

Lab costs have decreased greatly in recent years, and using dogs to ferret out bear poop can provide a broad diagram of a bear population.

With telemetry you capture perhaps 10 percent of the bears in a given area, then use mathematical models to try to figure out what an entire population is doing in terms of food selection, travel, and fertility. Also, one or two aberrant animals can skew the statistics.

With the scat-sniffing dogs, Wasser says, field crews can gather samples from most bears in a given area and never handle a grizzly. He conducted a study with the dogs in and near Jasper National Park in Alberta from 1999 to 2001, then compared his results to hair-snag stations, which allow scientists to identify and count individual grizzly bears, and to telemetry studies in the same area.

The dogs produced four times as many scat samples as the hair-snag posts did, and "the telemetry showed the same bear distributions as the scat, but at more than thirty-three times the cost," he says. Wasser's study cost thirty thousand dollars, compared to one million dollars for a telemetry study in the same area. And the trapping for the telemetry study killed two bears and injured another. The dog teams never even saw a bear.

But there are a number of things a scat sample cannot do, says Chris Servheen, grizzly bear recovery coordinator for the U.S. Fish and Wildlife Service. It cannot tell you how or where a bear died. It cannot define the age structure of a bear population or sketch out a bear's home range. And while scat samples can tell you where bears spend time and what they're eating, they can't tell you such things as where a bear chooses to cross a road. These are all things bear managers need to know, Servheen says.

Wasser says his techniques won't replace radio telemetry, but it could reduce the need for it.

"I'm obviously biased, but I think this is the wave of the future," he says. "There are huge values to long-term studies. But that doesn't mean you have to do it all with telemetry."

If he's right, that means scientists might not have to capture so many bears.

But telemetry studies aren't likely to end anytime soon.

Servheen says he sees promise in scat analysis, but it doesn't provide everything managers need to make good decisions.

"In a perfect world, where bears did not live in habitats filled with humans and human activities, our need for some of the specific types of information provided by telemetry would be minimal," he says. "But that is not the world bears live in."

And then there are the legal issues. Ongoing court battles have yet to resolve whether Yellowstone grizzlies should lose the protections they have under the federal Endangered Species Act. Servheen maintains it's time to take that step, that the Yellowstone area bear population has nearly tripled since the bears were first protected in 1975, that the population is recovered. Others maintain that is exactly the wrong stance.

"We are continually challenged by environmental groups in court to 'prove' with precise data what we know about bears, their sources of mortality, their physical condition, and how human activities impact them," Servheen says.

The demand for information dictates the methods used to gather it, he says.

"We aim for the maximum safety for bears and the least impact to bears," he says. Evolving technologies and techniques can help, but they don't provide all the answers.

———

Erwin Evert died in an area with plenty of grizzly bears. The Kitty Creek region is a focus of the delisting debate, a place where bear managers have to hustle from April to November, dealing with wandering bears, crowds of tourists, well-armed hunters.

Two days after his body was recovered, officials in a helicopter used the bear's radio collar to track the bear down and shoot him from a helicopter, about two miles from the attack. There was little choice in the matter, according to Servheen. Federal and Wyoming officials wanted to "err on the side of public safety."

It was more of a matter of government covering its own backside, according to Chuck Neal. If the bear wound up in any kind of trouble later, the government might find itself facing a lawsuit.

He says the bear that killed his friend didn't deserve to die. A sharpshooter could find it only because it wore a radio collar. Evert had left home that day hoping to meet the trappers, learn about their project, Neal says. But he wasn't looking to meet a bear. He found it only because it had been drugged, collared, and left alone, with the warning signs removed. Then the bear reacted in a natural way. Probably groggy and confused, it attacked with a flurry of bites and blows when Evert approached. It did not feed on his body. It went away.

For Servheen the attack might never be understood. Did it attack because it was coming out of a stupor, or did it attack because Evert approached too closely? Servheen says that question can't be answered.

As for the trappers, he says waiting for a couple of hours after the first signs of recovery is normal procedure. Trappers prefer to let the bear recover on its own terms; sleeping, lying around. In the field, judgment calls have to be made, and the team had another bear to work up.

"They followed the protocol as much as they thought it existed," Servheen said. "They didn't do anything egregiously wrong."

The trappers followed normal procedures, Neal says, and he sympathizes with the pain they displayed at Evert's death. He saw the tears. But the result is the same: a dead man, a dead bear, and a family in grief. Science didn't gain much on that particular day.

An investigation team of bear experts recommended some changes in how trappers, who already undergo extensive training, ply their craft. Warning signs should remain in place and areas should be closed for three days after trapping has finished. Cameras should be installed around traps and snares to monitor both human and bear use. This would help document how bears behave as they recover from drugs. When "possible and appropriate," trappers should use drugs that can be reversed with other drugs, to hasten recovery time. Press releases or other methods should announce bear trapping operations and urge people to avoid them.

Those measures will add to the workload of bear trappers, but they could cut the odds—already infinitesimal—of a repeat scenario of what happened to Evert. Bear attacks are rare enough. A case like this one—a private citizen coming across a recently drugged bear for whatever reason—had never happened before.

The story might not be over. As this book went to press, Evert's family had retained a high-profile law firm from Jackson, Wyoming, one that specializes in wrongful death cases.

3

Big Trouble in Banff

NOBODY KNEW WHEN OR WHERE THE BEAR WOULD STOP. IT MOVED through the cold night at the Lake Louise campground in Canada's Banff National Park, taking chunks out of Americans, Germans, and Australians as they slept.

The sow grizzly, traveling with a cub, hit them all in their tents at about 3:30 in the morning, ripping through the thin fabric and pouncing with tooth and claw. The attack—under a moonless sky, lit only by stars— would send six people to the hospital, scare a lot more than that, ignite lawsuits, and focus an increasingly bright spotlight on the beleaguered grizzlies of Banff.

❦

The bears hit the Germans first. Algis Povilavicius and his sister Tanya lost all thoughts of sleep when she woke up and told her brother, "There's a bear in the tent." It was pressing on the tent, putting weight on Algis's thigh. The siblings whispered: What do we do? Then the fabric tore, and the bear was inside, with them. Tanya scrambled for the car, but the bear grabbed the foot of Algis's sleeping bag and started pulling him toward the woods. After a few yards he managed to slip from the bag, and he, too, scrambled for the car. But the bear moved faster and was on him, pinning him to the ground with a paw on his left shoulder. "It was very silent, and the bear was standing on my arm," Algis says years later. He struggled, and the bear sank its teeth deep into his left arm. He moved again, and the bear bit his head. Tanya was in the car, yelling for help, but nobody mustered. Algis remembers the bear looming over him and stars glinting in the moonless sky. He remembers waiting, not knowing what to do. Finally, a car passed, its headlights illuminating the grizzly, and that was enough to start the bear moving. "It walked away silently," Algis says.

A couple from Germany came to help. They gathered Algis and Tanya in their car and took them to meet an ambulance.

Then the bears moved to the next campsite, where they shredded a tent belonging to two Montana women, Susan Olin and Laura Shearin, both of them summer naturalists in Glacier National Park.

"I heard huffing sounds outside . . . and then the bear was in our tent," Olin told reporters two days later from her wheelchair in a Banff hospital.

The bear went first for Shearin, who was lucky: She was sleeping with her pillow over her head, and the bear ripped away a big chunk of it, clawing her under the arm in the process. That was her only injury.

Then it laid into Olin, biting her back and chewing on her arm, clawing her face and her shoulders. She fought at first, then played dead while Shearin tried to make herself small in her sleeping bag. Olin would need more than fifty staples in her body and a row of stitches in her face to close the wounds.

Then came the Australians' turn.

Owen Hereford and his friend, Andrew Brodie, were still fast asleep when the bear tore the tent right off them. It grabbed Brodie's sleeping bag, chomped down on his arm and tossed him as if he were a toy. Hereford kicked at the bear, turning the attack toward himself. It ripped open his forearm and his thigh, chomping down hard on his rib cage. Brodie had escaped his sleeping bag by then and came to his friend's rescue, which brought him more injuries, with puncture wounds and gouges on his buttocks, knees, and feet. The bear finally backed off when he was able to bounce a large rock off its nose. The two men jumped behind a picnic table, but the grizzly kept circling them. Both men screamed at the bear.

Finally, somebody put them in a vehicle and drove them away.

Olin and Shearin had crawled through a hole in the tent and made it to their car by then, too. They discovered later that the bear had attacked the car as well, either biting or clawing the spare tire riding on the rear of the vehicle, hitting it hard enough to puncture the tire.

Steve Edgington was also in the campground, but he didn't wait for his turn with the bear.

"There was a lot of scratching and ripping, and it was close," he told a TV crew the next day. "So I just thought, 'Well, my turn's next.' I opened my tent, turned the other way, and just ran. I kept hearing all these people saying, 'Please just help me.' Loud screams."

In all, six people were mauled or battered. Two got off easy and were treated in hospitals and released. Others would need some time. It took ten hours for the doctors to stitch Algis Povilavicius together, and he stayed ten days in the hospital. Brodie would need six months to heal up. Some of the wounds festered in other ways for years. Clearly, Banff National Park can be a dangerous place if you want to hike or camp. But it's a lot more dangerous place if you're a grizzly bear.

When the sun came up that morning, September 25, 1995, park wardens loaded their guns, hunted down and killed a grizzly sow and its cub, and announced that the problem had been solved. Attacks on sleeping campers are incredibly rare, and even the most ardent bear advocate generally agrees that a bear that attacks people sleeping in clean campsites ought to be destroyed. After the bears were killed, the campground and trails reopened, and it was business as usual again in Banff National Park.

And what a lot of business there was to do. Banff is Canada's oldest national park, and you can't find a prettier place. If you haven't been there, you've probably seen its glaciers and crags and cataracts on TV or in a travel agency poster or a vodka commercial.

But Banff has problems, big ones that park promoters don't advertise, ones that are a lot harder to solve than the occasional rogue grizzly and, for most people, a lot harder to see. Its wildlife population is fragmented and in trouble, its water is tainted, and the park is too developed. Some Canadians have begun dismissing it as "Disneyland North," while others face being priced out of a trip to their own national park while rich foreigners are courted. Some scientists and academics wonder if the park will even exist for another century.

The scenery won't go away, of course, but it takes more than pretty vistas to make a national park. Will it be a nature preserve, the heart of an ecosystem where sometimes inconvenient and expensive critters such as bears and wolves have a home? Or will it be just another swell resort, the kind of place where elk are considered a golf hazard and there's a lot of Gucci luggage for sale?

This is a Canadian problem, and Canadians are working on it, or at least arguing about it. But there are lessons in Banff for Americans, too, especially those who care about the future of parks and wild land, who hope to make a living in a place where grizzlies live, who want to do it without killing the bear, who look to the Canadians for help with wildlife problems on the south side of the longest friendly border in the world.

To get a measure of the problems in Banff, it helps to compare it to Yellowstone National Park, about five hundred miles south along the Continental Divide and a place with plenty of problems of its own. Both are flagship parks, the "crown jewels" of national systems. They have much in common: mountains, lakes, grizzly bears, elk, hot springs, and world-wide fame. The areas around both parks are filling up fast with people, mostly moneyed ones from someplace else, and both parks face a wide variety of complicated problems and competing interests, many centered around the debate over the value of nature: Does it exist for the primary purpose of providing financial wealth, or does its highest value come simply from its existence? Or is it possible to have it both ways?

In Yellowstone scientists worry about the park's biological isolation in the larger landscape, that grizzly bears exist on a lonely genetic island. The grizzly population there is growing, but the amount of bear habitat near the park is shrinking, being gobbled by oil and gas fields, subdivisions, and ski resorts. That means the great bears, who avoid people and each other most of their lives, have less and less room to spread out without running into man, a creature even more dangerous than another grizzly.

Banff has similar problems, but they are multiplied by vastly greater numbers of people. Calgary, a city of 1.2 million people, lies within an hour of the park gate. The town of Canmore, just a few miles away, has become home to 20,000 people. The town of Banff, the park headquarters, is a bustling community of 8,700 people, a place anxious to keep growing.

And then there are the visitors. About four and a half million people a year visit the park, and millions more people pass through on the four-lane Trans-Canada Highway, which bisects the park along critical streamside areas, the kind of riparian habitat so vital to many types of wildlife. It's a road so big and busy that it needs eight-foot chain-link fences to keep the animals away from the rushing cars and trucks. Add to this a major railroad line, a golf course, three ski resorts, world-class hotels, lots of housing, and some dams. All of these things must be paid for, so you advertise the place all over the world, which brings a lot of people who expect a lot of services because Banff is expensive and they want some comforts for their money.

Having a major city only an hour away is not something Parks Canada could have done anything about. But what about the town of Banff?

It sought and got autonomy in 1990, negotiating a secession from the national park that lets the city lease the ground beneath itself from Parks Canada for the privilege of living and making money—sometimes lots of money—in the park.

Parks Canada regulations say the only people allowed to live in the park are those who provide "essential and basic services" to visitors. In Banff these services include a Hard Rock Cafe, a McDonald's, and selling Pierre Cardin neckties. The town has a shopping mall, real estate agencies (some of which advertise in Japanese), and dance music pumping from the bars on Main Street. It has a skateboard palace.

Even the tourists get overwhelmed.

"We can buy that at a Wal-Mart," one woman tells her companion as they dodge elbows among the trinkets in a souvenir shop. "There's a Wal-Mart here, isn't there? Where did we see a Wal-Mart?"

While there is no Wal-Mart in Banff (nearby Canmore has one), it looks like the kind of place where you might find one. That's something that really irks Brian Horejsi, a respected independent conservation biologist from Calgary.

"The bear population has virtually no hope," he says. "The Wal-Mart mentality and grizzly bears cannot coexist in the same place."

❦

There are maybe eighty to a hundred resident grizzlies in Banff National Park, a small number that many scientists say is just getting smaller, one that reflects the larger problem of disappearing bear habitat in southern Alberta. And the bears that mauled the Lake Louise campers on September 25, 1995, were not residents. And the bears the rangers killed afterward weren't even the ones that attacked the campers.

Nobody would figure this out for a while, though.

"We feel confident these were the bears involved," said Sheila Luey, park spokeswoman at the time of the mauling.

Then six months later Park Superintendent Charlie Zinkan acknowledged they were the wrong bears. DNA tests had shown the guilty bear and her cub had been trapped later and hauled to an area north of Golden, British Columbia, fitted with radio collars, and released.

The mistake may be understandable, since both sets of bears were captured near the Lake Louise campground the day after the attack. The guilty bear and her cub had been released near Banff earlier in the season after being captured in the Revelstoke, British Columbia, area, where they had become addicted to human food at the city dump, still unfenced at the time.

They worked their way to Lake Louise, and by the time they arrived, they were in the condition known as hyperphagia, a desperate, single-minded quest for prehibernation calories that often leads bears to trouble. There they wandered in an unfamiliar place where they didn't know where to find natural foods. So the bears applied the knowledge they had picked up at Revelstoke: Humans often mean food. The Banff dump had long been closed, but the campground was still busy, and to a bear's nose, no matter how clean you keep a place with that many people, a lot of enticing odors remain. It's a scenario that was repeated many times in Yellowstone in the 1960s and 1970s after the dumps were closed there. Bears that depend on garbage may become dangerously aggressive when they can't find the garbage anymore. And when bears become aggressive, they often don't live long.

Horejsi, the independent biologist, blames bear managers for the incident. You can't blame a bear for being hungry and following its nose, he says.

"Everything about the relocation was wrong," Horejsi says. "They were moved late in the year and were dumped into a strange ecosystem. It was a female with a cub. You can't think of a more stressful time to relocate a bear than in the fall, when it should be just fattening up. It doesn't know any of the food sources, and it presumably crossed into the park."

Horejsi isn't alone. There had been a handful of bear incidents in the campground in days previous to the attack. A bear had chased a bicyclist, one had knocked over a barbecue at a nearby residence, one had flattened an unoccupied tent a couple of weeks earlier, and one had ripped into an empty tent just a day or two before the attack. Banff chief warden Bob Haney said at the time that there are always bears around Lake Louise and the incidents hadn't been numerous enough to warrant closing the campground.

Hereford, the Australian, said if he had known of the earlier incidents he probably wouldn't have stayed in the campground. Susan Olin, one of the Glacier Park rangers, told reporters at the time that she had no reason to second-guess the wardens.

A year later she changed her mind and sued the Canadian government.

——

A naturalist who worked summers explaining Glacier to tourists, Olin was good at her job, her colleagues in the National Park Service say. But she found it incredibly difficult to go back to work in bear country the following summer. Glacier has lots of grizzlies, and if you spend much time outdoors there, you will see them. Olin was no longer able to do this kind of work.

Parks Canada "knew or ought to have known that the bear represented a danger to campers," Olin's lawsuit says, adding that the agency should have closed the campground or at least given explicit warnings to campers there instead of the standard admonition that everyone receives at the campground gate.

Glacier naturalists receive extensive grizzly bear training, learning how to conduct themselves safely in bear country and how to pass that knowledge on to others. Much of it can be boiled down to two words: Avoid grizzlies. Because of that training, Olin would not have stayed in the campground if she had known bears were attacking tents there, her suit says.

The attack meant Olin needed surgery, physical therapy, and counseling. She suffered from nightmares and didn't sleep well. The "emotional and psychological distress" took its toll. She suffered from fatigue, loss of energy, and loss of stamina and strength, along with continuing physical problems in her back, arm, and shoulder. Her face is scarred. She has had to give up hiking and camping. Her "heightened fearfulness and anxiety of bears following the attack" meant a probable loss of income, according to the suit.

"I had nausea on the trail. I had vertigo on the trail, and about August it became impossible for me to continue doing that job," she testified many years later. "The event took over my life for six months at least. I really could think of nothing else."

She demanded that the Canadian government pay at least $62,000, plus legal fees, expenses, and damages for "future loss of income."

The case was later settled on undisclosed terms.

It wasn't the first such suit. In 1980 Swiss tourist Remy Tobler was badly mauled in Banff, losing an eye and some teeth. He sued Parks Canada—and won—because the agency had announced that a bear that had killed a man a week earlier had been destroyed.

That one was the wrong bear, too.

The Lake Louise campsite where Olin and Shearin pitched a tent that night is in beautiful country, but you couldn't call it wilderness. There's a clutch of apartments nearby, and the restroom—which offers hot and cold running water—is only 120 feet away. The light above the restroom doors spreads just to the edge of the packed-gravel pad where their tent stood. The air smells of fir and pine, wood smoke from the campfires, and car exhaust left by people setting up at one of the 220 campsites or running to town for supplies. There are plenty of signs warning people that bears use the area, and most campers pay attention to them. Coolers left outside, strewn garbage, and dirty campsites that draw bears are rare enough to attract attention and frequently a ticket from a patrolling warden.

For most people screaming and fighting is a natural reaction when something pounces on you in the night. And when it's a bear that's pouncing on your tent, that's probably the best thing to do.

Bear behavior experts say that in *almost* all circumstances trying to fight a grizzly only makes things worse: They see you as a threat to a food supply or to offspring, as something that must be neutralized or intimidated. They usually treat people as they would another bear: Once you cease being a threat, they usually stop punishing you. If they want to kill you—as they very rarely do—they can make very quick work of it.

But bear experts also agree that having a bear in your tent is a different circumstance, one that calls for a different reaction. If that happens, it's time to fight. You have done nothing to surprise the bear, threaten it, or incur its wrath. Rather, it has come seeking food in your tent. You should fight, using a club or your voice and your hands and feet. You should do whatever you can to let the bear know that you are not the easy meal it is seeking. Luckily, this is a natural instinct for most people. If attacked on a trail, forcing yourself to hold still and shut up while a bear chews your head is an act of tremendous will. It's not an easy thing to do.

When attacked in a tent, when shaken painfully awake, coming up swinging, for most people, comes naturally.

The grizzly hit three tents and six people that night. Most of them said they fought back or resisted, screamed and yelled. One even smacked the bear with a rock. Although some were hurt badly, fighting may have kept them from being hurt even worse.

❧

While nobody can legally discuss the terms of Olin's settlement in public, plenty of people are talking about Banff and the agency and grizzly bears. The Canadian government, clearly embarrassed at what it has allowed to happen in Banff, organized a task force of academics, scientists, and business people in 1994. Its two million dollar report came out in 1996, one year after the attack, and it issued a bleak prognosis.

"Unless we take immediate action, the qualities that make Banff a national park will be lost," the task force said. It recommended no more growth and perhaps shutting down some tourist attractions. "If we continue along our present road, Banff cannot remain a national park."

In the town of Banff, the city council agrees the town can't grow forever, but it still wanted to expand its population by one-third and add several hundred thousand square feet of retail space. The bar owners association complained that proposed limits on the number of hotel rooms might hurt the liquor business. At Lake Louise plans proceeded to expand the ski hill and add another seven-story wing to the posh hotel there, leading Stephen Legault, campaign director for the Alberta Wilderness Association, to describe developments at the lake as "a persistent cancer eating away at both Lake Louise's ecological health and the very purpose of national parks. For many people, Lake Louise is little more than good shopping with a beautiful backdrop."

And with more commercial development comes the infrastructure to service it: roads, sewage systems, traffic. It all adds up to trouble for grizzly bears and big headaches for the people trying to manage them.

❧

One of the thorniest problems is the highway passing through the park. For much of its length, it parallels the Bow River. The road is big, noisy, and intimidating for such creatures as bears, especially sows with cubs. A number of animals have been killed trying to cross the highway, so the government is building stout chain-link fences along each side of it. The government also built a couple of overpasses in hopes that bears and wolves would use them, that populations on either side of the highway could mix their genes. At least initially, there wasn't much success.

"I have this picture in my mind of a Parks Canada employee in the middle of one of them on his knees," Horejsi says, "praying that some animal uses it."

Most scientists agree that for a grizzly population to survive, even in the short term, it must include at least one hundred bears. A very optimistic count of Banff grizzlies puts the number at that level now. For long-term genetic viability, you need hundreds of animals at least.

With the highway and the fences "we've broken the ecosystem into a couple of pieces," Horejsi says. "The overpasses are not functional ecologically. They're a fraud, expensive window dressing. They look good to the untrained eye, but they're a mechanical solution to what is an ecological problem, and things never work that way."

Outside the park, and the other parks that adjoin Banff, there are other big problems: Research has shown that wild, unhabituated bears—the safest kind to have as neighbors—avoid even small roads. That's hard to do around Banff. A vast network of roads surrounds the park on the east, the same roads that provide the oil and gas that has made Calgary a gleaming, prosperous city.

Horejsi says that if he were suddenly crowned king of the Banff ecosystem he would halt all development inside the park. Not another bedroom would be built. He'd close some of the highways. Instead of overpasses a couple of hundred yards wide, he'd bury a mile-long stretch of highway every five miles. He'd spend a pile of cash, buying privately owned developments and closing them. And he would stand on the park border and force changes and rehabilitation outside the park "so we could start managing the thing as an ecosystem. You have to have the idea that this is not an island. It can't function by itself. When you combine everything that's going on in the park with everything that's going on around, my gosh, it's just closing in. It's imploding. Road densities, continued development, the expansion of the oil and gas activities, the big mine they're going to build just out of Jasper Park."

But what would really happen if he became king? If he really had the power to make major changes in the way man and beast live in and around his nation's premiere park?

"I'd probably be lynched on the streets in downtown Banff, just for saying it."

— ⁓ —

Survey after survey shows Banff National Park, as it now exists, is not the type of park Canadians want. They prefer things a little more wild, natural, and affordable, places with bears in the woods. So how did all this happen in a place where, since 1930, protection of nature has had legal priority over development of commerce? The 1996 task force report, dominated by academics from Calgary and Edmonton, answered in soft language. It blamed "inconsistent application" of law and "weak political will in the face of a range of interest-based lobbying" and "a long and tangled history of ad hoc decisions."

Horejsi calls that caving in to the speculators and money-grubbers.

"The commercial and tourist lobby in Banff is exceptionally powerful," he says.

He blames a weak central government addicted to tax revenues—Banff generates $230 million a year in taxes (it's now $500 million, as of 2011)—and a system where the momentum belongs to the developers. Also, when government and business combine to make bad decisions, there isn't much average Canadians can do about it, he says, because the country offers limited access to the courts when people want to act on behalf of animals.

But what can be done about it now?

Bring wildfires and floods back to the park, the task force said. Shrink, relocate, or shut down some facilities. Stop stocking exotic fish. Close some roads. Limit hiking and climbing. Make businesses pay more for the privilege of a captive market. And make sure there is adequate funding to do the job right.

Horejsi maintains the suggestions don't go far enough, but even these were about as popular as cockroaches in Alberta, a friendly, conservative place with a strong oil- and gas-based economy and little tolerance for federal interference in business. The task force, again in soft understatement, predicts "constant political tension."

Meanwhile, the Parks Canada budget has been slashed.

Trying to restore ecological order to Banff will be incredibly difficult and expensive, the task force agreed, and some people will find the process "draconian," but the issue is too important to ignore.

"If this crisis is not resolved in Banff, it will spread throughout the entire national park system," the task force said. "We must find the political will to act decisively in the interest of all Canadians."

Americans would do well to pay attention.

The problems at Banff may dwarf the problems at Yellowstone or Yosemite, but the Canadians are arguing about issues similar to ones that polarize people surrounding American parks. Are bison a boon or a pestilence? Does Yellowstone Park owe you the opportunity to make a living renting snowmobiles just because you live next door? Should a national park be a playground or a preserve? It's the nation's park. How big a voice should locals have in its management? How many people and cars should be allowed through the gate?

When the task force began its work, it looked for help from the people who run parks in the United States and Australia. It didn't find much.

"These managers often look to the Canadian system for answers to their own problems," the report said.

South of the long, friendly border, bear advocates in the United States often look north, especially when they need a little help augmenting their own populations of animals such as wolves and grizzly bears. So far Canadians have cooperated generously. Horejsi advises Americans to focus on their own backyard. Don't look to Canada for solutions, he says, because the problems there are as big as they are in the United States.

❧

Other people involved in the debate over the future of Banff may lack Horejsi's scientific training, but they are just as passionate about the issues, including some who live and work in the town of Banff.

Leslie Taylor is the former mayor of the town and an advocate of capping growth sooner rather than later. She understands that keeping a population of wild grizzlies means saying no to a variety of people. Not surprisingly, she isn't mayor anymore. But she understands both her community and her surroundings. And she wants to make sure bears can survive.

"It would be more relaxing to go hiking if there were no grizzlies, and I'd probably sleep better in the tent," she says. "But there would be something missing. It would be like the difference between touring the castles in Europe, where people actually lived, and touring a castle in Disneyland."

Disneyland is a swell resort. It makes a lot of money, and it's a safe place to sleep.

But it's not a national park.

POSTSCRIPT

Brian Horejsi's predicted failure of the wildlife crossings didn't come true, exactly. By 2009 graduate student Mike Sawaya had documented eleven grizzly bears using the structures, including five females. Deer, elk, and other animals are using them as well. And the Western Transportation Institute has posted an online photograph of a sow grizzly with three cubs using one of the overpasses, raising hopes that bear populations severed by the highway will blend their genes. Encouraged by the apparent success, the Canadian government has built more overpasses and underpasses. Horejsi remains dubious.

"I'm even more skeptical now," he says, and occasional use by a handful of bears does not mean the ecosystem is being stitched together. "These little incidents are being pointed to as an example of how to solve the problems of continually expanding development. If you focus only on the five percent of bears that are using the overpasses, you might think that's pretty good. But what about the other 95 percent?"

And he remains worried about the grizzlies of Banff.

"I'm not optimistic about them," he says. "I don't think you can be. There's no evidence pointing to a light at the end of the tunnel."

Owen Hereford and Andrew Brodie, the two Australians mauled at Lake Louise, sued the Canadian government in 2010, seeking $75,000 apiece. A judge rejected their suit.

Sixteen years after the attack, Algis Povilavicius said it never occurred to him to sue anybody. But it frustrated him that Parks Canada refused to give him any information. They probably feared he would use the information against them in court, he says. Like the others who were attacked, he and his sister had been meticulous about keeping a clean camp, even pouring their pasta water in the toilet.

Tourism growth in Banff has leveled off, so promoters want to bring in more of them with extra attractions such as a via ferrata, which anchors steel rods and cables into cliff faces so people can scale things they couldn't normally tackle. Parks Canada is studying proposals that would allow "adventure" experiences such as nonmotorized hang gliding, kite surfing, and zip lines. Banff already offers dragon boat races and triathlons.

The town of Banff, now with 8,700 "essential" residents but concerned by a lack of tourism growth, is trying to lure well-heeled visitors from China and India. The fear is that without more paying customers infrastructure will suffer. Povilavicius says he has returned to Canada a couple of times and he remains fascinated with bears, worries about them running out of space. But he avoids places such as Banff, worries that the crowds there increase the chances of meeting a "spoiled" bear, like the one that nailed him in his tent.

Meanwhile, politicians still argue over just how big the town should get, and Gordon Stenhouse, one of Alberta's most respected bear biologists, is studying the causes of the "chronic stress" in which Banff's grizzlies live.

Alberta officials have nixed a hunting season on grizzlies for five years in a row, because of low populations all over the province, yet bears continue to die in the park: In the first decade of the twenty-first century, trains alone killed eleven of them.

4

A Bear of a Job

Ann Quarterman spent months pedaling a bicycle through the fetid jungles of Thailand and Malaysia, and that's a lot of work in anybody's book. Combine the intense heat and the bugs, the strange food, questionable water, and indecipherable languages, and it isn't hard to imagine an incredibly bad day every now and then. There were plenty of times when it would have been easy to just quit, to sit down in the shade and wait for the bus. Go to the closest city, the first airport, and get on the next plane back home to the cool green mountains of British Columbia.

But Ann Quarterman didn't do this. Love helped keep the pedals moving but so did a grizzly bear. These are powerful and strange motivators, and you don't often find them together—especially on a bicycle somewhere between Bangkok and Borneo.

❧

Ann traveled across Southeast Asia in 1996, but you could say the trip started in October of 1994, when she and a friend, Christine Bialkowski, drove from their home in Rossland, British Columbia, up to Revelstoke, where Ann was looking for a job. Revelstoke is about as far from the crowds and heat of Thailand as you can get. It's a sprawling railroad and logging town that straddles the Columbia River as it struggles south past the dams and levees that shape its pathway to the sea. The town has claimed a spot between the blue and green of the Monashee and Selkirk mountain ranges and filled it with quiet streets and noisy railroad tracks, with well-kept blue-collar Victorian homes, steep-roofed so the winter snows will slide off, so the damp forest in summer can't take root and move right inside.

The vast and fecund forest there is a living thing. Logging companies, mines, and ski hills have scabbed it up some, but still the forest moves. You see its seeds and roots growing on every flat spot. And every year, in the fall, the bears come to Revelstoke.

Grizzlies came to Revelstoke to forage in the dump until the town finally surrounded it with an electric fence, and they come to town in the fall looking for apples. Late-night party people sometimes bump into them—literally—after the bars close. And one Halloween the trick-or-treaters had to stay home because there were so many bears in town.

Bruce McLellan, a bear specialist for, at that time, British Columbia Forestry, says that in the ten years prior to 1997 120 "problem" grizzlies were taken from town to be shot or relocated. Three hundred black bears were killed in or near the town.

That is the kind of human interference that raises holy hell with a grizzly bear population, that fouls up home ranges and mating patterns and makes mothers desert their cubs. Yet there has never been a mauling in Revelstoke.

"I think we've just been really lucky so far," McLellan says. "It's probably just a matter of time before it happens."

~~~

Ann and Christine came to Revelstoke knowing it was grizzly country. In fact, if there weren't so many bears there, Christine probably would have stayed home.

The two women had been living as a lot of young British Columbians do: catching seasonal jobs, skiing in the winter, enjoying themselves all year. Ann was twenty-eight, tall and rangy. Christine, twenty-five, stands only five feet four inches but is athletic and strong. Both women liked working in the bush, doing outside work that built muscle and attitude. Christine did biological surveys, which means finding and counting animals. Ann cooked in backcountry work camps and lodges. Both had run into bears several times, and neither had any special fear of them.

The quest for work had brought them to Revelstoke. Ann hoped to spend the winter cooking at the Durrand Glacier Chalet, a backcountry lodge that caters to skiers in an idyllic spot tucked between Revelstoke National Park and Glacier National Park. There are two ways to get there if you aren't a paying customer: You can walk fourteen kilometers, or you can wait around for one of the infrequent helicopter flights and hope there will be enough room for you. A friend of Ann's had worked at the chalet the previous winter and advised her to walk to the job interview. It showed initiative, and the owners liked that, Ann's friend said.

It made sense to Ann. Christine wasn't looking for work, but she tagged along for company, for exercise, to see some new country. The trail doesn't get much use, it is prime grizzly habitat, and both women knew it is never a good idea to hike alone in grizzly country.

—∙∽∙—

The morning of October 2, 1994, broke chilly and damp. Driving east from Revelstoke on the Trans-Canada Highway, they found the Woolsey Creek turnoff, where the dirt road hugs the east border of Revelstoke National Park. There's a lot of water in this country and not much flat ground, a combination that means steep canyons and rushing streams, water so fresh off the glacier it's only a few degrees above slush. There was a highway crew working near the turnoff as Ann slowed her Ford Ranger pickup and headed up the old two-track mining and logging road, the kind of route where, if you meet another vehicle, somebody has to back up, maybe for a long way. Carved along the waistline of a steep canyon wall, it climbs steadily through dense green forest. To the left Woolsey Creek tumbles through the rocks a couple hundred feet below. On the right mountains rise almost straight up.

On rainy days like this one—snow in the high country, no doubt, with real winter coming on soon—the mountains often draw the mist to them like a soft shawl, tucking it in close around the collar and shoulders, tight up under the chin. Wolverines live in these cold wet canyons. So do cougars and lynx and grizzly bears. The forest is lush and verdant and thick. It's not very often that you can see very far.

At the end of the road, Ann backed the small pickup into the little parking area and the two women prepared to climb through the steady drizzle, toward the clouds. They had backpacks, rain gear, and some food. They planned to stay overnight at the chalet.

It didn't take long before they found bear scat on the trail. They knew enough about bears to tell it was nutritionally poor, that the bears were feeling the effects of the small berry crop that year. They kept walking, making plenty of noise so they could alert any bears to their presence, especially when they had to hopscotch across the noisy creek. They didn't want any surprises. Signs of human traffic were few, and they briefly lost the trail a couple of times.

About three hours into the hike, after scampering up a small rock face—steep and tricky but not a real challenge—the women stopped at a ridgetop. They had just climbed out of the conifer forest and stood spellbound by what they found. The habitat had changed entirely, from pine and fir trees to dense brush and small, scattered deciduous trees, each one sparkling with a different color and shining with wetness. It was the kind of scene you expect in Ontario, not in British Columbia. Christine remembers brilliant red leaves highlighting the rest of the colors.

They admired the view for a few minutes, then started walking down into the panorama.

That's when they saw the bears, a sow with two cubs just a few months old. The women felt no particular alarm. They had both seen lots of bears, and these animals were three hundred meters away. Ann saw them first.

"Look," she said. "Bears."

"At first all we could see were brown dots," Christine recalls. "A couple seconds later, we did a double take. Those brown dots were charging us."

The women yelled at the sow. They waved their arms and did everything they could to make her aware of them, trying to make her realize they were human, that they were neither food nor enemy.

"She didn't flinch. Nothing. She stayed focused on us," Ann recalls.

As the bears came closer, Christine bolted momentarily and ran a few steps. Ann told her not to run, and Christine slowed to a fast walk. By then Ann was right there with her, moving fast. This bear looked serious and getting out of its way seemed like an excellent idea. There were no nearby trees big enough to climb, but the women wanted to get behind a small ridge, to at least be out of the bear's line of sight. Maybe that would make her stop.

"We dropped behind the little rise and couldn't see her any more," Ann says. "Neither of us really thought she was going to do anything, but I thought I'd better get ready, so I got my pepper spray out.

"I turned a little bit, and her head popped up over the rise, about twenty-five feet away. So I just stood there, with the safety off my bear spray, ready, knowing I had one good chance."

The bear charged fast, running over the rise that divided her from the women and lunging upward on her hind legs when she was about four feet away.

"That's when I sprayed her, full face."

But the spray didn't act the way it should have. Designed to blast a thick fog of fiery pepper, it spat only a thin dribble. The can was at least three or four years old, possibly past its expiration date. So it didn't stop the bear.

Instead, it dropped to all fours and ran past Ann. Her immediate reaction was relief. She thought the spray had worked. But then, before a sigh could pass her lips, she turned and saw what the bear was doing to her friend.

"The bear just picked her up by the left elbow and started shaking her as if she were a rag doll. I knew I had to do something. It was just total instinct. I ran over and sprayed the bear again, while she was biting Christine."

"She was throwing me around like a dog would," Christine says. When Ann sprayed her, "she threw me into a small tree."

That was good for Christine but not so good for Ann. Despite the face full of fiery red pepper, the bear turned again to Ann, grabbing her first by the right arm and biting down several times, her teeth reaching the bone but not breaking it, shredding the flesh on biceps, triceps, and forearm.

"We were kind of wrestling on the ground; I was trying to get my arm out of her mouth, and I did. But she bit it again."

Ann tried the pepper spray again. The can was empty, and she thought surely the jig was up.

"I thought I was going to die."

The bear carried a horrible stench, a foul combination of wet dog and rotten meat, of filthy hamster cage and musk and musty decay. "Only ten times worse," Ann says.

She told herself she had to quit fighting and play dead, so she rolled onto her stomach. The bear grabbed her arm, rolled her back over, and let go. Ann rolled onto her stomach again, and the bear sank its teeth first into one side of her torso and then into the other. Ann's backpack deflected some of the damage, but the bites were still hard, the jagged teeth punching holes and making bruises.

Then the bear used its claws, the tools that can rip apart a tree trunk, dig up a ground squirrel, or shatter the ribs on a bull elk.

"She scalped me with her paw. One swipe of her paw."

The wound began at her left temple, no more than an inch from her eye. The claws raked across the top of her head almost all the way to her right ear, severing her scalp from her skull, from the brow back. Ann was screaming throughout the attack, even while she thought she was playing dead. At some point she realized she had to quit screaming if she wanted the bear to think she was dead.

Ann laughs when she tells that part of the story. So silly. But she wasn't laughing then. She thought her life was over.

But Christine wasn't out of the fight yet.

"The bear was chewing on her arm and had swatted her on the head," Christine says. "In my mind neither of us had anything to lose. I thought we were both goners, and that's when I found myself kicking it in the head. I think I kicked so hard that I landed on my back."

So the bear started chewing on Christine again. It bit down hard on her lower left leg, but she kept kicking, fighting back. Finally, she curled up her leg and kicked straight out, as hard and fast as she could, the bottom of her hiking shoe catching the bear on the end of the snout.

That got the bear's attention, made it hop to the side and quit trying to immobilize the fast, strong legs. Then it sank its teeth into Christine one last time, biting the side of her hip. It didn't shake its head, it didn't chew, it didn't rip away the flesh. It just bit once, released her, and ran away.

Much more quickly than it had begun, the attack was over. The bear was gone.

———

After a moment Christine rose and came to Ann, just a few paces away. "Are you okay?" she asked. "How bad is it?"

Ann didn't know where the bear had gone and was concentrating on playing dead. She tried to explain this to Christine, but it came out all wrong.

"I'm dead," she said. "I'm dead."

She laughs now about that part of the story, too. Ann Quarterman laughs at her own mistakes quite a bit.

It's hard to say how long the attack lasted. A minute or two, perhaps, maybe more, probably less. That's a long time, as bear attacks go. They usually start and finish in a flash. The attack also was unusual in that it gave the women plenty of time to prepare for it. They saw the bear coming from three hundred meters away. They had time to move fifty meters. They had time to get the bear spray out, get it ready, and use it. They did everything they could to avoid the attack, but the bear kept coming.

They have often puzzled over why. So have others.

"We all stood there and wondered why a bear charged from that sort of distance," says J. P. Kors, a bear management specialist for Parks Canada. "It's like the weather. It's hard to predict."

Clearly, unless the women vastly misjudged the distance when they first saw the bear, it was not a surprise encounter. The bear almost certainly saw them first, ignored their attempts to defuse the situation, and came after them.

It was a poor year for natural foods, the bears were hyperphagic, and a black bear had been seen in the same area a few days before. Perhaps the grizzly had been defending its meager food sources from the black bear and treated the two women as the same type of interloper. Perhaps the bear had bad eyesight. Maybe it had a carcass stashed nearby.

"Maybe she was just naturally an aggressive bear," Ann says. "We really don't know for sure. I don't believe she wanted to kill us, because if she had we would not be here today. She was telling us to get out of her territory. Which we did, gladly."

Christine agrees. "She just wanted to turn us around."

Getting away was no easy job.

Both women were badly hurt. Ann's head was bleeding hard. So was her right arm. Christine's arm and hip were pouring blood, too, and both women were bruised and battered and torn. It was raining. They needed help, and there was nobody around but them.

Ann wrapped a shirt around her head to staunch the bleeding, pulled the first-aid kit from her pack, and bandaged the worst of their wounds. They felt no pain—that would come later—and argued briefly about which way to go.

They were about halfway between Ann's truck and the chalet, but the chalet was uphill, and getting there meant crossing a glacier in bad weather. Once there, a helicopter would have to be summoned to take them to a hospital. Walking back to the truck seemed a simple, logical choice. But there was a big problem with that option: The bear had gone in that direction.

After the attack the bear had run downhill, meaning that somewhere between the two women and their best source of help was a mother grizzly with the taste of their blood in her mouth.

"That was our big fear, that the bear was down the creek and waiting," Ann says.

"Or that another bear would be there," Christine adds. There were almost definitely other bears around, all of them likely to be hungry and crabby.

"That was not the only grizzly in that valley," says Kors. "I can say that pretty much unequivocally. It's not a huge area, and we have known there to be up to eight grizzlies in there at one time."

But they started walking toward the truck anyway. It made the most sense. Each had an arm in a sling and the stench of the bear traveled with them. It permeated their clothes and skin and hair. They would smell it for weeks whenever they used that clothing.

The women shouted out. They sang the A&W Root Beer theme song. They talked about the symptoms of shock. They vowed never to go to the backcountry again. Then they changed their minds. They vowed to live forever and do whatever they wanted, wherever they wanted. They talked and talked, and sometimes they wondered if they would make it. Ann fell once, hard, and the bandage slipped from her head. She asked Christine to pass her love to her sister. Most of the trail was downhill, but there were a few little rises, and the uphill stretches were brutal. They wondered what they should do if one of them collapsed and could go no farther. They would spend the night together, they decided. Nobody would spend the night on the mountain alone. Nobody would be abandoned here.

"This woman came after that bear when it was attacking me," Christine says of Ann. And Christine did the same thing for Ann, armed only with her size-seven shoes and the knowledge that her legs were the strongest part of her.

"We decided to stick together."

It took three hours, but the women made it. Reaching the truck was a milestone, but it wasn't the end of the road. Ann bent to lock the hubs on her truck and engage the four-wheel drive for the treacherous drive out. She was wearing a raincoat, and blood had pooled in the sleeve. Bending over sent a torrent of blood gushing to the ground.

She had been hurt and bleeding for a long time, probably in shock. Now she freaked out. The big puddle of blood spelled out how serious things had become. It was three hours after the attack, and she was still bleeding hard. Five miles of soggy dirt road lay ahead of them. The truck had a stick shift, which means you need two functional hands to drive it, and that is something neither woman had at the time.

So they tackled the job together. Christine operated the steering wheel and the pedals. When she pressed the clutch with her mangled left leg, Ann used her left arm, the good one, to shift gears.

The Woolsey Creek road is an unforgiving one. On the uphill side a little drainage ditch separates the road from the mountain. This is good erosion control, but it makes an easy place to get stuck if you drift into it. On the downhill side there is thick timber growing on the almost sheer face. If you went off the road here, a tree probably would stop you before you hit the creek two hundred feet below. But that is little comfort when you gaze over the edge, still bleeding, knowing you need help and need it soon. There is very little room for error on this road. There are switchbacks and hairpin curves, places where you have to stop and back up to make it around the corner. There are places where the shoulder has crumbled away.

━◆━

When Ann and Christine got close to the highway, they remembered the work crew they had seen earlier. Would the workers still be there? If not, could they double-team the truck to the hospital in Revelstoke, twenty miles and a mountain pass away?

Then they saw a man running a chain saw. He had his back turned and couldn't hear their truck pull up. What would he say when they told him they'd been mauled by a bear? Would he believe them?

There wasn't much problem with that. Ann's face was caked with drying blood. "I looked like I was wearing a mud pack."

The man with the saw took one look at the women, turned white, and ran for help. The road crew was still nearby, and they radioed for an ambulance. Then they approached the women.

"We just started crying," Ann recalls. "Because, up until then, we really had to keep it together to survive. Once we found people to take care of us, we just kind of lost it."

The radio message for help had been garbled, leaving the impression that somebody on the work crew had been mauled, that a dangerous bear was still close by. Wardens from Parks Canada showed up. Conservation officers from the British Columbia government. The Royal Canadian Mounted Police. Most of them were armed, thinking they were going to have to kill a bear.

One of the men—Ann isn't sure who—asked her if she wanted them to hunt down the grizzly bear and kill it.

"We said no. She was just following her instincts. We were in her territory, in her house, basically. I couldn't really have any bad feelings toward the bear."

And then they were in the ambulance, heading toward a hospital where a young doctor who had recently trained in an inner-city emergency room went to work on them. Using the suture techniques he had practiced on flesh torn by knives and bullets and jagged metal, he put the two women back together. He reattached Ann's scalp, didn't even have to shave her head, and the hair remained thick and shiny. He gave her a sedative when she hallucinated, when she thought she saw the bear in the hospital. Then the adrenaline ebbed, and the pain and the stiffness set in.

"We felt like we'd been hit by a Mack truck," Ann says. Reporters kept calling. A TV crew wouldn't take no for an answer and reduced the women to tears once again.

Then a visitor came. It was the woman who owned the chalet. A helicopter had flown there to deliver the bad news, and the woman had a question.

"Do you still want the job?" she asked.

Ann said she'd have to think about it.

~⌒~

She didn't think long, though. Out of the hospital in a few days, the two women and their dozens of stitches went back home to Rossland, an old mining town just over the American border from Washington State.

Christine went back to work counting ungulates, but Ann concentrated on healing before she started the job at the chalet just after Christmas that year, flying in on a helicopter this time and working a schedule of three weeks on and one week off. There, during her third week of work, she met Keith Robine, a tall, dark-haired teacher from Colorado who was skiing the Canadian Rockies. The crowd was small that week, and Keith and Ann had time to talk. Then they kept up the conversation during Ann's week off.

"I had the week off, and Keith was just traveling around. . . ."

"By the end of the second week, we knew," Keith says. "We were pretty much committed at that point."

Later Keith moved to Canada, and they traveled together to the Far East, where they made the bicycle trip, and where Ann learned that she had redefined what makes a bad day. "Some days were just really tough," she says. "But it wasn't really anything compared to what I'd been through with the bear."

Ann says being mauled by a bear brought out a lot of good things in her. She is stronger now, and she understands that strength. The mauling made her adjust her priorities and focus on what is important. And it may be what made her relationship with Keith possible.

"The bear attack put me in a place where I was ready to be in a committed relationship, and where I met Keith."

Christine, too, is stronger because of the attack.

"It's changed my way of thinking quite a bit," she says. "Life is rich, and life could be very short. I'm much better at rolling with the punches now."

Christine and Ann both remain strong supporters of letting bears be bears. And that means teaching people to respect both the bears and their habitat. In parts of southern British Columbia, bears are so common that people often tend to disregard them, Ann says, so both women have talked to groups of schoolchildren, showing their scars and warning them that bears can be dangerous.

"It's easy to get complacent about bears," Ann says, "especially when you live in a place like this. You go for years and years and years, and nothing happens even though you see bears all over town. I think it's good to give a reminder that bears are powerful and that they can hurt you and they can kill you. Respect them."

They tell the kids about simple things they can do to keep bears out of town, to save their own lives and that of the bear: pick up apples as soon as they fall from the tree; put the garbage out in the morning instead of the night before the truck arrives. And be careful. Give the bears room.

Biologist McLellan says that is the kind of message people need to hear if they want to keep a healthy bear population in such places as Revelstoke.

"Changing human culture is what we're really asking for," he says, even if it's as small a thing as taking out a fruit tree that your father planted.

Capturing and moving "problem" bears, the ones that wander into town, is becoming less and less attractive as an alternative, he says. Road building and logging continue to grow in British Columbia, and that means there are fewer and fewer places to put bears where they won't just get into trouble again.

"I have a feeling we're going to be doing more killing than we used to," he says.

Ann and Christine both remain happy that the bear that mauled them was left undisturbed. They say the experience gave them an increased faith in bear spray, even though the bear continued mauling them after she was sprayed.

"I think she left a lot quicker than she would have if we hadn't sprayed her," Christine says.

Ann says if she ever were attacked again, she would play dead first, then use bear spray only if the bear kept chewing. Christine has read a lot about bear attacks since she was mauled. She says she's glad she didn't read about them before the attack, didn't read all the advice about playing dead; she's glad that she fought the bear, even if doing so fetched her some nasty extra wounds.

She wonders about some of their choices, though.

The women left all their food at the scene of the attack. It wasn't an easy decision to make. All their backwoods training told them to pack out their mess, but they didn't want to smell like bait. Still, they didn't want to leave the bear a food reward, to teach it that aggressiveness pays off in peanut butter.

Self-preservation won out. They left the food on the ground. Christine left her backpack as well.

A friend of Christine's walked the same trail the next year and found a water bottle, Christine's pack, and the empty pepper spray bottle, all bearing the teeth marks of a bear or some other large animal.

J. P. Kors, the bear warden for the nearby national parks, says deciding whether to leave the food was a tough call.

"Who am I to comment on what people should or should not have done?" he offers. "You can argue both sides of it."

~ ~

A few months after the attack, Ann and Christine lost touch with each other for a while. Christine left Rossland and moved to Nelson, a relative metropolis about an hour away. Both traveled overseas, found new jobs and new relationships. Life moved on, the women didn't see each other for a year and a half, and the bear attack shifted to the mental back shelf, became something you cannot throw away but you can put into storage. You still own it, but you don't look at it every day.

Then Christine found herself in the hospital again, in the fall of 1997. She was awaiting some minor surgery in a hospital in Trail, British Columbia, just a few miles from Rossland, and was thinking hard about Ann. She hadn't been in a hospital since the two had shared a room in Revelstoke.

Then, outside the room, Ann walked right by the door. She was working her new job in the hospital's kitchen. She caught a glimpse of the small woman lying on the bed inside. Could that be Christine?

It was.

The women embraced, caught up. They had saved each other's lives, and they wanted to know what had happened with those lives. Ann was to marry Keith in two weeks. Would Christine come to the wedding?

"I was thinking of her at that very moment when she walked past my door," Christine says. "Regardless of what happens, we still have a link. I think we'll keep on connecting at important times of our lives."

~ ~

Ann Quarterman and Keith Robine married on September 27, 1997, not quite three years after the attack.

"It was everything we wanted and more," Ann says.

The weather was a little dicey for an outdoor ceremony in their yard, and the clouds pulled wary eyes skyward. But then, as the ceremony started the clouds broke, and the sun shone down on Keith and Ann and all their friends. Christine was there, too, smiling and smiling with everybody else.

POSTSCRIPT

Ann Quarterman and Keith Robine remain married and are the parents of two young girls. They built a new home and remain in Rossland, where Ann worked a few years as part of the town's Bear Aware program, which teaches people how to live safely among bears, how to manage or remove the garbage and apples and other things that can attract bears. Now she runs children's programs at a ski resort.

Though she's still missing some muscle from one arm, the grizzly attack on Woolsey Creek didn't etch into her too deeply until after the birth of her second child, in 2002. The physical stress of that event helped things bubble up and trigger some post-traumatic reactions, a phenomenon that left her in a "constant state of fight or flight." But counseling helped with that, and she's fine now, and she doesn't spend a lot of time puzzling over the attack.

"We were just in the wrong place at the wrong time," she says now.

And she still lives among bears, though mostly black bears.

"They're in our yard all the time," she says.

Christine Bialkowski says the bear attack hasn't changed what she does in the woods, though motherhood and a new career as a physiotherapist keep her at home in Nelson more often. But the attack did change how she prepares for a hike, a ski, a bike ride. She brings a first-aid kit, keeps her eyes open, doesn't go alone, discourages others from doing so. She carries pepper spray. "Accidents happen, even to you," she says. That's the lesson from the attack.

She's a little philosophical about it. If something terrible was destined for her, "then I'm glad it was a bear. If it was a human attack in an inner city, you'd have no idea what their motives were. Then you have to live among people afterwards."

The two women still see each other, though less often as the years pass. Life brought them good things: new careers, children, mates. They're busy. They're fine.

The town of Revelstoke is now a better place for bears and people, according to biologist Bruce McLellan. The town organized its kids to help find abandoned fruit trees, the kind nobody had pruned or tended for decades, that produced woody fruit that people didn't want but bears devoured. Most of those trees are gone now. And people do a better job with their garbage.

In the backcountry "the overall (grizzly) population is doing pretty well," McLellan says. That's mostly because the country is so rough that few people venture into it. While hunters nail a few bears illegally, and most of those shootings go unreported, more and more people are willing to do what it takes to live with bears.

"A new generation is coming in that is more aware, more willing to listen, more caring" about bears, he says. "It's a cultural change. People in Revelstoke are happy to live there. They're very proud of their mountain home."

5

In the Box

ROLLIN BRADEN HAS A CARDBOARD BOX AT HOME, ONE THAT HE DOESN'T open all that often.

It's got some power inside and some strong memories: grizzly bear teeth, a mashed watch, a busted compass. A piece of his scalp, pickled in a jar. Some gory pictures. A ragged handkerchief.

Braden lives in Soldotna, a busy little town on Alaska's Kenai Peninsula, a place defined by fish and bears, glaciers and ocean, rivers and moose.

Braden is a wiry man with a lot of determination. He started his own business—an auto parts store—when he was nineteen years old, and by the time he reached his early forties, he was thinking about partial retirement. He's got all the toys to help take advantage of Alaska's prodigious hunting and fishing: a cabin on the Kenai River with a private fishing hole right there, four-wheelers, snowmobiles, horses.

Braden loves to hunt, but there are things he doesn't do anymore. He doesn't go into the thick brush alone. He doesn't sneak around in the woods much. He's gotten pretty good with a moose call. These days, he much prefers to let the moose come to him.

—◆—

Alaska has about forty thousand grizzly bears. It's also got a lot of people who spend a lot of time in the bush. That's why most people live there. They like to hunt, fish, hike, climb, or just get away from people. And then there are the tourists, lining up elbow to elbow on the salmon streams, hiking the trails, and camping on every sort of flat spot they can find.

It's amazing, when you think about the numbers, that bear attacks aren't more common. Drive around the Kenai, and you find overflowing dumpsters and sandwich shops set up in travel trailers, with barrels of fetid refuse out back. People clean fish in the crowded campgrounds. They feed bears. They leave pet food outside. They make dirty camps.

In places like Yellowstone or Glacier National Park, where grizzlies are almost always at least a little hungry, these things would be bear magnets, drawing hungry bruins from many miles. But in the Kenai the bears are fat and life is easy. The grizzlies here—referred to as browns when they live this close to the ocean—get huge, up to a thousand pounds, fattening up on the abundant berries and the incredible runs of salmon. Alaska and bears were made for each other. For several months in the summer, Alaska explodes with life in the twenty-hour days of sunshine. Fish, plants, and animals grow like crazy. Then come winter, the country shuts down. It's dark and it's frozen and people often get a little nutty. But not the bears. The bears don't go nuts. They just go to sleep for a few months, and when they wake up, the season of abundance is at hand again.

The attraction of rank garbage and dog chow and bird feeders usually can't compare with fat-rich salmon, especially when the unnatural foods are usually associated with people, who, from a bear's point of view, are dangerous.

Still, in Alaska, when it comes to grizzly bears, lots of people just don't screw around. Thousands of people are armed every time they go into the woods. Fishermen pack shotguns or pistols. Campers lug big-bore rifles. And for many of these people, if a grizzly acts the least bit aggressive, or even if it is only trespassing, they start shooting.

Between 1900 and 1996 there have been only 144 grizzly bear attacks in Alaska serious enough to require hospitalization, according to state epidemiologist Dr. John Middaugh. Only twenty-one of those people died. By comparison, Alaskan dogs killed almost twice as many people in half as many years.

Dogs, mostly sled dogs, have killed thirty-six people since 1939, which is as far back as the records go.

Still, Alaskan bears can be dangerous, especially the small proportion of grizzlies that has learned to associate people with food. And when you push those bears, even unintentionally, the consequences can be awful.

Rollin Braden was moose hunting on September 19, 1984, in the Caribou Hills in the southern part of the peninsula. He and his family had hunted there for years and, like dozens of other Alaskans, had built a hunting shack on public land there, partly to provide a little protection from bears.

The hunt had gone well for everybody but Rollin. His brother and his father had bagged their moose a couple of days earlier, and his hunting partner, Darrell Rosin, had killed a bull about five o'clock that afternoon. A little anxiousness on Rollin's part is easy to understand. Moose season would close the next day, and Rollin hadn't gotten his animal. It had been a good hunt, with lots of good company and laughs. But Rollin had other things on his mind, too.

Halfway through the weeklong hunt, he had had to drive a four-wheeler back to the truck, then take the truck to town so he could appear in court and finalize his divorce. That's the kind of mental shift that can take the edge off your concentration when you return to the bush.

Rollin helped Darrell field-dress and skin his moose, and the two were walking on the trail back to camp when they heard noise in the thick brush. They stopped and listened. Twigs snapped. Branches moved. Darkness was coming on fast under the gray sky, and it had been raining. Water dripped from the branches.

"That's my bull," Rollin said.

So he took off into the brush, moving slow and soft, "Indianing," he called it, trying to get a good look at the moose before it saw him and spooked. He kept up the excruciating pace for about fifteen minutes, moving less than one hundred yards as he practiced the hunter's gait of one baby step followed by a good look around, baby step and a good look around.

"I would walk for a ways, hear the noise, and walk that direction. Then I would stop and listen and hear it in another direction. Then I would go that direction."

Finally, he stepped around a tall spruce tree and the world changed.

"The first thing I saw was two brown bears, charging at me at full speed."

Braden was packing a .338 Magnum, a gun big enough to knock down anything in North America. He stepped around the tree, swung the gun from his waist, and pointed it at the bears, which were still coming.

"They were blowing: whoosh, whoosh, whoosh, coming fast around the tree. The moss and dirt were just flying from their feet."

When they got within fifteen feet, Braden pulled the trigger.

"I missed. They didn't even flinch."

Braden made a partial turn and the bears hit him in the back, knocking him to the ground.

"I was thinking there's some areas I've got to protect," he says. "I was laid straight out. My hands were up along the side of my face. I was trying to keep them from getting their canine teeth into my eyeball socket or my ear.

"They were biting anything that moved. If I tried to resist in any way, move my arm or my leg, they'd bite it. So I decided I'd better not move. I'd better just lie there still."

There was a three-hundred-pound grizzly on either side of him, one at his head and one near his feet, and their bites came all over, in the legs and arms and back. There was a bad one on his butt.

"They bit me in the head a lot. They weren't adult bears. Their mouths weren't big enough to fit around the circumference of my head. So they would just bite, and when they closed their jaw, it would just rip the scalp. They did that four or five times on the back of my head. They would hit, and then their teeth would just scrape."

One bite crushed the crystal on his watch, halting the hands at 7:33 p.m.

"I had a compass in my pocket, one of the liquid-filled ones. They bit through that and busted it. I had a handkerchief wadded up in my back pocket. Later on when I unfolded it, it was just all full of holes. I was wearing a black-and-white wool plaid shirt that had belonged to my grandfather. It was kind of my special hunting shirt. It got ripped up pretty bad."

Other than a few grunts, the kind that come with exertion, the bears made no sounds. Braden noticed no odor, but he worried that the bears would start fighting over him, turn him into the rope in a game of tug-of-war. He thought about his children; he wondered if the bears would kill him. And he thought about trying to lie still while bear teeth raked his head and body.

"I was pretty much focused on just surviving and getting through it somehow. I was trying not to move and to protect my face. I was worried about my ears. Anything they could have hooked on to and pulled could have been pretty disastrous. I thought that at the time. I think I was very alert through the whole thing, but I didn't feel a lot of pain while they were ripping my head up. I didn't feel like screaming out with pain."

Then the attack stopped. The bears backed off. Braden raised his head and saw them standing together about ten feet away.

"Just standing there and looking at me. And when our eyes met, they came right back and chewed on me some more. I told myself, if they ever quit chewing on me again, I was just going to lie there for a few minutes and give them time to move off."

And that's what happened.

When Braden raised his head again, a big piece of his scalp was hanging over his right eye and there was blood in both eyes.

"So I put my scalp back up and was wiping the blood out of my eyes so I could see."

He got to his knees and still could see no bears.

He stood. Still no bears.

He took his shirt off and wrapped it around his head.

"I was trying to hold my head together, because I didn't know at that point whether my skull was broke or not. Cause it sounded like it was breaking when their teeth would hit it and scrape along it.

"I made four or five steps backward and realized maybe I'm not going in the right direction. I wanted to go back to where my partner was, and at the same time I sure didn't want to bump into these bears again, wherever they were."

"I hollered for Darrell. No answer. Then I hollered again. I hollered a third time, as loud as I could, and he yelled back. Then I knew I was going in the right direction."

Rosin, sensing trouble, walked into the woods and found his friend.

"I told him I just got chewed up by two bears. I said, 'I've got to get to town. I've lost a lot of blood, and I hope I can make it.'"

The attack didn't last long. Maybe thirty seconds from the time he first saw the bears until they stopped chewing on him the first time. The second attack was even more brief, Braden said. But getting from an isolated hunting camp to a competent surgeon was an adventure in itself.

"It was kind of a fiasco," Braden says.

He and Rosin walked and jogged back to the shack. On the way they found his brother, who had just returned from a spaghetti dinner at another camp.

"I took my shirt off my head and boy, they turned white," he says of his brother and his friend. "Probably ten minutes later my dad shows up. He couldn't hardly speak and didn't know what to say."

Then things started happening.

"We wrapped a bath towel around my head, and I put on a winter parka with a hood. It was getting kind of cold."

The hunting party had come in on all-terrain vehicles pulling gear in trailers. Braden's brother's machine wasn't there, so he used Rollin's, an outfit he hadn't driven before, to go get a trailer, traveling through the darkness by then. On the way back, excited and moving fast, he busted a trailer axle.

Another trailer had to be rounded up. A foam pad was laid in the bed for Rollin, while his dad and brother rode the ATV.

After breaking one axle, Rollin's brother knew he had to slow down with the second trailer if they were going to make it to the truck. The trip took an hour, but they made it over the logs and through the bog holes that could easily stall a vehicle.

Rollin says the pain still wasn't too severe except for his wounded butt, which bounced on a can of Copenhagen all the way to the truck.

Which had a flat tire.

Then once in the village of Ninilchick, local rescue workers put him in the back of an old Suburban being used as an ambulance, a vehicle icy cold on the inside, and three women stripped off his clothes.

"They got me down to my underwear, and I just started shaking. I was freezing."

About halfway to Soldotna a real ambulance met the Suburban and took Rollin back to the closest hospital. But no doctor would touch him.

"It was like, if this guy's been chewed on by a bear, he's got lots of infection and needs to go to Anchorage."

Airplanes are almost as common as cars in parts of Alaska, and a local company had a contract to fly all medical evacuations to Anchorage. But nobody at that company could be reached, so a plane had to come from Anchorage to get him.

"So I sat in Soldotna for three hours, waiting."

It took five hours to get Rollin Braden from the scene of the attack to a surgical table in Anchorage. It could have been a lot worse, considering the size and isolation of Alaska, but it seems like a long time to a man waiting for help.

Doctors needed more than an hour just to clean the sticks and dirt and dried blood from Braden's skull. It took two hundred stitches and a few weeks of railroad tracks on his head, but his hair came back, and within a few months he carried no outward signs of the grizzly bear attack.

His family returned to the scene of the attack and gathered his gun, his hat, and his binoculars. Rollin's father marked the spot with brightly colored flagging, so it could be found again. One of the party found a piece of Rollin's scalp—about the size of the bottom of a drinking glass—and brought it to Anchorage. That was three days after the attack.

"It was too late to do anything about it. If I'd had it with me at the time, they could have pieced it in. I've got it at home in a jar, in formaldehyde."

Braden turned thirty in the hospital. Tubes connected to a suction sack at his waist ran underneath his scalp and drained the fluids. He stayed there eight days. The worst part was when a doctor, not the one who had put him back together, pulled the tubes from beneath the skin on his head.

"He grabbed my head with one hand and the tubes with the other hand and just pulled. He had a hell of a time getting them out. It just hurt like hell."

Braden now believes the bears that attacked him were three-year-old or four-year-old siblings, recently driven away by their mother. For several years bears had been breaking into hunting camps in the area, being rewarded with food.

Braden believes, and there are plenty of similar cases in all parts of bear country, that the bears had been taught by their mother that cabins were a good source of food, especially late in the year when the fish and berries are gone.

About a year after the attack, two hunters using a nearby cabin returned from a hunt to find the contents of a cooler they had left on their porch strewn all over the yard.

"So they cleaned up the mess, and later that same day, while they were there at camp, these two bears came back. And they shot and killed them both. I never did see the two bears personally, but my dad took pictures of them."

Because of the bears' behavior, the location, and the size of the animals, Braden believes they are the ones that attacked him.

"They were juvenile delinquent bears and were tearing cabins up. And they stayed right in that area."

A skull was left behind. A friend of Braden's later went by and pulled four teeth from it. They are in Braden's cardboard box now.

On the day Braden was mauled, the bears may have been lurking in the area, hoping for an easy meal in one of the cabins. Braden believes they may have been further intrigued by aromas from the carcasses of the three moose his party had killed. When he followed them into the brush, they backed off for a while, moving perhaps a hundred yards as he approached. But there came a point when they would go no farther.

"When I think about it now, what I was doing was pushing these two bears away from these three kills that we had. They wanted to get on the kills and I was pushing them away from them.

"I don't think they thought they were being hunted," Braden says years later. "I think they were just being made to do something they didn't want to do. I pushed them for ten or fifteen minutes, and I think they just decided that they'd gone far enough and were going to stand their ground."

Braden is still an avid hunter, although he prefers a horse to a four-wheeler these days. For a while he dreamed about the attack, but most of the dreams turned out better than the reality did.

"I've dreamed of being charged by four grizzly bears. But I got down on my knee with my rifle, and I shot every one of them before they got me."

Like anybody who knows the Alaska bush, Braden always had a healthy respect for grizzlies and at least a little fear of them.

"But I guess I wasn't quite as afraid of them as I am today. Then, I would go out by myself in the woods, through thick brush. I remember many times just lying down in the middle of a hot afternoon and taking a nap underneath a tree. I don't do that anymore."

He usually takes a large pistol along when he hunts, though he's not positive it would be much help.

In the days before he was attacked, he and his party had often seen fresh grizzly tracks, usually left there during the night. A couple of hours before the attack, while he was in a tree stand, he thought he heard a dog barking in the distance and kept expecting to see a hunter and a dog coming up the trail.

"I never gave it too much thought. I kind of waited for this hunter to come by with his dog, and it never happened. Maybe I should have thought it wasn't a dog and was a bear. They can sound like a dog sometimes. If you're out there and you hear noises you aren't familiar with, grunting or barking or something, you probably need to pay more attention to it."

When he and his girlfriend hunt on horseback, they do a lot of talking back and forth.

"If there's fresh tracks right in front of me and we know there's a bear nearby, we'll start talking louder. We'll just start making noise of some kind. Because we don't want to surprise that thing."

And if he hears noises in the brush, does he investigate?

"Not by myself," he says.

One box full of bear souvenirs is plenty.

POSTSCRIPT

Rollin Braden achieved his dream of an early retirement and that freed up a lot of time to hunt, fish, and trap. But after the attack Rollin Braden made a decision not to hunt alone anymore. He brings his wife, a friend, or a Karelian bear dog.

Bred in Finland to hunt bears and protect people from bear attacks, Karelians are fast, smart, and tenacious. In Montana, biologists use them to teach bears to leave developed areas and stay away, a process called "aversive conditioning."

They also make great companions, Braden says. When he goes to the woods and lies in wait for a moose, he usually has a Karelian on a leash beside him.

"He's definitely more aware than I am all the time," he says. "If there's something nearby, he knows about it. I'm hunting with a dog for protection."

At home the dogs chase moose and bears off his twenty-acre property. In the bush, he says, the dog will provide a few extra seconds of warning, time that can be critical. He carries a .44 Magnum pistol, in case a bear gets past his dog and comes at him. As for bear spray he's not a believer and has never owned a can.

His wife, Susan, breeds Karelians for sale. The breed isn't for everybody, she says. For instance, her website warns that they can and will bark at a squirrel all day long. Braden says they can be pretty rough on cats and chickens, too.

"I've heard her talk people out of buying them," Braden says of his wife. But he's glad he has one of his own.

6

Red Hot Chili Pepper

It had been a pretty good day for Mark Matheny and Dr. Fred Bahnson. There had been no elk so far, but the two men had dropped a nice mule deer buck that morning, each of them putting an arrow in it, up on a high ridge in Montana's spectacular Madison Range north of Yellowstone National Park. It was a nice piece of teamwork.

The two friends felt pretty good, walking down the trail. The buck had been field-dressed and hung in a tree, and they were walking together, talking quietly, keeping an eye and an ear open for one of the bull elk jousting for their harems in the area. But the day was a success even if they didn't find an elk. The two friends planned to come back the next day to pack out the buck's meat and head.

Then about noon Matheny started shouting.

"Bear," he yelled. "Bear."

The grizzly sow and her three cubs had been relaxing about thirty yards above the trail the men were traveling and the meeting was a big surprise for everybody. Both men wore camouflage and they were trying to be quiet, hoping to jump an elk. The sow may have been lying on her back, utterly relaxed and nursing the cubs when the hunters surprised her. But that changed fast. Matheny heard a noise, looked up the hill, and saw baby bears flying through the air as the mother jumped to her feet and charged.

All four of the bears came fast. Bahnson told investigators he remembered seeing a "herd" of them coming at them. Matheny was focused on the big sow in the lead, the one coming at him so incredibly fast.

"I saw her coming and glanced for a tree. I said to Fred, 'Get your spray, it's a bear,' and I backpedaled toward him so he could spray the bear.

But he dove off the trail because he had a homemade leather holster and couldn't get it out very quick."

Matheny dove then, too, clambering over a down log, and spun toward the bear as she lunged at him. He held his long wooden bow in front of him and yelled, "Get out of here." The bear swatted it to the ground with one swipe of a paw and sailed over the log in the same easy motion. Then she bit him on the throat, ripping away his saliva gland and a big piece of jaw muscle. Then she bit again on his face, leaving a gash in his cheek he could stick his tongue through.

"The next thing I knew she had me down on the ground. I've got my head in her mouth and she's crushing my skull."

One tooth punched a hole in his skull, and another scraped a deep, four-inch-long rut across the top of his head. The sound, he says, reverberated through his entire body.

"It felt like she was crushing my skull, and I made one last plea for my life. I said to Fred, 'She's got my head. She's killing me.'"

Then Bahnson charged, armed with his bear spray. He yelled at the bear, she dropped Matheny's head, and he gave her a short burst of the fiery red pepper spray. Right in the face. But it wasn't enough to send her away. Rather, she attacked this new threat.

"The bear just mowed him over," Matheny says. She sank her teeth into Bahnson's back and his right side and knocked the spray from his hand.

"I was scurrying away on all fours and that was probably good because it took her off of Fred. She swapped ends and just pounced on me."

Bahnson wasn't finished, though. He had lost the eyeglasses he needs badly but somehow found the canister of bear spray without them. By then the bear was chewing on Matheny's arm so hard that he thought she would rip it right off, though he had quit struggling by then. Then she let him go, almost gently, and turned toward Bahnson. He emptied the rest of the four-ounce can into her face and the bear ran away, her cubs in pursuit.

"She took off gasping for air and breathing really heavily," Matheny says.

The two men then had to make it another mile back to the trailhead, where somebody took a picture of Matheny, his lacerated skull, his torn jaw and ripped throat, his face covered with blood. When they got to the hospital in Bozeman, Montana, Bahnson, a plastic surgeon who had sewn up a mauling victim before, put off treatment of his own injuries until he put Matheny back together. It took four hours and over one hundred stitches.

The photograph taken at the trailhead would be an important one. It would help put Matheny in the bear spray business and give him a label as the "poster boy" of that highly competitive industry. It's a job he relishes. It was September 25, 1992, and Matheny's life, you see, had just changed forever.

◆─◆

The intense pain lasted for a long time after the attack, and Matheny, at thirty-nine, was losing interest in his prosperous construction business. He knew he had to get his life back together, but it wasn't easy. Part of the job meant returning to the scene of the attack nine days later. He and a friend brought a rifle, a shotgun, a video camera, and more pepper spray.

"It was a terrifying trip back in there. But it was real good for me to do that. I didn't want that bear attack to create an irrational fear of bears. I wanted to get back on the horse that dragged me around and kicked me, so to speak."

His injuries healed eventually. Bahnson had done good work in the emergency room. The scar on his left cheek will always be there, and he's glad to let a visitor run a finger over the dent in the top of his head, the place where the bear took out a piece of skull. For a couple of years, going out in the woods was "nerve-racking," but he's hunting again, although he prefers to do it in places where grizzlies don't live.

"It just taxes me too much. Especially hunting alone. Spending the night up there and stuff. I just don't enjoy it too much."

Hunting has long been a passion for him, but it's taken a back seat to a new obsession: putting as much bear spray as possible into the hands of as many people as possible. He's become an apostle of hot pepper spray. He talks about it all the time. It is his business, his mission, his role in life.

"The spray helped us tremendously in that situation," he says. "We could have been injured a lot worse or maybe killed."

The active ingredient is capsaicin and related capsaicinoids, which are extracts of chili peppers, combined with a propellant and carried in a powerful aerosol can. Police departments around the world have used it for years. Spray it in a violent thug's face, and he finds it hard to see and breathe. The throat constricts, the eyes gush tears, the skin burns like fire.

In most cases it brings a man to his knees as effectively as a nightstick or a gun, lawmen say, and the perpetrator heals up a lot faster. After a couple of hours of misery, he's fine. Recovery from a bullet hole or a busted skull takes a long time, if it happens at all.

The same theory applies to bears, although you need bigger doses of spray. Grizzlies have twice the muscle density of humans, making them twice as strong, pound for pound, as a well-toned man. Also, they're a lot bigger, so it takes more spray to divert them. The better brands of pepper spray are designed to spew a cloud of pepper gas a dozen feet wide and propel it about thirty feet, to create a barrier between you and a charging bear. And as in police work, the spray doesn't kill anybody. The bear goes away upset and in pain, but at least it goes away. That's the theory, anyway. And that's what Matheny is selling.

Shortly after the incident he went to work selling bear spray for a Kalispell, Montana, company called Counter Assault, a pioneer in the bear spray business. But he had a falling out with the company and within months branched out on his own, eventually building a shop behind his rural Montana home and hiring a crew to build holsters, package the pre-filled spray cans, and ship them to retailers around the country. He markets the stuff under the label UDAP, which stands for Universal Defense Alternative Products, a company whose name is also a pun: UDAP. Adapt. Get it? The acronym sounds almost like the word.

"I chose to adapt," Matheny says. "I was ingrained into a traditional gun as a way of defense. You adapt to a new way of defense. UDAP."

Bahnson said shortly after the attack he was glad he didn't have a gun.

"I could have hit Mark or made the bear more furious," he said.

And the bear survived the attack as well. In the Yellowstone area, where grizzlies are protected by the Endangered Species Act, each one is important, especially a breeding-age female such as the one that attacked the hunters that day.

"It was total surprise and motherly instincts," Matheny says of the attack. Neither man blames the bear for what it did. Still, it isn't something they want to live through again.

———

Bow hunters are at particular risk of grizzly encounters. They break all the rules of safe travel in grizzly country. They sneak through the bushes. They wear camouflage and do everything they can to disguise their scent. They stay as quiet as possible. They favor the hours of dawn and dusk. It's a prescription for a surprise encounter, and in the forests around Yellowstone, they run into grizzlies almost every year. In Montana and Wyoming it's legal to carry a handgun while bow hunting, and most who do so choose a .44 Magnum, a hand cannon that will blow a hole through almost anything. Almost every year in the Yellowstone region, a bow hunter kills a charging grizzly with a handgun. And those numbers add up: In 2010 fifty bears died in and around Yellowstone at the hands of humans, many of them by hunters who felt threatened.

But a charge doesn't always mean an attack. Grizzlies often bluff-charge a potential threat, sometimes stopping just a few feet away. Bear advocate and author Doug Peacock says he's been bluff-charged thirty-four times and stood up during all of them. But few people have Peacock's skill or his stones, and for most of us it's hard to tell when a charging bear is bluffing, when the bear intends to cuss you out, and when it means business. It's likely that many of the bears killed in recent years were bluffing. But because they got big bullets instead of pepper spray, nobody will ever know. Those bears won't charge again. Nor will they reproduce. A bullet might teach a lesson, but it's the last one a bear will learn.

Dave Moody, a bear manager for the Wyoming Game and Fish Department, says he's sold on pepper spray. "No doubt about it in my mind," he says. "It's more effective than a gun."

＿＿

Some rifle hunters are beginning to carry pepper spray as well. Perhaps more of them should. Tom Smith, a biologist at Brigham Young University who researched bears in Alaska for sixteen years, analyzed dozens of bear attacks and found that relying on bear spray instead of a gun boosts your chances of going home in one piece.

He took a close look at seventy-two incidents in which people defended themselves with pepper spray against aggressive grizzly, black, and polar bears and published the results in the *Journal of Wildlife Management* in 2008.

Of those bears fifty were grizzlies and eighteen were aggressive toward people before they got a dose of spray. (In the other cases the bears were curious, raiding garbage, or causing other trouble.) In all but two of those cases, "bear spray stopped the bear's aggressive behavior," Smith's study found.

But the spray also prevented serious injury. In one incident the bear charged through the fog but halted three feet from the person with the spray before it ran away. In another case the bear still nailed the person, but the damage was relatively light: some claw marks that needed stitches on one leg. But in every incident the people walked away and so did the bear.

In a previous study Smith found that firearms were effective only 67 percent of the time, and a survey of U.S. Fish and Wildlife Service lawmen has found that, "since 1992, persons encountering grizzlies and defending themselves with firearms suffer injury about 50 percent of the time."

Bears don't go down easy, even with powerful guns, and wounded bears can do a lot of damage.

Hunters often engage in vigorous debates about the merits of bear spray versus firearms. And the right person with the right firearm can often, but not always, kill an attacking bear. People argue about techniques, calibers, and "what if" scenarios. But the debate often misses a crucial point: Hunting involves a lot more than stalking and killing your prey. Once that job is complete, a lot of work remains. The animal must be gutted, processed, and taken from the field, sometimes over great distances. Anybody who's done this with large game, such as elk or moose, knows it can be a backbreaking chore and one you can't do with a rifle or shotgun in your hands.

And there is increasing evidence that grizzly bears are learning to see autumn big game hunts as a buffet of guts, bones, and hides. Usually, bears wait until hunters leave before scarfing their leavings.

But sometimes they don't.

—◆—

On the day before Halloween 2001, Tim Hilston left his Great Falls, Montana, home and drove about one hundred miles to the Blackfoot Clearwater Game Range, a stunning stretch of forest and meadow near Seeley Lake, Montana. It's grizzly country, but Hilston was there for elk. He found the elk first, then the bear found him.

Investigators did their best to piece together what happened: the fifty-year-old hunter probably arrived shortly after dawn and started hiking. Before long, he shot a cow elk, then followed the mortally wounded animal for a few hundred yards. Knowing he would need some help to retrieve the animal, he put out some pink flagging to mark the location so he could find it later. Then he filled out his tag and bent to the heavy task of gutting the five-hundred-pound animal, a task that requires fairly close attention if you're going to do it properly. He didn't know it, but a mother grizzly with two cubs had followed the same blood trail that took Hilston to the carcass. He was busy, and his rifle was a couple of steps away when the 375-pound mother bear decided she wanted the elk. She might have nailed him from behind, or he might have tried to scramble away from her. If so, it didn't work. About twenty feet from the elk carcass, investigators found Hilston's checkbook, all ripped up. They also found shreds of the rubber gloves he'd worn to gut the elk.

The day before, a search-and-rescue team with a tracking dog had found his body, bitten and chewed from head to thighs. He'd made it 130 yards toward his truck before he laid himself down, on his back with his knees bent and his feet on the ground, the position of an exhausted man. That's where his life drained from him. The bears hadn't followed him or consumed any of his body.

Before bending to his labors, Hilston had placed his gun on the ground, where it would be safely away from his messy chore. It was a prudent step, one that conscientious hunters take all the time. But the rifle was too far away to be of any use in a sudden attack. He had no sidearm or bear spray.

It's possible he tried to fight the bear, given that his thin rubber gloves were shredded at the attack scene. If that is the case, a weapon would have helped. A powerful pistol might have saved his life. A can of bear spray on his belt might have done the same. And it might have left the bear with a powerful lesson. Other hunters had seen her eating gut piles earlier in the season, and she was suspected of stealing at least one other carcass. A big dose of red pepper might have taught her to delay such behavior until all the people go away. (Hilston's widow later sued the state of Montana, alleging its practice of disposing of livestock carcasses in the area, well away from people's homes, created an unreasonable risk. The Montana Supreme Court denied her claim.)

Hunters aren't the only people who sneak around in the woods. Some of them are the same people who tell you to sing and clap your hands out there, to travel in groups, to make yourself visible and audible so you don't surprise any bears. Some of the biggest violators of these rules are park rangers, who also have the job of catching poachers in the national parks.

"We preach all this," notes Bundy Phillips, a former ranger in Yellowstone's wildlife-rich Lamar Valley. "But with the job we have, to try to catch the bad guys, we can't do it. We are out in the woods in the fall, crawling from bush to bush, trying to catch poachers in the park."

Phillips and fellow ranger Dave Hubbard were patrolling the backcountry along Yellowstone's eastern border in early October of 1997, keeping an eye on two camps of hunters just outside the park. One party had killed two big bulls about two hundred yards from the border a few days after the season opened, leaving the bones and entrails on the ground. As with the bear that killed Hilston, things like this make irresistible bear bait, especially in the fall when bears are hyperphagic, and the rangers knew it.

"We saw no bear sign whatsoever, but we were still being cautious," Phillips recalls.

On the cold morning of October 7, they were walking toward the carcasses, still some distance away, and facing a stiff wind when Phillips's ears perked up.

"I heard this thundering, it sounded like four or five horses or elk stampeding behind us."

He called to Hubbard and they stepped into some trees, expecting to see a herd of elk run by.

"The next second, two big bears were barreling down on us. They were about a hundred yards away when we first saw them. It looked like probably a sow and a two-year-old. The sow was probably about four hundred pounds, and the two-year-old was about three hundred pounds."

The two rangers were carrying both .45-caliber pistols and large canisters of bear spray. They chose the spray.

"Neither one of us even thought about drawing a weapon. We just hit the bear spray first."

Then the bears were there, charging hard at a slight angle, the bigger bear in the lead. When they got within fifteen feet, the sow veered toward the rangers and came within five feet.

"We both sprayed and she came right directly into the spray. Then she veered off and went back toward the other bear, about thirty feet or so, and came barreling back in on us, within about three feet. We sprayed again, pretty much emptied both of our bear canisters, and she turned and left. Both bears ran away almost as fast as they came in. The whole encounter lasted about ten seconds."

Phillips says he can't say for sure that the spray deflected the charge. He knows the stuff is powerful because his training once required him to take a faceful of it.

"It's just phenomenal. It puts you to your knees right now. And it takes twenty minutes with a full-force hose to get over it."

But did it turn the bears?

When the grizzly charged, it made no sounds. It wasn't snapping its teeth or woofing or growling.

"It looked very intent on getting to us or bluffing us. When it ran into the pepper fog, it looked unaffected." He noticed no sneezing, coughing, or rubbing of the face. But he was also preoccupied.

"We were doing our holy mackerel thing."

But the bears left. They didn't attack, and that's the important part.

"Had we not sprayed, she might have done the same thing. Just bluffed us real close," Phillips says. "That's pretty close for a bluff charge, three to five feet away. But probably not out of the ordinary."

Also, there was a steady wind of at least fifteen miles per hour that day, making it harder to assess the effectiveness of the spray.

Nevertheless, Phillips is glad he had it with him. Clearly, it did no harm and might have saved the rangers a huge amount of pain.

Both of them were almost out of spray by the time the charge was over.

"I had about a spritz left. Dave had about a microdrop."

That knowledge was enough to help the rangers make a decision: It was time to go home. The closest road was twenty-five miles away, through a lot of bear habitat, a hike made longer by the fact the rangers were out of bear spray.

For the rest of his career in the Park Service, whenever Phillips did any more covert work "sneaking around in the bushes," he made sure he had two cans.

❧

As a trained ranger Phillips knows that bear attacks can happen almost without notice anywhere in grizzly country. So he made it a point to keep his bear spray handy all the time, in camp or on the trail, usually wearing it in a holder on his chest where he could grab it in an instant. But most people lack his training, his backcountry lawman's sense of constant wariness. And that's a potential problem with bear spray: Some people think it's brains in a can.

If carrying the spray creates a false sense of security, then it's probably a bad idea, says Dr. Stephen Herrero, a University of Calgary bear specialist who has researched hundreds of bear attacks and coauthored Smith's research paper.

"If a person can still maintain a high level of alertness, of what's going on out there, their actions, the changing habitat, then it's an additional backup," Herrero says. But in all cases paying attention and avoiding an encounter is the best defense.

Smith agrees. Caution and alertness are the best defense, he said. But sometimes, even that isn't enough. And that's when the spray comes in handy. When it spews from the can in a dense orange fog, it makes a considerable whoosh. That alone might be enough to make a bear pause for a second thought.

Some people worry the spray won't work on windy days. Smith says that's probably not a major concern, since most surprise encounters happen in places with dense forest or brush that shed the wind. Also, the spray leaves the can at an average speed of seventy miles per hour.

Others worry that they'll disable themselves with the spray. While that's a possibility—author Mike Lapinski, who is built like a linebacker, was reduced to a snotty, drooling mess when he volunteered to be doused by Mark Matheny—it's a dim one in the field, Smith found. Of all the cases he studied, a few people felt the burn, but nobody was disabled.

And there's one more advantage: While the spray isn't brains in a can, it might provide people with the nerve to stand their ground in the face of a charging bear. Most experts say that is the best response, that running is always the worst thing you can do. While that is hard advice to follow, the spray could act as a spine stiffener.

"When you stop and plant your feet, that makes them stop," Smith says of charging bears.

— ~ —

The bear spray business has become intensely competitive, with a handful of companies all claiming to be the best. The Environmental Protection

Agency regulates the industry, and its website lists approved manufacturers, who must meet standards on how much pepper power the cans pack and how forcefully they shoot. Smith's study was too small to tell if one brand works any better than another, and Chuck Bartlebaugh, executive director of the Center for Wildlife Information, says the differences in various brands aren't great. All of them contain between 1 percent and 2 percent capsaicin and related capsaicinoids.

"The variance in potency is negligible, and all will affect the eyes, nose, throat, and lungs of a bear," Bartlebaugh says.

Use of the spray on a bear remains uncommon—about three times a year in Alaska, Smith found—but if you're going to carry it, know how to use it. Make sure it's on a belt or pack strap where you can grab it in an instant. And pay attention to the expiration date.

When a grizzly attacked mountain biker Kirk Speckhals near Jackson, Wyoming, in 2004, his friend Tom Foley rushed into the fray and doused the bear in the face with bear spray. The bear halted the attack, and Foley believes the spray helped, even though it exited the can in a sputter. But the bear didn't show much reaction. Rather, it stood still, opened its eyes wider, and stared at Foley.

"His head was down, and he was looking at me like he was going to kill me," Foley says of that summer day. When another man and a barking dog showed up, the bear took off.

Only later did the men realize the bear spray was out of date.

"Semieffective" might be a good way to describe the way the spray helped Fred Bahnson and Mark Matheny. Matheny has worked hard to come up with what he calls a better product.

Bahnson had only a four-ounce canister, the kind designed for human predators, that September day in the Madison Range. Matheny markets big ones—including a 7.9-ounce canister and a 13.4-ounce "magnum"—for people worried about bears rather than muggers. And then there are the accessories. He sells a specially designed neoprene holster that keeps the canister from falling out when you bend over but still lets you pull it in a jiffy. If that's not quick enough, it's designed to let you shoot from the hip. And he sells a lot of bear spray, as many as four thousand canisters a week during peak times.

That's where the picture of his bloody wounds gets important, the one taken right after the mauling. It appears on his pamphlets and on his packaging and his Facebook page. A big laminated enlargement of it travels with him to gun shows and trade fairs, where he sells the spray. It appears on the sleeve of a video he helped create, during which he reenacts the mauling for the camera, holding what looks like a stuffed bear head to his throat and screaming as he thrashes on the ground. He shows that picture all over the place, even when people are laughing at him. Gun show patrons are particular skeptics, he says. People stop at his booth and don't recognize the tall, well-groomed man there as the same one so horribly mauled in the picture. His scars healed well. His posters tell people to be prepared.

"Yeah, it helped that guy," the wiseacres quip. "I'll be prepared with my .44."

"I get that response all the time," Matheny says.

⌒

"Capitalize and make some bucks. I guess it's the American way," Kevin Frey, a bear management specialist for the Montana Department of Fish, Wildlife and Parks, says of Matheny. He investigated the Matheny/Bahnson incident and found that the spray may have saved the hunters from worse damage. Or the bear might have decided on its own that it was time to leave, that it had neutralized the threat it thought the men posed to its cubs.

"The big kicker is he quit kicking and fighting," Frey says of Matheny, who played dead when the bear nailed him the second time. "That's when she dropped him."

"It's an alternative protection method," Frey says of bear spray. "It may keep you from getting chewed on. Or it may lessen the severity. But it's not some kind of guaranteed force field."

It could be particularly helpful in situations where a bear approaches, perhaps dances on his front feet, slobbers, or shows some other sign of agitation but hasn't quite decided whether to attack or not.

"If you zing him then, it will damn sure benefit you and probably help the bear in the long run," Frey says.

The memory of the burning spray may help the bear decide, the next time it comes close to a person, to make a hasty retreat.

But judge your distance carefully. It only spews for about thirty feet. You don't want to run out of spray before the bear even enters the danger zone.

The spray is a little like seat belts. They save a lot of people, but they don't save everybody. And they do no good at all if you don't wear them properly.

"I don't think people school themselves" in how to use the spray, Frey says.

They often carry it in a pack, forget it in the car or at camp, or just forget they're wearing it. They don't read the directions, they fail to test the can, they don't remove the safety clip. Frey says bow hunters, in particular, should be able to reach the spray instantly, at all times, without looking at it.

──◦──

According to some reports, some people even think the bear repellent works like mosquito repellent and start rubbing it all over themselves, thinking that will keep bears away. They usually don't do that more than once.

Other people apply the mosquito repellent theory even more broadly, smearing the stuff on their seaplanes and boats and even an outhouse to keep bears away. It doesn't work that way. Tom Smith documented cases in which the spray even acted as an attractant, if used improperly. Infamous grizzly advocate Timothy Treadwell tried spraying it around a tent one time and said bears treated it "like a salt lick." Smith has documented cases of grizzlies rubbing their heads or rolling around on ground doused with the spray, seeming to enjoy it.

It might help to compare pepper spray and grizzlies to Tabasco sauce and people: You sure don't want Tabasco in your eyes but it makes fried eggs smell and taste great. Used correctly, the pepper spray can halt a charging grizzly, but use it like mosquito spray, as a prophylactic measure, and you could have more trouble than smarting skin and eyes. The spray is for emergencies, for when a bear is too close. Use it then and only then.

Surprise encounters happen incredibly fast. Grizzlies have been clocked at forty-four feet per second. That means if you surprise a bear at fifty yards you've got three seconds to lay out a mist between you and the animal. And you've got to have the presence of mind to wait until the bear is almost within range or the vapor barrier will dissipate before the bear reaches it.

Still, this gives you more latitude than you have with a gun, especially for people who lack experience with firearms.

Bear spray is less intimidating than a gun for many people, it projects a cone of spray that is a lot bigger than a bullet, and it doesn't take the dexterity and training required to fire a gun accurately, especially when an angry grizzly bear is after you and you've got to think and act fast.

Matheny's promotional literature calls the picture of his fresh wounds "the grizzly attack that created UDAP Industries." As with many other mauling victims, the attack was a seminal event in his life, perhaps more so in his case. He collects news clippings about bear attacks and underlines any mention of bear spray. He tried, without success, to start a support group for mauling victims and solicits testimonials from users for his website. The "poster boy" label doesn't seem to bother him much. He knows he's capitalizing on misfortune, but at least it's his own misfortune. And his product could save somebody's life someday, as well as the lives of a number of bears.

"What was I supposed to do?" he asks. "Become an alcoholic and lie in the gutter? Life gave me a lemon, and I made lemonade."

POSTSCRIPT
Mark Matheny says UDAP sales keep growing every year. He's branched out, with new spray products designed to fend off muggers, and he sells portable electric fencing, meant to keep grizzly bears out of your camp.

He's focusing on other species, too. Though he's not ready to spill any details yet, he's working on a product he hopes will deter poisonous snakes.

"It's something to keep them out of your yard," he says.

7

A New Kind of Scared

DAN BOCCIA THOUGHT HE SAW A MOOSE JUST A LITTLE WAY THROUGH the trees and knew right then it was a good time to be someplace else. When he realized the big brown animal moving in the woods was a grizzly bear, he lost all doubt. His hair stood on end, his muscles tightened, and his breath came in shallow gulps. The bear was eating something, ripping chunks of meat from a carcass, and Boccia had an image of the bear doing the same thing to him. He was close, maybe sixty feet away, and he was in a jam. He wanted out of there and he wanted out of there now.

The bear hadn't seen him yet and Boccia was trying to slip away as quietly as he could. He watched his footing, trying to place his steps with care, but watching your feet is not easy to do when something as compelling as a feeding grizzly bear is a million times closer than you want it to be. He took three quiet steps and then he blew it: One of his stiff new boots thumped against an exposed tree root and the bear was on its feet. It growled once. Then it charged. Then it mauled him. The attack lasted only a few seconds, but it changed forever Boccia's life and the way he looks at bears and at wilderness. And it changed the way he looks at fear. He knows it better now and says he's a better man for it.

"The experience was very awesome," Boccia says, two years after the attack. "I feel fortunate to have had the experience. And I'm 100 percent physically, so I consider it one of the better experiences in my life. Who's stared a bear in the eyes from two feet away? Nobody."

A rangy, good-looking redhead, Boccia is an engineer for the Alaskan Native Tribal Health Consortium in Anchorage, Alaska, where he designs water and sewer systems for isolated native villages. When he's not working, he's a self-described "fun hog" who rides mountain bikes, climbs cliffs, and skis the backcountry. The fun keeps him busy enough that in the summer he rarely gets six hours of sleep a night. He's taken some long falls while strapped to cliffs hundreds of feet high, and he's been caught in avalanches and major storms while skiing, alone and a long way from help. Those things scared him, too. Plenty. But nothing compares to an attack by a five-hundred-pound bear.

It's a different kind of fear, one you have not embraced, one you can't control no matter how good your equipment, no matter how vast your training. You can only react. You don't have much time to make a choice; whatever you decide will change the rest of your life; and you can only hope you do the right thing.

On skis or at the end of a climbing rope, the moments or hours of fear, however real, involved a sense of adventure, he writes in an essay detailing the bear attack. "A chance to push my physical, technical, and psychological abilities to their raw edges, knowing that any small error, lack of concentration, or physical weakness could lead to disaster."

In short, he was scaring the crap out of himself on purpose. It's the adrenaline rush common to people who jump out of airplanes or shoot white-water. (The more placid among us may seek similar sensations in horror films.) It's a competition between yourself and nature, one that you have calculated and measured to give yourself a maximum thrill, with a real but manageable chance of death or dismemberment. And then there's the sense of accomplishment, of testing yourself, of learning your abilities.

But going nose to nose with a grizzly bear, unarmed, is a different thing. It's a very real danger in a situation you may have created, though not purposely. There's a chance you may die, and your survival depends partly on you and partly on the bear, an intelligent creature—and at this point an excited one—that makes choices of its own. It's almost a sure thing you will bleed and suffer. You could lose your face or an eye or a limb. You could get scalped. The bear could shake you by the neck like a rottweiler does a kitten.

"Never before had some other living, breathing creature, man or beast, threatened my existence," Boccia writes in the essay. "This was easily the most fundamental fear I have ever felt. There was no element of adventure, nor potential for accomplishment."

It wasn't any fun, this kind of scared.

～～

Boccia was attacked on May 15, 1995, in Chugach State Park near Eagle River, Alaska, where he had gone to photograph wildflowers, normally a low-adrenaline pursuit. Strong sunlight sliced between the trees and a brisk wind blew across the canyon. Just a few miles downstream lay the town of Eagle River, where upscale subdivisions steadily gobble up more and more bear country.

He had crossed a bunch of beaver dams and was between two branches of the stream, walking into the wind, looking mostly to his left and watching for good photographs. Then he glanced to his right, and there, that mere sixty feet away, he saw a brown form through the trees.

"I thought, oh, it's a moose. There's probably a calf around, so I'd better get out of here."

Moose are a definite hazard in the Alaska bush, and sometimes even on city streets. The giant ungulates are everywhere and can be foul tempered. They attack people more often than grizzly bears do.

Boccia paused while he considered which direction to take. Then he looked again and noticed "something kind of going up and down. I looked closer and realized it's a bear feeding on something, with its head going up and down, tearing off pieces of meat."

Since the bear showed no sign that it knew Boccia was in the area, he decided to try to go back out the same way he had come in.

That's when his boot clunked against a tree root, which was all it took to get the bear's full attention.

"The damn thing heard the tree root, jumped way up in the air, turned around and landed, just like a linebacker. His front legs were really wide apart, trying to make a big profile."

It growled once, real loud.

"I looked at the bear and the bear looked at me and a couple seconds later it charged. I just stood there and watched. I didn't know if it was going to bluff or what was going on."

When the bear was thirty feet away and still coming at full speed, Boccia knew this was no bluff charge. He had a four-foot-long tripod in his hand and briefly considered trying to clout the bear on the nose. But that, he decided, would only anger the bear even more. So he lay down in a thick patch of small birch trees and tried to put his head between a couple of them. There was no time to climb one, and the trees were too small anyway. So Boccia played dead.

The bear ran right past him, stopped, and did "a weird dance. He was just moving his front paws up and down as he looked at me." Boccia spoke to it, said "No, bear," and repeated the words three times, softly.

Boccia said he didn't think about what he was doing, didn't flash back to the books and other information he had read about safety in bear country. His gut, his instincts, guided him. So far, his instincts had been good. Moving the front paws like that is a sign of agitation, bear experts say, but the animal had not yet attacked. It may have been trying to decide whether Boccia posed a threat. Speaking calmly, avoiding eye contact, making yourself look small and unintimidating can sometimes convince a bear to go away.

Then Boccia made what was probably a mistake. He looked the bear in the eyes, and the bear made up its mind: Boccia needed a lesson.

"I looked in its eyes, and it looked at my eyes. Then it came up to me, obviously to attack. I just laid my head down, flat on the ground, face down."

The first blow came from the bear's paw and felt like a hard punch in the ribs. It shoved him roughly across some exposed roots. Then the bear lit into his back with its teeth, delivering a terrific butt with its snout and ripping off a piece of meat.

"It felt like it took a great big chunk out of my back. But what hurt most was the impact of its big head hitting me."

Then the bear jumped over him, back to the trail, and Boccia looked up to see the bear do its weird dance again. After the first growl, it made no sounds other than occasional small grunts, "like somebody getting out of a soft couch."

When Boccia looked at it the second time, the bear came back to him, and "I kind of blacked out, turned black inside, for a couple seconds. I thought, this is it. It didn't run off. It's going to thrash me for good.

"The first thing it did was rake me all along my right side, from my armpit all the way down to my right knee."

Remarkably, the long claws, the tools that can rip apart a tree or turn over huge stones, did little damage.

"It just shredded my clothes and left a couple claw marks on my skin. Then it clamped down really hard on my left calf and just shook the hell out of me, a vigorous three or four shakes of the head. It didn't lift me off the ground. It just shook me hard on the ground."

Then it bit his other leg but didn't shake him.

"Immediately after biting me on the right calf, it took off right over the top of me. It didn't step on me, just went right over me and went crashing through the brush. And that's the last I ever saw of that bear."

Boccia lay still for a moment, wondering if the bear had left enough muscle to allow him to stand. His leg hurt like hell, and he had no idea where the bear was.

"I decided it was time to go and I stood right up. I really couldn't believe that I could do it. And then I ran about two hundred yards, running pretty fast, wanting to get the hell out of there."

But running didn't work. He was seeing stars and hyperventilating, probably in shock. So he rested a while before walking back to the parking lot at the visitor center, almost a mile away. He babbled all the way.

"Oh, I'm lucky. Oh, I'm lucky. Oh, he messed me up. Oh, he messed me up. I just kept saying these two phrases over and over and over. I figured there was a bear behind every tree, and I was scared to death. I could still hear the bear in the brush, and it was difficult, with the wind, to tell if it was coming closer or if it was going away. And I was coming back by a different route than the way I went in. That made me nervous. I was deep in the woods, and there could have been another bear."

His mind was targeted on his vehicle, seeing it as a refuge.

"I wanted to touch my truck. I just had to get to my truck because then I knew I could get in the damn thing and nothing could get me."

It took him about fifteen minutes to get to the parking lot. He left the trail and scrambled up a bank, through the brush, to reach pavement.

A couple in their late thirties walked by, looked him up and down, and kept walking.

"I had sticks poking three feet out of my hair. My clothes were barely on me, they were so shredded up. I was filthy. I was a sight. And I couldn't believe these people just walked right by. I thought, you've got to know that something's not right here."

Then another man approached Boccia and offered to take him to the hospital in Anchorage. Boccia said he would drive himself to town. But as soon as he touched his truck, the "rabbit's den, the squirrel's nest, the place of protection and comfort," the pain took hold and his entire body stiffened.

"I said, Jesus, I can't drive anywhere. I'll drive off the road and then I will be killed."

He turned to the man and said he might take that ride after all.

Boccia's wounds were minor, as far as grizzly attacks go. The hole in his back was substantial and had to be packed with gauze every day for weeks. His leg hurt for a long time, as did his entire chest cavity.

"He just hit me so damn hard with his nose."

But doctors treated him in the emergency room and sent him home. A couple of days later, a friend took him back to Eagle River to get his truck. A ranger there interviewed him, and managers decided not to pursue the bear. It was reacting in a normal way, protecting its food from a surprise visitor, and wasn't particularly aggressive.

Boccia backed up that decision all the way.

"It wouldn't have taken very much effort on the bear's part to snap my head off. People say, 'Oh, you should go shoot that bear.' That's the last thing I'm going to do. They should shoot me. I'm the one that screwed it up. I wasn't making any noise. I wasn't paying any attention to where I was going, and I ended up right in its kitchen, basically. I would have expected any animal of that nature to have reacted exactly the way it did."

Looking into the bear's eyes, while it is a rare experience, probably wasn't a good idea, he agrees.

"If I hadn't kept eye contact, I wonder if it would have left me alone. That's a threat to anybody. If I stare you in the eyes, you're going to get nervous. If I stare at an animal, it's going to get nervous. When it bit me the first time and backed off, I made eye contact with it again. I wonder if that might have been a mistake."

He says he's had a few dreams that weren't much fun, but they passed soon enough. Other things lasted longer. Spur-of-the-moment hikes by himself are a thing of the past. So is mountain biking solo.

"I'm a bit jittery in the woods, now, especially if I'm by myself. If I hear something in the woods, I want to know what it is. I'm uncomfortable riding around here by myself on my mountain bike, so I just don't do it. You move too fast on them, and bears don't have a chance to get away. It's too scary. If you ran into a bear on the trail up here, you'd get your tail clobbered."

On a trip to the Okanogan Valley of Washington, where there are no grizzlies and black bears are scarce, the jitters set in "even knowing full well there was nothing to worry about."

His father gave him a 12-gauge shotgun to take on things such as boat trips. He carries bear spray at other times. Since the attack, he has seen lots of bears.

"In every case they get my full attention, without a doubt."

He's a little uncomfortable giving advice and says his own story is a positive one only because his injuries were slight. But he does tell people to be careful: Make noise. Carry a gun if you want. Bear spray. Dogs. Bear bells. Bring friends. Pay attention, and be aware.

Boccia had returned from a three-week biking trip in southern Utah just a few days before he was attacked. When he had left Alaska for that journey, it had still been winter. As he started his stroll along the Eagle River, he thought about bears, wondered idly if they were out of their dens yet.

"I thought, well, maybe there's a bear out now. But I dismissed it. I just wasn't used to preparing mentally for going out. When I go out now, I prepare myself mentally."

The preparations necessary for outdoor fun in Alaska, all of which is bear country, can be a hassle, Boccia says.

"There's so many of them around here that they're kind of a pain in the neck. You feel like you're in the army or something. You've got to get all ready for battle when you go out."

But he does it.

"I had a couple dreams about what it might feel like to really get bit hard and mauled, like some of these people. Chewed on the face and the neck and thrashed all around. Late at night I'll just get up and think about it a little and then go back to sleep."

There's a message in the dreams, he says.

"Pay attention. My body is telling me to pay attention."

POSTSCRIPT

Sixteen years after the attack, Dan Boccia remains dedicated to getting all he can from living in Alaska. At forty-two he still skies hard and climbs the tough stuff, crashing through the brush and sloshing through streams if that's what it takes to reach the right cliff. But he doesn't do that alone, not in the months when grizzlies prowl, and he makes plenty of noise.

He's choosy about the paths he takes, and he knows he's a little different from his companions, people who've never had his kind of experience with a bear.

He still has fun, but the attack changed something, increased his focus. He knows a bear could pop up almost anywhere.

"I never really turn myself off when I'm out there."

8

A Picture to Die For

THE SUN WASN'T QUITE UP YET, AND JEFF HENRY WANTED TO TAKE A quick sweep along the banks of the Yellowstone River. Maybe the driver of the suspicious car had gone fishing and come to grief. Maybe there was a tackle box or a fishing pole, footprints or some other clue. Maybe he had fallen in, filled his waders with water, and been swept downstream toward the big waterfalls in the Grand Canyon of the Yellowstone. Maybe there was something, anything, that would prove his nagging feeling was wrong, and maybe Henry and his German shepherd search dog, Hoss, could find it.

The idea of a drowned man, one likely dashed to pieces in waterfalls, is not a pretty image. But it wasn't as disturbing as the dark thought chilling Henry and the other Yellowstone National Park rangers in the field that morning. A car had been parked haphazardly along the road and left there for three days, drawing the attention of rangers, who ran a check on the plates and found that its owner—normally a responsible guy—was overdue at work in Great Falls, Montana. Also, a grizzly bear had been hanging out nearby for a few days, and the signal from her radio collar said she was staying in one spot, not moving around as much as she should have been.

"We had a pretty good idea there was a grizzly bear involved before we even started searching," Henry says.

Henry and Hoss returned from their quick exploration along the riverbank and joined the rest of the search party just as the sun came up on that chilly October morning. They'd found nothing.

John Lounsbury was the district ranger at Lake Village in Yellowstone, and that made him the man in charge of the search. It was October 7, 1986, a Tuesday, and he had risen especially early that morning. A party was going out at first light, and Lounsbury wanted to know where bear No. 59 was before he sent people into the field, looking for somebody injured or maybe dead. He, too, had a nagging feeling about how the search would turn out, and he didn't want to make it worse by putting his people in danger, by sending them on a collision course with a grizzly bear. Almost everybody who lived in that part of the park knew No. 59. Rangers had moved her away from Canyon Village just a few weeks earlier, not the first time they had done that chore, but the 255-pound grizzly had made a hasty return to her home turf at Canyon. It wasn't that she had ever been an aggressive bear, but she did have some pesky habits. She was what rangers call "habituated." She tolerated people, tried to swipe a little human food when somebody gave her a chance, and spent too much time around developed areas. Rangers had moved her often, fearing that it was just a matter of time before she wound up in serious trouble.

Lounsbury and ranger Mona Divine carried with them that morning a device they thought would be a big advantage: a handheld radio receiver designed to pick up the constant series of beeps emitted by the bear's radio collar. Some independent researchers in the park had picked up her signal just the day before and told rangers she'd been lingering in the Otter Creek area for at least three days.

By October in Yellowstone, grizzlies are preparing to enter their dens, packing in as many as twenty thousand calories a day, beefing up the layer of fat that keeps them alive all winter. Doing that usually means covering a lot of country, unless a bear finds a carcass or kills a large animal.

"What's holding that bear?" Lounsbury wondered to himself when he heard what No. 59 had been doing.

Rangers had first become concerned Sunday morning, after a twenty-three-year-old Chevrolet sedan had stayed in a picnic area parking lot for twenty-four hours. They ran a check on the plates and found it belonged to William Tesinsky, a thirty-eight-year-old mechanic at a Chevrolet dealership in Great Falls, about 250 miles to the north. At first they thought the old car probably had broken down and Tesinsky had gone to fetch parts. But when it was still there Monday, rangers got concerned.

Nobody answered the phone at Tesinsky's home, but rangers snooped around and figured out where he worked. They called the shop.

"He should have been back," Tesinsky's boss said. He was worried. Tesinsky's girlfriend worked at the same dealership. She was worried, too. He was a frugal guy, a hard worker. It wasn't like him to miss a day's work, especially without calling. They said he was a photographer who specialized in wildlife.

And No. 59 was in the area.

Lounsbury didn't like the way things were adding up. He got busy and organized a search party for the next morning.

Bear managers and researchers rely heavily on radio equipment when they work with "management" bears such as No. 59, the kind of bear that has done something to earn it a capture, a relocation, an ear tag, and a radio collar. Though more modern collars with global positioning systems have become commonplace since 1986, at that time the plastic and leather collars each carried a fist-size transmitter that has its own radio frequency so individual bears can be identified from afar. At any given time a few dozen bears in the park wear collars of one type or another. The radio collars transmit beeps that, to the person listening to a receiver and waving an antenna in the air, become louder and more frequent as the searcher comes closer to the animal. The receivers often provide the only way to find a specific bear in Yellowstone's 2.2 million acres of forest and canyon and meadow. But the receiver wasn't working that day and because of that failure, Lounsbury and Divine nearly stumbled on the bear in a dangerous situation, one that might have occurred, ironically, because the bear was wearing the collar in the first place.

It was the sad, eerie croak of a raven that brought the rangers up just short of disaster.

They had left their homes at about four in the morning and picked up a signal from the Canyon area, fourteen miles to the north, while it was still pitch dark. From there they started moving south on foot, past a long-abandoned campground at Otter Creek; past the site where a band of Nez Perce Indians had killed some of Yellowstone's earliest tourists in

1877; past the place where, until World War II, grizzlies had dined on the slops from the Canyon Hotel as bleachers full of tourists giggled and gasped. They climbed some small hills and moved steadily across a broad, sloping meadow, still within sight of the highway, picking up nothing but silence as daylight began to inch across the valley, a place of sage and grasses and scattered groves of pine trees. Good grizzly habitat.

Then the raven croaked.

"I looked down the slope and saw the raven in a tree," Lounsbury remembers, more than a decade after that day. "I stopped walking and looked closer. And there was the bear, a little farther down the slope, about twenty-five yards away. We made eye contact, and that sort of chilled me."

The rangers had been headed directly toward the grizzly, nearly invisible in the predawn gloom. A few more paces and they could have stepped on her. They backed off and marched to the patrol car to fetch binoculars and a rifle with a telescopic sight. Then they came back and watched the bear through their optics. They didn't like what they saw.

The bear was eating a person.

"We could see a tennis shoe and a little bit of a leg she was feeding on."

Lounsbury got on the radio and told the rest of his crew the search was off. They'd found what they were looking for, and nobody was happy about it. Lounsbury thought about what had almost happened: He had nearly walked right into a feeding grizzly bear, an animal that will fight to the death to protect its food. And this was no ordinary feeding area: The bear was eating a person. He had relied on the radio signal to alert him and Divine, but it didn't work as well as did the raven, a creature the Indians of the Northwest see as a messenger.

"It rattled me," he recalls. "That raven might have saved my bacon."

Other rangers arrived quickly, and radio messages were relayed to park headquarters at Mammoth Hot Springs. Kill the bear, ordered assistant chief ranger Gary Brown.

Two rangers laid their crosshairs on the bear as she continued to eat. They shot simultaneously. The bear took a step or two and fell dead, her role in Yellowstone at an end.

Lounsbury kept most of the crew away from the scene.

"I knew there was a big investigation coming, and I didn't want to muck it up with a bunch of footprints."

They would find bits of Bill Tesinsky scattered around the hillside. The bear had been feeding on the body, but there was a coyote nearby, waiting its turn, just as the raven that warned Lounsbury had been doing. The bear had been working on the body for three days, and she had been thorough; it was dismembered, with parts buried in mounds. The lower half of the body was almost untouched, still clothed, but the torso was gone, and rangers remarked that Tesinsky looked as if he'd been cut in two, just above the belt. The bear had treated him just as she would have treated an elk or a bison—as valuable calories to be buried, saved, and guarded from other scavengers. Yellowstone managers will tolerate a lot from a bear, but they will not tolerate this. And that is why she died.

Gary Brown, now retired from the National Park Service, said the decision to kill the bear was easy to make and one he never regretted, even after rangers pieced together what led to the death. He is a big fan of bears. He wrote *The Great Bear Almanac,* an exhaustive compendium of bear knowledge, and another book about how to travel safely in bear country. The bear was feeding on a human being and that could not be allowed, Brown says. From then on the place would be known among rangers as Tesinsky Meadow.

❦

Bill Tesinsky was the divorced father of two teenage daughters and a younger son. He specialized in automatic transmissions, and in his off hours he took on extra projects, fixing cars in a frigid garage and using the money to finance hunting, fishing, and photography trips. He trapped. He skied and snowshoed. His bedspread was a soft tanned elk hide. As a youth he had raced cars and motorcycles, but it was on his feet that he excelled. A native Montanan who grew up on a ranch in the foothills of the Belt Mountains, he was a prodigious walker and a determined hunter. His brother, Ron, tells of elk hunting with Bill, tells stories of the times when, driving to a hunting spot before dawn, they would find elk tracks crossing the road.

The brothers would sit in the truck for ten minutes, "until he'd get anxious and say let's go. And we'd track them, with flashlights, until daylight." Sometimes Bill would track animals for twenty-four hours or more, catching a few hours of sleep under a tree somewhere. His prey rarely escaped him, Ron says.

Photography was a relatively recent passion for Bill Tesinsky, but it was one he embraced with his characteristic enthusiasm: As in all things, he was competitive, tenacious, and anxious to get the job done.

He prided himself on pictures of truly "wild" animals and looked down on photographers who did most of their work in national parks, where the wildlife tends to be more tolerant, where a person can get an excellent shot from the side of a road. He rigged up contraptions of rope and wood he could tie to the bumper of his pickup truck and lower himself off the edge of a cliff to take pictures of eagles. He had shots of big herds of elk, all bulls, in snow past their bellies, the famous Chinese Wall of the Bob Marshall Wilderness in the background. He had pictures of bighorn sheep in snow so deep that only their heads and necks stuck above it.

"He was right there among them," Ron Tesinsky says.

He was finding some commercial success as well. A handful of galleries around Montana sold his work and he was beginning to build a reputation. And he did it even though he had only an inexpensive camera and didn't own a lens longer than 200 millimeters, the one he was using when he died. He relied on his knowledge of animals and the outdoors, his ability to stalk, to get close enough for a picture.

But there was a serious hole in his portfolio. He had photographed most of the animals of the Northern Rockies, but he had no grizzly bears, a hot seller for many photographers. Like most people who want such pictures, he knew that meant going to a national park. He didn't have the money for an expensive photo safari to Alaska, and he lived about halfway between Yellowstone and Glacier National Parks, both strongholds for grizzlies, a handful of which will tolerate photographers. He decided to go south to Yellowstone, where he found such a bear, No. 59.

(On the same day Bill Tesinsky died, Idaho photographer Tim Christie was treed by a sow grizzly in Glacier National Park. She followed him up the tree—the story that grizzlies can't climb trees is a myth—and grabbed him by the tennis shoe. His foot slipped out of the shoe, he made it to the top of the tree, and the bear descended. If he had been wearing hiking boots, "she would have pulled me right out of the tree," he says. The bear went away after a few harrowing minutes.)

Bill had talked to Ron about his Yellowstone plans at a family gathering.

"He said, 'The only thing I don't have is a grizzly,'" Ron says. "So he took a drive into the park. He went there for a reason, and that's what it was."

The conversation was cut short, though. Their mother was approaching, and Bill didn't want her to know what he was planning.

"He said he was going to the park," Ron says. "Then he hushed me because he knew our mother would be just frantic about that."

No. 59 was one of the most photographed bears in Yellowstone, one that often appeared in magazines and film documentaries. That's because she was so easy to photograph safely, for people who observe the limits: She was a willing or at least uncaring model for people who kept their distance. She first showed up at the Canyon Village area, a complex of stores, restaurants, cabins, and a campground, in 1980. She was a two-year-old, recently separated from her mother. Worried that she would learn that people meant rewards of cast-off sandwiches or untended garbage, rangers captured her and released her more than thirty miles away. She was back within days.

The next summer, 1981, she displayed what the Park Service calls "increasing habituation," which means she was losing more and more of her natural fear of people, so she was hauled twenty-five miles away to a new location. It took five days for her to find her way back.

She bred for the first time in 1983, bore two cubs in her den the following winter, and lost one of them while it was still tiny. The second cub lived another year but had disappeared by June of 1985, victim of a fall, a drowning, another bear, or one of a thousand other dangers that can beset even the best-protected babies in the park.

In 1986 she was spotted with new cubs again, teaching them to hunt elk calves early in the summer in the Antelope Creek area north of Canyon but returning to the developments there by July.

In August she was grazing in the employee softball field and walking near the campground, attracting big crowds of people on a regular basis and displaying no aggression to anybody.

She did have an appetite, however. She once tried to raid a freezer illegally placed outside an employee's trailer home. The owner woke up, approached within six feet, and sprayed her with a fire extinguisher. She turned tail and ran.

By September 4 of that year, rangers had decided to move her and her cubs one more time and took them twenty-two miles to the southeast. That meant being hauled in a culvert trap. She was back at Canyon within two weeks, without her cubs.

"When she came to, she bolted back to the Canyon area and left her cubs behind," Jeff Henry recalls. The cubs were frequently seen along the park's east entrance road.

"They undoubtedly starved," Henry says.

It was a poor year for natural foods in 1986. The pine nut crop had failed, meaning grizzlies had no squirrel caches to raid, and like all the park's other bears, No. 59 was hyperphagic, desperate to put on weight. Also, being handled and moved may have worsened her physical condition. That was the situation Bill Tesinsky marched into on the last day of his life.

─── ───

Rangers painstakingly reconstructed the death scene.

Tesinsky's car was parked "haphazardly," they say, indicating he had parked quickly and left immediately. He probably spotted No. 59 from the road, pulled over, grabbed his camera, and took off after her.

Henry, aided by the keen nose of his search dog, retraced Tesinsky's steps. He found that he had walked up the hillside to his death, following along the right side of a small draw and leaving tracks from the distinctive tread on his tennis shoes. On the left side of the draw, a hundred feet or so from Tesinsky's tracks, were grizzly footprints and places where No. 59 had been digging the succulent roots of yampa and melica, along with an occasional pocket gopher. The first digging site was less than 150 yards from the road, and that may be where Tesinsky saw her first.

"It looked like he was paralleling that bear up the draw," Henry says.

The bear moved up the hill, past a power line, and over a small rise to a place in a little bowl where she was barely hidden from the road. That's where Tesinsky died.

It's impossible to tell from the tracks whether he paralleled the bear up the slope, as Henry believes, or he followed her up the draw later. There was a second feeding site about one hundred yards closer to the road from the death scene and visible from the road. He may have spotted her working there and pursued her. If so, she probably had crossed the small knoll by the time he caught up with her. He was walking into the wind and crested the small rise within forty yards of the bear, possibly surprising her. Then he moved even closer. Rangers hoped his pictures would provide some evidence but there was no help there; the film in his camera had no images of bears. But that, too, is consistent with the situation and with Tesinsky's personality.

He wanted pictures of a wild grizzly, and No. 59 wore a radio collar, which sticks out like a sore thumb in a photograph. He also liked "full-frame" pictures, shots that contain a lot more animal than background, the kind that force you to get close. If the bear held its head just right, the collar would be hidden, and that's probably the kind of picture Tesinsky was waiting for, conserving his film until he got it.

The camera did show, however, that Tesinsky got much too close to the bear. His Pentax 1000 camera was on a tripod and bore an 80-millimeter to 200-millimeter adjustable lens. It was set at 120 millimeters when the rangers found it, matted with blood and hair, one of the tripod legs bent and twisted, dirt thrust into the flash attachment as though it had been mashed into the ground. At that setting a bear would appear full frame at somewhere between thirty and fifty feet, and that is much too close, even for a tolerant bear such as No. 59.

Seeing the radio collar might have been a surprise for Tesinsky. If he spotted her close to the road, he probably saw the collar and then decided to follow her, to try to manipulate a good photograph. But if he saw her at the far feeding site, and her head was down as she dug roots, he probably couldn't see the collar, even with the binoculars on the car seat beside him. Once within shooting range, possibly frustrated at finding the collar, he may have whistled or yelled, trying to make her turn her head so he could get the shot he wanted. Nobody knows how long he was close to the bear; it was long enough to set up his tripod and a shutter-release cable but not long enough for him to get cold. His gloves were in his pockets when he died that chilly morning.

After trying without success to photograph grizzlies in such places as Montana's Bob Marshall Wilderness, he must have been excited to get that close to a bear. Habituated animals like No. 59 have learned that people usually pose no threat to them and will allow a much closer approach than will a bear that has rarely or never seen people. It's a situation manifested in many species in national parks, where all wildlife is legally protected. Such animals have mentally reduced their "safety zone," the amount of separation they require before running away or attacking. But the dimensions of the safety zone are elastic; they vary according to circumstances. A bear that lives near a roadway rarely runs away at the sight of a car, even if it stops and shutters start clicking. But if the same bear moves to a place where people rarely go—such as the small meadow where Tesinsky died—the fight-or-flight instinct can arise when a threat is still distant. A human may not seem to be a threat in a parking lot but can look dangerous in a relatively isolated meadow. The park's bison and elk act the same way. A noisy, smelly snowmobile can stop twenty feet from a resting elk and the animal rarely rises to its feet, as long as the machine and the rider stay on the road. But cross-country skiers who leave the trails very rarely get that close to an elk because the skiers are in places the elk don't see them every day. With their safety envelope penetrated, they move away. Animals, like people, like things to be predictable.

No. 59 provided an excellent example of how flexible the safety zone can be. When a man approached within six feet of her as she tried to raid his freezer, next to a trailer in a residential area where she fully expected to see people, she showed no aggression. She ran away once she got a dose from the fire extinguisher. Two months later, when Tesinsky came within fifty feet, in a place where she probably had never seen a person before, she attacked even though he was several times farther away than the man with the extinguisher.

"She had shown remarkable tolerance," Henry says. "She'd been closely approached a number of times."

By analyzing tracks, blood, and other evidence, rangers could tell that she hit Tesinsky first as he stood close behind his camera, probably triggering what would be Tesinsky's last picture: an unidentifiable dark blob, possibly an out-of-focus close-up of the ground. Bear hair stuck to the tripod legs. Tesinsky probably tried to run, back up the little rise and toward the road, but he didn't get far. Ten yards from the camera, rangers found large amounts of blood on the ground and on the grass. Then she dragged him back downhill, away from the road, pulling him across his camera and tripod and leaving large amounts of blood in the drag trail, indicating that he was still alive for some time. The elk bugle—a long plastic tube—that he had carried on a string around his neck was snagged on a bush, the string soaked in blood, the bugle mashed and torn.

Using devices like an elk bugle can make it easier to get close to an animal, but they are illegal in Yellowstone: They're used to call in animals, and they disrupt natural behavior. But Tesinsky had one anyway. He also had an unused predator call in his car, another indication of how he manipulated animals to get pictures.

After he was dead, Tesinsky made his last transition: from possibly dangerous annoyance to food. Tesinsky had invaded the bear's safety zone, had become a perceived threat. He may have tried to fight the bear, which in most cases only intensifies the attack. There wasn't enough left of him to tell precisely how he died. The autopsy listed cause of death as "injuries inflicted by a bear."

"Then, once he was dead, she realized he was meat," Henry says.

Three days later, rangers found what remained.

❧ ❧

"He pushed it, and he got caught," Gary Brown says years later of Tesinsky. "A lot of people push it and don't get caught."

Henry agrees. He is also a wildlife photographer and left the Park Service after seven years to ply his craft full time. Like anybody else with a few years' experience in the park, Henry and Brown can both tell stories of tourists doing incredibly stupid things: feeding bears, approaching bears, acting as if the animals are pets. Invariably, they complain if the critters turn aggressive. With more than three million visitors a year, and the type of behavior some of them display, it's remarkable that only five people have been killed by grizzly bears in the park's 139-year history.

Dealing with the Tesinsky case, trying to gather as much evidence—and as many of his bones—as possible, made for an incredibly long and emotional day for the rangers.

"It was just a nasty job," Lounsbury says.

But as the day wore on, evidence mounted showing how Tesinsky had followed the bear, how he had ignored Park Service warnings to stay at least a hundred yards from all bears.

"I felt for the guy, and I felt for his family," Henry says. "But it was pretty clear to me that the guy had pushed it too far."

❧ ❧

Tesinsky knew a lot about animals, but he didn't know much about grizzly bears, his brother says.

"Grizzlies were unknown to him and me both," Ron Tesinsky says.

After his brother's death, Ron began reading widely about grizzlies, learning how unpredictable they can be, that a habituated bear is still a wild and potentially dangerous animal if you push it too far. He says it gave him a shiver to recall the times he had camped in Yellowstone as a young newlywed, traveling on a motorcycle with his wife, Gail, taking no special care to keep a clean camp or use other bear precautions.

"We had bears roam the camp area, in sight of us, many times," Ron says. "We never even gave it a thought. After Bill died, it was one of the first conversations Gail and I had about this. God, all those times we did that. I wouldn't do it now for anything."

He believes his brother probably tried to fight the bear, almost always a futile exercise, especially if a person is alone. A punch or a kick may distract a bear, especially if the bear is trying to keep its eye on someone else at the same time, but in most cases it only serves to anger it further.

Tesinsky understood black bears; the brothers had run into them a number of times on hunting trips. "But they were timid," Ron says. "They took off like rabbits."

Grizzlies often run away, too. Or else they hide when they see somebody, crouch down and wait for them to pass by. Those bears tend to live long and are rarely photographed. But there are thousands of excellent bear photographs in the world.

Where do they come from?

"The first thing you do is get a really big lens," advises Tom Murphy, a renowned wildlife photographer and author from Livingston, Montana, who has shot polar, grizzly, and black bears all over North America. He also teaches photography and nature workshops in Yellowstone and for many years was the man his hometown search-and-rescue team called in when the search dogs had given up on a lost hunter or hiker. He knows bears, and he knows backcountry.

He recommends a lens of 600 millimeters or more, a piece of advice that, if Tesinsky ever heard, he ignored. Rangers found a 1,000-millimeter lens in his car, one he had borrowed from a friend. He left it behind when he went after No. 59.

"The technique to use for Yellowstone grizzly bears is probably to drive around early in the morning in a car and hope you can get something along the road," Murphy says. "To walk across that country, the chances are almost nil that you're going to get a good shot. They either run like crazy in one direction or they'll run up and knock you down. That's my experience. They view man in vehicles as a benign presence, not as a threat and not as a source of food. Somebody on foot, they don't know. That's the problem."

Sneaking up on an animal in a place like Yellowstone also doesn't make much sense, Murphy says.

"Don't fool yourself that an animal doesn't know you're there, although you can surprise them. With animals my experience is that they know you're there. They pay attention to sound, they pay attention to movement, they pay attention to smell a lot more than we ever will."

Bears read body language, Murphy says, and if you are trying to stalk a bear, the animal is going to interpret that as a threat. You're acting like a predator, after all.

"Anytime you're stalking, it's aggressive behavior, and you don't want to do that with something that can knock your head off," Murphy notes. "Some people have this new-age thinking that bears can read your mind, that you're benign. That's bullshit. They're reading your body language, not your mind.

"One technique that I use, if I see an animal stop and start looking at me, sometimes I'll turn and start walking the other way. Then my body language is not as a predator. It's just a casual passerby. I've seen predators like coyotes do the same thing."

Reading the body language of a grizzly bear is a complicated affair. Bears use posture, the position of their ears, movements, the way they hold their heads, to send signals of warning, submission, fear, or anger. People with vast experience among bears maintain they can read these signals, but it takes years of practice and the experts admit that body language is only an indication of attitude, not a sure sign of what the bear will do next. And reading a bear's body language is not something the average tourist, or even most outdoors professionals, get a chance to practice.

Some photographers get lucky, however.

Frans Lanting is a world-famous photographer, celebrated for his work for *National Geographic,* for his up close portraits of lions and elephants and bears. In a December 1997 interview in *Outdoor Photographer* magazine, he explains how he does his work and uses an Alaskan grizzly sow and her newborn cub as an example.

He got the shot, but what he describes also can be a prescription for disaster, a situation that can easily result in mauled people and dead grizzlies: He tells the thousands of amateur photographers who read the magazine—people like Bill Tesinsky—how to help turn a wild bear into a habituated and perhaps more dangerous animal.

It was early summer, mating season for grizzlies, and the cub was still tiny, Lanting told the magazine. An aggressive male had left the mother "freaked out" that morning, but Lanting decided that didn't matter: He said he "felt really drawn to her" and set out in pursuit. He and his companions followed her all day, but she wouldn't let them get closer than one hundred yards, not close enough for the kind of "intimate" work Lanting wanted to do.

The next morning they were able to approach within seventy-five yards. Then the bears lay down beside a creek for a nap.

"I knew that creek would provide a psychological barrier," Lanting told the magazine. "She would feel safer and allow us closer because of it. So I had all of us move to the other side of the creek, just twenty yards from the bears. And her behavior showed she felt safe with us there."

Like Murphy, Lanting stresses that you must never startle the bear and shouldn't try stalking them. Rather, show yourself and make sure the bear knows you're there. Let the bear make the decisions.

Unlike Murphy, Lanting then pushes his luck incredibly hard.

After the sow fell asleep, he and his party crossed the creek, eliminating the "psychological barrier."

"The cub approached us," he says. "And Mom let her do it. We finally had our pictures."

And they walked away unharmed, no doubt exhilarated. But what kind of bear did they leave behind?

"My favorite approach," he told *Audubon Magazine* later, "is to habituate animals to the extent that they ignore me."

In short, he robs them of a little wildness, shrinks the safety envelope they need to survive in a world of dangerous humans. When this happens in a place such as Yellowstone despite the best efforts of sincere people, it's sad. When somebody like Lanting does it on purpose, just to get a photograph, it's pathetic.

Lanting doesn't say where in Alaska the incident took place; he only calls it a big treeless valley with no other people in it. When they started following the bear, she was wild, unapproachable, leery of people, following her survival instincts. When they went away, she'd been taught something she'll never forget. Will she now begin approaching humans, even those who want to keep their distance? What will happen the next time an ambitious photographer approaches, somebody like Bill Tesinsky? She might let him or her come quite close. But her safety envelope will never go away, will always be an elastic thing that expands and contracts according to circumstances. Will the next photographer be as lucky as Lanting? And what happens if the cub approaches another photographer? Will the mother attack? Will she then be killed by bear managers reacting to political pressure?

Lanting's impact isn't likely to be limited to one bear family. He does what he can to spread his method around.

The same issue of *Outdoor Photographer* also carried a couple of advertisements from camera maker Nikon. One offered a video. If you can spare forty minutes and $29.95, you can travel to Africa with Lanting "and learn his secrets of wildlife photography." The second ad features a Lanting photograph of an African lion, looking at him, wary, close enough that the big cat's eyes reflect his flash.

"You can almost hear the photo editor purr," the advertisement says, noting, of course, that the picture was made with Nikon equipment.

That's probably the sound Tesinsky was hoping to hear.

~ ~

Charles Wayne Gibbs provides a good example of how dangerous it can be to pester a grizzly bear, to push its safety envelope. It also shows the danger of Lanting's type of thinking—that you can get "intimate" with a grizzly bear.

Gibbs and his wife Glenda were hiking in Glacier National Park in late April 1987, just six months after Tesinsky died. Gibbs spotted a sow with three yearling cubs on Elk Mountain and decided he wanted pictures of them. So he sent his wife down to the trailhead and took off after the bears.

It worked. Gibbs got some nice shots. Then the bear killed him. It attacked him, chased him eighteen feet up a tree, dragged him to the ground, and killed him.

Like Tesinsky, Gibbs was an accomplished amateur photographer, a man who sold some photographs but kept his day job as a bus driver in Libby, Montana. Also, like Tesinsky, he lacked good pictures of a grizzly.

"Chuck really loved the bear," a neighbor and fellow outdoor photographer told reporters shortly after his death. "He believed he was for the bear, so the bear wouldn't hurt him."

Rangers developed the film in his camera, which bore a 400-millimeter lens. He had taken about forty pictures of the bears, followed them long enough to finish off one roll of film and part of another. Several of them show the bears looking at him, and the last clear shot was probably taken from about fifty yards. It shows the sow moving toward him. Clearly, he had violated her safety zone.

Most of his wounds were in the front of his body, indicating he had faced the bear instead of lying flat or curling in a ball.

He also had a .45-caliber pistol with him, a violation of federal law in Glacier at the time, but there was no indication that he fired it.

For those purists who believe an animal can read their thoughts, the pistol probably would indicate some tainted thinking on Gibbs's part. Realists who deal with grizzlies all the time—such as the rangers in Glacier—say it probably just made him cocky. A .45 isn't likely to stop a charging grizzly. What it will do, says Alan O'Neill, assistant superintendent at the time, is create a false sense of security, let you feel safe enough to take chances you wouldn't normally take.

———

Eleven days after Bill Tesinsky's death, there were no photo editors purring in the conference room at Yellowstone headquarters in Mammoth Hot Springs. All the evidence had been gathered, and a somber board of inquiry had assembled. It included Park Service administrators and bear specialists from outside the agency, including Dr. Stephen Herrero, one of the world's top experts on bear attacks.

No. 59 had been "approached and photographed at close range on hundreds of occasions," the board found, and had displayed notable tolerance. But Tesinsky approached her in a place where people almost never go. He had acted, in the bear's eyes, in an unpredictable way while she was foraging natural foods. "In such a situation, bear Number 59 probably would not tolerate as close an approach by people as she would when in developed areas where people would be expected by the bear."

The bear was clearly habituated, and that's why Tesinsky was able to get so close, the board found, but that's not why he died.

"We believe that Number 59's habituation allowed Mr. Tesinsky to approach, but that due to his desire to get good, albeit dangerous photographs, he approached too closely and was attacked and killed. The circumstances do not suggest that the bear attacked and killed Mr. Tesinsky with the intent of preying on him. Rather, the circumstances suggest that Mr. Tesinsky approached and provoked the bear to attack."

Ron Tesinsky isn't so sure. He says he doesn't hold the bear responsible for the attack. He knows his brother may have been too aggressive.

"He may have pushed for a photography shot," Ron Tesinsky says. But he also believes the bear was "on the prod," that her frequent handling and drugging, possibly the recent loss of her cubs, may have given her a bad attitude.

"I don't hold one thing against bears at all," he says. "I think they're magnificent animals. As far as the bears in the wild and protecting them, I'm all for it."

And he realizes how difficult it is to keep animals from becoming habituated and therefore dangerous, even without Frans Lanting's advice.

"It's hard to have an area like that, with so many tourists going through there. They can't live as a natural animal out there with all those people. But I don't like the idea of people handling them like that. I think it's wrong. Drugging them, hauling them in culvert cages. Even domestic animals handled that way get wild. All that stuff has to have an effect on them."

At least one bear expert said Ron Tesinsky might have a point.

"Nobody can answer the question: If you handle a bear, does it start to hate humans?" says Barrie Gilbert, a man who was terribly mauled in 1977, then went on to study bears for 35 years.

The board of inquiry didn't see it that way.

"There is no indication or evidence that the bear's physical condition, its history of handling, drugging, and monitoring, or the low levels of the whitebark pine nut crop in the Yellowstone ecosystem were directly related to the incident," the board found.

The bear's habituation was a factor, however, even though the Park Service had tried to break her of it. The agency's job gets harder, and bears get more dangerous, when people like Lanting preach to amateurs on how to undo its work.

—◦—

The whole Tesinsky family was deeply saddened by the death, and Ron built a sort of monument to his brother in the basement of his home. It includes some of his photographs, his cowboy hat, his funeral notice. Bill's daughters were angry, Ron says, and briefly considered suing the Park Service. But that didn't happen.

Jeff Henry, who also has many years of experience around Yellowstone grizzlies, says he disagreed with the Park Service's decision to kill the bear.

"I didn't think it was fair," he says. "If it made sense to kill that bear, then it makes sense to kill all bears. Any bear would have reacted that way in a similar situation."

He does understand the fear of a lawsuit, however. If the bear had not been killed, and if she had hurt another person later, the Park Service could have found itself on the losing side of a court battle, he notes.

It's happened before. In 1972, twenty-five-year-old Harry Walker, of Anniston, Alabama, and a friend camped illegally near Old Faithful, unwilling or unable to pay campground fees. There was food strewn around the camp and that lured in a grizzly, which killed Walker as the two men walked into camp after dark. His family sued and won $87,000 from the Park Service. The ruling was overturned on appeal, but park managers remain wary of such cases.

Gary Brown still maintains the decision to kill the bear was the correct one.

"The decision was made on the fact that a bear was dragging this person. It was based on respect, and not for the bear in this case."

Tom Murphy also feels bad that No. 59 had to die.

"The bear was trying to ignore this guy and go about her business."

Murphy knows that experience well. He's been charged four times by grizzlies.

He tells a story about escorting Bob Bennett, formerly President Bill Clinton's personal attorney, on a hike through the Hayden Valley, just a few miles south of where Tesinsky died. Bennett wanted to see some bison and Murphy agreed to show him some. The two men crested a small rise and spotted a bison carcass about sixty yards away. Murphy knew that grizzlies often feed at such sites for days and wanted to leave right away.

"We went about ten steps away from the carcass and this head pops up, a grizzly bear's head. Fortunately, she was facing into the belly of the bison and didn't see us. I pointed it out to Bob and said, 'We've got to get out of here.'"

They started moving toward a herd of bison, trying to put the shaggy giants between them and the bear.

"We got about 120 yards away and she saw us. She just went nuts, racing back and forth all around the carcass. She was digging, throwing dirt on the carcass, wanting to protect her food. Then the three little cubs woke up.

"As soon as she panicked, I stopped, set my tripod down, and got down, trying to minimize my threat.

"Then she got down on all fours and came running at us full blast, through the sagebrush, the three cubs racing after her, trying to keep up. I thought, oh shit, this is going to hurt.

"So I stood up, trying to look as big as I could. Bob's a pretty good-size guy, too, and he was standing right beside me, which helps. If you've got a couple people, you stand side by side so you look as big as possible.

"She kept coming. It was going through my head that at about fifty yards I would raise my arms as high as I could and yell. At about twenty yards I would drop down and curl up in a ball."

But at eighty yards the bear spun around and ran out of sight, her cubs trailing behind her.

"After a while, I got my heart working again."

Murphy and Bennett survived that charge because they did several things right. They moved away when they saw the carcass, trying to put at least the recommended one hundred yards between them and the bears. They shrank down, minimizing the threat when the bear first showed signs of agitation. They stood up, looking as big as possible when the charge began. They were ready to play dead if the attack continued.

None of these things are easy to do when an angry grizzly is charging. It takes a cool head and considerable knowledge of bears. Murphy was charged once in Alaska after he and three other professional photographers surprised a bear during a midday nap. Murphy froze and tried to look as big as he could. The others all ran away and left him standing there. Luckily, the bear did the same thing.

Did Tesinsky do any of that? No one can say for sure, but it seems unlikely, given his limited knowledge about grizzlies, his aggressive nature, and his brother's certainty that he would have tried to fight the bear.

"When people hang around a grizzly long enough, eventually, she's going to catch somebody doing something stupid," Murphy says. "And she's going to be blamed as a violent bear. I hate it."

Just being in grizzly country can be incredibly exhilarating, Murphy points out, even if the bears are at a distance. You don't need to get close to get the feeling.

"The thing that I really like about traveling or hiking in country where you know there are grizzly bears is that your hearing improves, your eyesight improves, your sense of smell improves. You're paying attention a lot more. You're a lot more alive if you're paying attention to bears."

And if you're not paying attention, you can wind up a lot more dead.

Postscript

Twenty-five years passed without another fatal bear attack in Yellowstone. But on July 6, 2011, Brian and Marylyn Matayoshi surprised a female grizzly with cubs while hiking in the park's Pelican Valley. They tried to back away, but the bear charged and the couple tried to run. The mother bear caught Brian and killed him quickly. Marylyn played dead and survived without serious physical injury.

The Park Service took no action against the bear.

9

Bear Whisperers

PEOPLE CALL THEM BEAR WHISPERERS.

They know how to handle grizzly bears, live with them, approach them, survive in their close presence. They do things that would scare the wits out of most people: approach within arm's length of a grizzly, follow them through the woods, live with them. Most of them issue warnings. "Don't do this at home" is the message they often give. Too many people don't listen.

Timothy Treadwell and Jim Cole were men of this type, able to work closely with bears for many years. Both had great affection and respect for the bears. It wasn't enough: Treadwell was killed and eaten by a bear. Cole had his face torn off and lost an eye.

———

Treadwell was the better known of the two. Made famous in the documentary movie *Grizzly Man* by Werner Herzog, Treadwell died on October 6, 2003, in Katmai National Park, Alaska. It wasn't pretty. Even worse was the death of his girlfriend, Amie Huguenard, who put her faith in what Treadwell said he could do, which means she put her life in his hands. His hubris and stubborn delusions killed them both.

"I will die for them," he once said of Katmai's grizzlies, speaking into his own camera. "But I will not die at their claws and paws."

As it turns out, he was wrong on both counts. A bear did kill him. At least two bears died because of him, and there could be more to come. Time will tell.

Treadwell's life story is a familiar one in the world of bear enthusiasts. He grew up in Long Island, New York; moved to California; and tried to be an actor. That didn't work, and by his own account he wound up drinking too much and taking a lot of dope, enough that he figured it would kill him someday.

Then he wound up riding a motorcycle to Alaska and ran into a grizzly in close quarters, and the bear did what most grizzlies do: It looked him over and ran away. But for Treadwell this became an epiphany, a gift. As with so many of us, the grizzly's power mystified and enthralled him. That this one—like almost all bears—decided not to injure or kill him, gave Treadwell the wake-up call he'd been looking for. He was thirty-three years old and realized grizzlies were pretty cool but decided they needed his help, which meant he had to quit drinking and get focused. For thirteen summers he came back to Alaska, taking pictures and videos of bears, then returning to the Lower Forty-Eight to speak to schoolchildren about the gentle nature of bears and solicit donations to finance another trip.

The story goes on, and you can read about it in the book he coauthored, *Among Grizzlies,* or you can see more in Herzog's movie. Mike Lapinski also wrote an insightful biography of Treadwell called *Death in the Grizzly Maze.*

Treadwell appointed himself the true protector of grizzlies in Katmai. He worried about intrusions by ecotourists; indifference by the National Park Service; and, especially, poachers, though as a national park Katmai was already protected, and officials said poaching hadn't been much of a problem there.

Treadwell didn't buy any of it. He'd read of atrocities committed against bears. Greedy fools lust for an illegal trophy or sometimes slaughter them for their gallbladders, which fetch huge sums in the traditional apothecaries of East Asia, where some people believe they cure diseases ranging from impotence to liver ailments. Treadwell tried to convince the world that if the bears of Katmai were to avoid senseless death, he had to be among them, provide a human presence benign to grizzlies yet fearsome to wrongdoers or people who infringed on his turf.

He ran around acting like a bear, sneaking through the brush, huffing at people who arrived in boats to look at the bears he considered his own. A lot of people thought he was nuts. Treadwell thought he was special.

"Come here and camp here, try to do what I do here, and you will die here," Treadwell told the audience he envisioned, speaking into his own camera shortly before he died. "They will get you. I found a way to survive with them. I love these bears enough to survive and do it right."

In the early years Treadwell took a lot of chances, but he also took some precautions. He brought bear spray and gave one particularly troublesome bear a heavy dose in the face. For a time he strung electric fencing around his tents to keep the bears away. Later, he spurned both those common protective devices.

As the years progressed, he seemed to lose touch with reality, to think that he had become a bear.

Lapinski reprinted one of Treadwell's final letters, a note to one of his financial backers.

My transformation is complete—a fully accepted wild animal-brother to these bears. I run free among them—with absolute love and respect for all animals. I am kind and viciously tough.

People—especially the bear experts of Alaska—believe this cannot be done. Some even bet on my death. They are sure you must have some sort of weapon for defense—pepper spray at the least, an electric fence a must. And you cannot hope to make it in a flimsy tent under thick cover among one of the earth's largest gatherings of giant brown grizzly bears.

People who knowingly enter bear habitat with pepper spray, guns, and electric fences are committing a crime to the animals. They begin with the accepted idea of bringing instruments of pain to the animals. If they are that fearful, then they have no place in the land of this perfect animal.

Three weeks later the bears ate him.

The dark humor arose almost immediately. Wags in Alaska quipped that Katmai's bears were "fed well by Treadwell," and the Internet still buzzes with mockery on YouTube videos. But German filmmaker Werner Herzog, whom some people accuse of having a death fetish of his own, saw a real story there. But it's not likely the story Treadwell would have told.

The film, excellent in a macabre way, uses Treadwell's own footage to show him taking increasing risks with the bears: swimming with them, touching them, cooing his love in his childlike voice, issuing profane rants against the National Park Service because it didn't like his breaking the rules about approaching bears and camping illegally.

On his website Herzog calls Treadwell's life "a tangle of passionate environmental activism, idealistic half-truths and outright lies."

Before his death, Treadwell convinced a number of people he was doing good and appropriate work. He attracted a lot of press, got donations from movie stars, became the closest thing there was to a celebrity in the small world of people who work closely with bears. Herzog's film documented the deceits, the exaggerations, the self-aggrandizement, and vanity of Treadwell, his crocodile tears, his increasingly loose grip on reality.

Huguenard, too, worried over his mental condition during their final summer.

"Amie called him hell-bent on destruction" and planned to leave him for good, Herzog says in the film.

But she hadn't left yet. She still had enough faith in him to return for a final week to the place Treadwell called "the grizzly maze" and do so late in the year, when the salmon had nearly disappeared, when new and unfamiliar bears had arrived. There, in a tent that contained no bear spray, unprotected by electric fencing, a bear attacked and killed them both. It hit Treadwell first. While it was thrashing him, he called for Huguenard to help, to attack it with a frying pan. Then he urged her to run away. But the bear got her, too. The final six minutes were all recorded, but only on audio: The lens cap remained on the camera.

The couple had been scheduled to leave the next day and when their pilot arrived he found a bear jealously guarding their bodies, eating voraciously. The pilot backed off and called park rangers, who approached with shotguns and pistols. When a huge bear charged to within twenty feet, they killed it. When a second and smaller bear charged, they killed that one, too. That's what often happens when the government sends its people to clean up somebody else's mess: The rangers understandably don't want to add their own names to the roster of the dead.

The impacts of the deaths rippled. Treadwell's friends eulogized him as a champion of the bear and its wilderness. When a new edition of his book came out two years later, an introduction by coauthor Jewel Palovak says he died "in the field among the bears he devoted his life to," but it doesn't say how he died, and it says nothing about Huguenard, who died because she trusted him. It notes that "in 2004, the first summer without Timothy's presence, six bears were poached" in Katmai. But it doesn't point out that the poaching took place dozens of miles from the places where Treadwell camped.

He founded an organization called Grizzly People that still exists, or still has a website anyway, though its Internal Revenue Service documents listed no assets and no revenue for 2004. The website says it is devoted to "preserving bears and their wilderness habitat." It tells people not to feed bears, never to run from them, and to stay at least one hundred yards from them, then offers video of Treadwell within a few yards of a grizzly, playfully offering it fishing advice.

The celebrity Treadwell courted in life expanded after his death. But not for Huguenard. She remains a footnote in most accounts of Treadwell's life. The Grizzly People website barely mentions her. At least Herzog gave her some attention and respect. So did Lapinski.

Chuck Jonkel thinks Huguenard's family should have filed a wrongful death lawsuit against Treadwell's estate.

"I thought they could do it and win. And I would certainly testify" for the family, says Jonkel, the dean of North American grizzly bear experts. "They could have gone after him and his organization."

Now eighty years old and with more than five decades of experience with all sorts of bears, Jonkel remains a staunch advocate of letting wild bears be wild bears.

"I'm still angry at [Treadwell] and the things he encouraged," Jonkel says. "He was out there playing with bears and inventing things to get his picture in the paper."

And he spawned imitators.

"Now we've got half a dozen Treadwells out there," he says, people encouraging others, through their photographs and videos, to take too many chances, approach bears, and put themselves and the bruins at risk. Whether they like the label or not, these people, like Treadwell, often are called "bear whisperers."

"I see red every time I hear that," Jonkel says. He maintains that, no matter how clear a bear whisperer's message may be, how explicit the warnings, there are people who just don't listen.

Some are good enough to get away with it, maybe forever, in a place like Katmai, where the bears are mostly fat and tolerant and happy. Others just think they're good enough.

"You've got to count on there being a bunch of idiots out there that are going to go out and misuse the information, and then the bear gets blamed," Jonkel says. "You're going to get the bear in trouble, and the bear's going to be dead, and it's going to be your fault."

The Katmai Coast is a popular place for watching grizzlies for the simple reason that so many of them gather there, to feed on sedges in the spring and on runs of salmon in the late summer and early fall. Treadwell often tried to give the impression of incredible isolation, but anybody with a valid credit card can book a photography tour there. It can get a little crowded.

The bears generally cooperate. Since they live in unusually high densities, the bears grow accustomed to seeing other bears. They learn which ones pose a threat and which ones don't. And since this gives them more social skills than most bears, they learn to ignore people, mostly, if the humans behave themselves.

Photographer Buck Wilde, whose website calls him a bear whisperer, leads tours there every year. He often crossed paths with Treadwell.

"We were anything but friends, most of the time," Wilde says. "He wanted these places to be all his private turf. So he'd act very weird and manufacture stories about what I and other people were doing. He did not have both feet on the ground, emotionally."

Wilde maintains that, as with animals such as horses or dogs, people with the right training can learn to understand the bears' body language, their motivations, the threats they pose. You have to understand how to make sure the bear views you as something nonthreatening, nonaggressive. But that's a unique set of skills that most people lack.

Treadwell had those skills, according to John Rogers, owner of Katmai Coastal Bear Tours.

"His knowledge and understanding of bears was equal to the experience of any commercial bear-viewing guide or bear specialist in Katmai National Park, better than most," Rogers wrote on his company's web page.

But Treadwell's behavior and his contradictions puzzled him, as well.

"I'd say Timothy cared about them as much as any bear enthusiast or commercial operator along the coast of Katmai, but this was second place to his own fascination about himself as a so-called 'bear whisperer.'"

Treadwell claimed to want to educate people about bears, to undo myths about their ferocity, but "when major film companies like the BBC came to create documentaries that would educate millions, Timothy disrupted their filming by yelling and charging up and down streams to scare away the bears," Rogers wrote. "Encounters between us became frequent and hostile."

And he noted, while Treadwell maintained he was protecting the bears, he was doing so "in the largest bear protection area in the world."

Both Lapinski and Rogers say they believe the bear that killed Treadwell and Huguenard was a fairly small animal, not the thousand-pound male the Park Service killed first. That giant probably stole the human bodies from the smaller bear, which rangers killed a few minutes later when it charged them in the growing darkness.

The season was late, salmon were scarce, and hibernation loomed, with its constant prods to find more calories. The bear could have been attracted by smells from the couple's tents as they prepared their gear for departure, Rogers writes.

"The bear was probably curious about it all, approached the tent, and Timothy confronted it with his usual reaction of dominance toward a curious bear: making noise, hollering and running toward it," Rogers writes. "This situation, especially if the bear was unknown to him, along with the poor weather conditions, which make it difficult for bears to use their sense of smell and hearing, likely triggered the attack."

Once they were dead, Treadwell and Huguenard became food. So did the bears the rangers killed. A storm kept investigators from flying to the site the next day, but when they were able to return, they disemboweled the big bear and removed human remains. Other grizzlies had eaten almost all of the smaller bear, so there wasn't much the team could learn from that carcass. Eventually, bears and other scavengers ate the big bear, too.

Two dead people. Two dead bears. It's the last thing Treadwell wanted. But it's what he got. And he wanted fame. He wanted to be the star of his own documentary. He got that. But it wasn't the movie he thought he'd be making. Treadwell wanted to talk about bears. Herzog talked about how they killed him, how his obsession and self-absorption led to his own death and that of Huguenard.

Treadwell thought he had special skills. Maybe he did. Maybe it was just one mistake, or a series of them.

Wilde said the bear had been sending Treadwell signals before the attack, with bluff charges and stare downs.

"This bear had been trying to send a message for five days," Wilde says. "Timothy fell into the trap of thinking he was special enough to win that bear's heart. If he had kept his ego in check, he'd be alive today."

The bears would be, too.

Jonkel worries that it will happen again. No matter how good your skills are, you can't read a grizzly's mind. Not every time, anyway.

Treadwell proved that, at least.

<hr />

When photographer and author Jim Cole died, an obituary ran on the front page of his hometown newspaper, the *Bozeman Daily Chronicle*, in Montana, on July 30, 2010. It included a quote from Cole's book.

Grizzly "attacks are defensive and they're not out there stalking us," the paper quoted him as saying. "They're peace-loving animals and they're just the most fascinating, interesting animals I've ever known."

On the same front page ran another bear story with a very different message. This one included a picture of a woman in a hospital bed. She'd been attacked a couple of days earlier in her tent by a grizzly bear, an animal that was treating her an awful lot like a potential meal, one that killed and consumed a nearby camper later that night.

"It was hunting me," said the banner headline, quoting Deb Freele, the woman who'd been chewed on.

So which story was right? Maybe both of them. When it comes to grizzly bears, things often get complicated. Contradictory, even. They almost always avoid people. But sometimes, even the savviest among us suffer at their teeth and claws.

The summer and fall of 2010 were busy years for grizzlies in Montana. They attacked and killed two people near Yellowstone, the first such incidents in a quarter century; grizzlies were spotted far into the Montana prairies; a poor year for natural foods sent the bears wandering, and nearly eighty of them would die at the hands of humans in the greater Yellowstone area; and photographer, author, and bear advocate Jim Cole died. Having survived two grizzly maulings, one of which took out an eye and ripped off half his face, Cole died at home, in his bed, apparently from a heart attack, at the age of sixty. The ink was barely dry on the first edition of his new book.

If he'd lived long enough to see the headline on the Freele story, it probably would have given him fits. He hated that kind of coverage for his beloved grizzly bears.

A Midwesterner who never lost his Chicago accent, Cole bristled with energy and enthusiasm, especially when it came to grizzly bears, the animal to which he had dedicated twenty years of his life: watching them, taking pictures of them, following them in the woods, trying to teach people that, almost all the time, they try to avoid trouble with people.

He was a prodigious walker who thought nothing of covering twenty-five backcountry miles in a day. He maintained he had tallied over twenty-seven thousand of those rugged miles, enough to circumnavigate the globe and still hike from the Rockies to the Atlantic.

"Humping a 40-pound backpack and camera up and down relentless switchbacks for hours was a good workout but not a big deal," he wrote in his third book about grizzlies, *Blindsided: Surviving a Grizzly Attack and Still Loving the Great Bear.*

That book detailed both of the maulings he endured. The first came in Glacier National Park in 1993, when he spooked a subadult bear from its day bed alongside a trail. By the time Cole saw it, it was only a few feet away and in full charge. It took him down and chomped his hand, his skull, and his camera holster before companion Tim Rubbert distracted it, then unloaded his pepper spray in its face. The bear disappeared, but Cole still faced a ten-mile walk to the hospital.

As bear attacks go, that one was relatively mild. After the doctors put a few stitches on his head and a sling on his arm, he convinced them to release him that day.

There was nothing mild about the second attack. Cole was hiking alone that snowy morning, about three miles from the highway, off-trail, in Yellowstone National Park's Hayden Valley. The date was May 23, 2007, and as always, he was hoping to see grizzly bears.

"I'm not interested in just a hike," he wrote. "I've hiked thousands of miles in Rocky Mountain National Park (in Colorado) but it doesn't hold my interest because it doesn't have grizzlies."

He found bear sign that morning, none of it fresh. He kept walking, glassing hillsides with his binoculars, looking for grizzlies he knew were in the area because he'd seen them just a few days earlier. It seemed there were no bears to watch that day, so he turned east, toward the road, and crested a small rise topped with a line of thin sage.

Then, wham. Kapowya. The bear was on him. As with the first attack, he saw the bear from just a few feet away. Unlike in the first attack, this animal was a mature female with a new cub to protect, not an immature bear just trying to get away.

"There was nothing I could do except go down quickly, grab my bear spray and cover my head," Cole wrote. "I did a poor job across the board."

The bear dislocated his right shoulder when it tackled him. Then it planted one massive paw on his right arm, the one that was wiggling for the bear spray. With its other paw it raked his face repeatedly, breaking his jaw and most of the other bones between eyebrow and chin, destroying one eye and shredding the eyelid on the other. Nose, lips, and ear were destroyed. He kept reaching for the spray, which he saw as his only hope, and the bear kept raking him. He tried to cover his face with his left arm, but it didn't do much good.

"My feeling at the time was that she was purposefully tunneling her head under my body to inflict additional facial damage," he wrote.

That's possible. Bears trying to neutralize a perceived threat often attack the face. They treat people like they do dangerous bears: They try to neutralize an opponent's most fearsome weapons, the teeth.

Then Cole quit moving, and as quickly as she attacked, the bear left. Cole was three miles from help, alone, and in a lot of trouble. He'd told nobody where he was going. One eye was demolished, and with the other he could see only though a slit the bear had torn in the eyelid. Somehow, stumbling through rough country, bleeding hard, he made it to the highway, then an ambulance, then a few weeks in the hospital and several rounds of surgery.

"She had literally 'defaced' me," Cole wrote.

But he lived, a testament to his tenacity and physical vigor. His surgeon in Idaho Falls, a man who has treated six mauling victims, said Cole's case was the worst he had ever seen.

Cole described the attack as purely defensive in nature. He hadn't warned the bear that he was nearby.

"So, with all my years of experience, my attitude might have been a bit complacent on that morning," he wrote. "I may have assumed that because I had not seen any sign of bears so far that there would not be any, which is always a big mistake."

Cole never blamed the bear for the attack. She saw him as a threat to her cub, neutralized the threat, and went away. And he never lost enthusiasm for bears. As he healed, he went back to work writing songs about bears, planning to take his message of tolerance and affection beyond the greater Yellowstone area to a bigger audience. He remained rightly convinced that grizzly bears are misunderstood, too often seen as random killers or vermin. He even saw some advantages in disfigurement.

"Without the drama inherent in the attack and its aftermath," he wrote, he would have remained a bear advocate anyway. "But it would have been far more difficult to gain a national audience. In a very real way, the attack has made it possible for me to fulfill my life's purpose in a way that would not have been available to me before. I suppose my eye was the price I had to pay for that gift, and although it's not like I had a choice, I'm really okay with that."

He said he looked forward to decades of teaching people about bears. Unfortunately, that didn't happen. He died just a few weeks after his last book was published.

❦

Cole said he was happy with his life, that he wouldn't change a thing. But a number of people weren't happy with Jim Cole. Even before the second mauling, he had a growing reputation for pushing the limits with grizzlies. In July 2004, Yellowstone officials in an airplane spotted him within twenty yards of a family of grizzlies. Rangers issued him a citation that could have meant banishment from his beloved Yellowstone. Cole admitted he was close to the bears but said he approached them unknowingly, took a few pictures after he spotted them, and moved away slowly. A judge found him not guilty, but in the wake of the incident, the National Park Service changed its rules.

"Under the previous law you could not knowingly approach within one hundred yards of a bear," Yellowstone Bear Management Specialist Kerry Gunther told the press after Cole died. "After [the Park Service lost] that case, because the government couldn't prove he approached the bear, his method was that he would crouch down and let the bears forage past him. [In order to ban that practice] the law was changed to say you cannot knowingly approach or remain with one hundred yards of a bear."

Crouching down and letting bears approach is a common tactic among photographers shooting the numerous, well-fed, and relatively docile bears of Katmai, where Treadwell did his controversial work. If Cole continued to employ this technique in Yellowstone, he never got caught. But he had a reputation for pushing the envelope.

"He thought he knew everything the biologists knew, but he wasn't a biologist," says veteran biologist Chuck Jonkel, a revered figure in the world of bear people. "He was getting too close to bears. I was kind of leaning on him about it, and he was resisting. The next time I saw him I was really going to come down on him, but the bear came down on him first."

In his defense Cole maintained that he never had any trouble with a bear that he spotted before it saw him. He also acknowledged that he would trail bears into the woods, though he insisted he did it, mostly, without bothering them.

In his book he quotes a naturalist from Canada's Jasper National Park: "He confided to me that the only real way to learn about an animal's life was to safely follow it to get a firsthand look at 'what it eats, where it travels, and how it interacts with other animals.' I never forgot that advice."

And he practiced it, something that disturbed even his closest friends.

"I thought he encroached on bears, he really pushed their limits," said Michael Sanders, a close friend of many years. "I told him I didn't want him to end up like Treadwell."

Cole insisted that he was careful, that he knew how to get close enough for great pictures of Yellowstone grizzlies without endangering them or himself.

"The difference between me and other people is that I understand bear behavior and keep my cool," he said in his book. "Still, I don't recommend what I do to anyone. It takes experience and a great deal of discipline to minimize the dangers to humans and bears."

He acknowledged he should have been paying more attention and making more noise the day he was attacked. He didn't acknowledge breaking the standard admonition against traveling alone in grizzly country. Rather, he boasted that he'd probably spent more time alone, on foot, in grizzly habitat than anybody alive.

Like Treadwell he maintained that his special knowledge kept him safe. He might have been right, up to a point. His specialized skills let him approach bears for years, and he took a lot of incredible photographs.

Then, on a chilly morning when he wasn't expecting to see a bear, when his camera was still in its holster, an event of incredible rarity happened: a second mauling, one of perhaps three in all of North America.

"Anybody can be in the wrong place at the wrong time," he wrote.

True enough. But following the rules can help you get home from that place in one piece.

POSTSCRIPT

Timothy Treadwell and Jim Cole had at least a passing acquaintance. Both had spent a lot of time in Alaska, and they shared a love of bears and a capacity for endurance. They even exchanged Christmas cards.

"Are you going back to Denali?" Treadwell wrote to Cole in 1994. "It must be wonderful to study those beautiful bears for such a long time and so close!"

For his part Cole was dismayed about the impacts of Treadwell's death.

"There must have been some big arrogance [t]here," Cole wrote to a friend in 2004, adding that bear spray could have saved Huguenard and the bears. "He always said that if something ever happened to him, no bears should be killed/prosecuted. That is a stupid and or naïve statement because we know that after an incident like this, bears are often killed."

10

Grizzly RoboCop

AT SIX FEET NINE AND 385 POUNDS, THE BIGGEST BIKER WAS ABOUT THE size of a grizzly bear. Along with a couple of friends, he was doing everything possible to put Troy Hurtubise in the hospital for a long time. The big guy had a splitting maul, a second man had a two-by-four, and the third had a baseball bat, and they were all whacking Hurtubise as hard as they could.

Hurtubise stood up to the punishment for a long time before one of the big guy's mighty swats flattened him in the poolroom parking lot, tipping him over backward like a tree. Then the big biker kept working like a berserk logger, trying to take the limbs off him, chopping on his legs until the head fell off the maul, keeping it up until the hardwood handle shredded, leaving him with a handful of splinters.

Hurtubise, cocooned in his Ursus Mark VI bearproof suit, didn't feel a thing.

"I heard somebody banging away out there," he said, once a couple of his buddies pulled his helmet off. "Like a woodpecker."

Then he danced a clumsy little jig.

It was the final test. The suit of titanium and plastic, flameproof rubber, air bags and chain mail, the bubble-headed contraption that would eventually cost him everything while turning him into a minor celebrity, had weathered all sorts of beatings, as well as a stroll through a bonfire. It—and Hurtubise—had endured the sort of punishment suffered by the coyote in the old Roadrunner cartoons: tumbles off 150-foot cliffs and a few collisions with a three-ton truck going thirty miles an hour. Wearing the suit, Hurtubise survived a smack from a three-hundred-pound log-on-a-rope that dropped forty feet onto his chest and face. The suit stood up to sharp arrows from a hundred-pound bow, slugs from a 12-gauge shotgun.

Now, Hurtubise said, the suit was ready for a grizzly bear. It was time to go find the Old Man.

＞⌣

That was in August 1995. Hurtubise had been looking for the Old Man—his name for all grizzly bears—since one had let him walk away unharmed but dumbfounded in 1984.

Twenty years old at the time, he had been panning for gold in a remote part of central British Columbia called Humidity Creek. Already a seasoned prospector and no slouch as a salesman, the high school dropout had organized an expedition of greenhorns willing to pony up a few thousand dollars apiece to come with him. But a solid week of rain had washed the gold from his customers and Hurtubise was alone in the bush, where things were getting weird. There was a bad feeling out there, a "presence" that had joined him, an ominous, invisible thing that would come out of nowhere and seize him by the mind, leave him gibbering with fear and flinging tiny, useless bullets into the trees. It would grab him at work in the daytime or in his tent at night. Too scared to leave the tent, he'd grab his .22-caliber rifle and start pumping rounds in all directions. But he didn't chase away the presence and he didn't do much for the tent, either.

"The presence was there," Hurtubise insists. "I wouldn't even get out of the tent. The fear was too much. I just laid out round after round."

Or he'd be panning for gold, standing knee-deep in cold water, and a flock of ravens would break from a dead tree. There was no apparent reason for the sudden rising, but Hurtubise grabbed his rifle—it had a sawed-off barrel and a sixteen-shot clip loaded with .22 shorts, a combination that made it inaccurate past a few feet—and started tossing lead.

"I didn't know what was behind me, and I didn't care. I must have used 90 percent of my ammunition, just shooting at nothing."

In retrospect he knew it made no sense, but he was a young tough guy, skilled in martial arts, not quite as independent as he'd thought he was, and a long way from anybody. Too proud to leave and too scared to stay, he was learning how much he didn't know about the bush.

"It was like somebody watching you. But the last thing I thought of was an animal, especially a grizzly bear."

At that time of year in that part of the world, there are a handful of prospectors around, and that's about it. They don't trust each other much, and Hurtubise rattles off all kinds of bad-guy-in-the-bush lore.

"If a man comes into your camp this far out, it's not because he got lost and his Winnebago's broken down. He's either gonna kill you and take your supplies, or he's gonna sit down and have a cup of coffee."

Hurtubise says his practice was to point his gun at all strangers at first sight, just to make sure all they wanted was coffee and conversation.

"They understand," says Hurtubise, a man who fires out all his stories as if he's still squeezing the trigger on a semiautomatic weapon, spitting a profanity-laced spray of bear lore, self-aggrandizement, and quotes from academic journals and bad movies.

The tension was getting to him, there on Humidity Creek. He'd had only four hours of sleep in the past three days, and prospecting is no walk in the park, sluicing tiny flakes of gold from huge amounts of sand. Then, one mid-August afternoon, exhausted by hard work and no sleep, he was trudging back to camp, bent under a heavy load of prospecting gear. He had a rucksack on his back; carried an aluminum sluice box in one hand, the rifle in the other; and towed an inflated one-man rubber boat with his head, letting it rest on his back.

He believes that "any mountain man worth half his weight in spit" always carries a brace of long, razor-sharp knives. On his shoulder he wore a long, double-edged dagger, butt down so he could grab it quickly. On his hip rode a bowie knife, nine inches long and sharp enough to shave with. Such weapons can save your life in any number of ways, he says. But they almost got him in big trouble that August day.

He had just entered a small meadow when he got the feeling again, felt the "presence" that had so agitated him for days. Years later he would compare it to the feeling rape victims talk about: They can't see anybody, but they know they're being followed, stalked. Even if they're wrong, it's a bad experience, and they often go to somebody like Hurtubise for martial arts lessons.

He looked up, a little breeze blew the boat off his head, and he saw the grizzly, leaning over a stump. A white beard adorned his chin, labeling the bear as "the Old Man." Hurtubise had never seen a grizzly before, and this one looked so calm, so human. In the face of Hurtubise's trigger-happy panic, his sweats and nightmares, the bear's placid demeanor was a damned insult. He finally knew what had been hassling him for three days, what had made him turn a perfectly good tent into Swiss cheese, had deprived him of sleep and interfered with his work. And he lost his temper about it.

"If I had picked up the dinghy and kept walking, he wouldn't have done a damn thing. But I went nuts on the bear. I was ranting and hollering, saying, 'Come on, you son of a bitch, let's go.' And man, he came."

The bear tucked his head and charged, hitting the brakes a few feet away and skidding on the slick grass, finally halting close enough that Hurtubise could feel his hot breath, could taste the stench coming from him.

"Right then is when I shit in my pants," he says. "I pissed in them, too."

The bear popped his teeth together, growled, danced back and forth on its front paws. In short, it gave all the classic indications of a really agitated bear, and it was about three feet away. Then it smashed him in the chest, giving him a tremendous butt with its snout, sending sluice box, rifle, and Hurtubise flying in three directions. Troy landed on his ass, his knapsack holding him almost in a sitting position.

"If I hadn't had a knapsack, I probably would have played dead, probably would have instinctively gone into a fetal position. Just closed my eyes like a child under the blankets."

But he didn't. What happened next is hard for him to describe. The fear that made him fill his pants disappeared, replaced by something else.

"A calm came over me that was unbelievable. It just flushed through my veins. I knew right there I was going to die."

Then the tranquility disappeared, too. The anger was coming back. It's a martial arts thing, he says, a mental process where anger replaces fear.

"I thought about that four-hundred-pound bear raking me with claws and teeth. I said bullshit, that's not going to happen."

The bear was just a quick lunge away but had become still. The two stared at each other. Hurtubise slipped his arms from the backpack straps and drew the blade from the shoulder sheath. The bear didn't twitch. So he drew the other blade. He stood. He yelled at the bear.

"I'm so pissed off with all the bullshit you put me through," he shouted. "I'm going to take both of these, as sure as God made little green apples, and I'm going to shove 'em both right up your ass. And that's a fact."

The bear took this loud announcement with remarkable calm. It turned around, then swiveled its head back to look at the rash, loud fellow with the big knives.

"And if a bear can smile, the Old Man did it."

It ignored the impertinence. It granted an indulgence. It walked away, slowly, and never looked back.

"He knew he could kill me if he wanted to, but he decided it wasn't worth the effort," Hurtubise says. "From that day forward I've never figured out why it happened."

—◦—

Which brings us back to the bikers in the parking lot.

Hurtubise had asked them nicely if they wouldn't mind clubbing him for a while. It was his father's idea. You see, Troy was having a little credibility problem by then, and he thought the bikers could help.

After he met the Old Man, he'd broken camp as fast as he could and stayed away for a couple of weeks. When he returned to get the stuff he'd been too scared to pack right away, he ran into a British Columbia conservation officer who thought the whole story was downright hilarious.

"'You dipshit,' he said. 'You were a hundred feet away from a scratching pole, right in the middle of his territory. He was a three-year-old, maybe a four-year-old. An old one probably would have killed you dead and ate you in the field for acting like that. It was nothing more than curiosity for this bear. For three days he was probably thinking, who is this guy? What is this thing? And he was probably out there sneaking around corners, watching you. He was probably in your camp a dozen times at night."

Hurtubise later came to agree with the conservation officer. It was a curious young bear, just a teenager on his own, trying to behave himself in a tempting and curious world. The bear was a lot like Hurtubise at the time: It minded its manners and caused no damage but didn't want to be insulted. And it changed Hurtubise's life. The bear would put the man in the headlines and in the movie theaters. Troy's name would come up in Parliament. It would bring him admiration and mockery and bankruptcy.

As soon as Troy got back to civilization, he started reading voraciously about grizzlies. He talked to psychologists and dream analysts and a Lakota medicine man, who told him he'd been knocked on his butt because he was impertinent to the bear. He ordered books about bears in Russia, in Japan, in America in the days of Lewis and Clark. "I wanted to know everything that could be known about grizzly bears." He eventually collected "maybe nine hundred pounds" of books and technical documents, but the more he learned the more he wanted to know. So he went back to high school at the age of twenty-two, and a year later he began a program in natural sciences at Sir Sandford Fleming College in Lindsay, Ontario, the school the conservation officer in British Columbia had recommended for anybody who wanted to spend a life in the bush.

"You get to do what you like, and you get paid for it," the CO had said of his job.

Then in November of 1987, his first year of college, Troy's life changed again. This time it happened in a movie theater: On the screen was the Hollywood mass-carnage thriller, *RoboCop*.

He bolted from the theater, his brainpan cooking.

His reading on grizzly bears had left him with one solid conclusion: "We really don't know nothing about the grizzly bear. Okay, we know about the eyesight, how fast it can run, the ferocity and stuff like this. But behavior-wise, the conclusion was that we can't get close to the damn things. It's impossible. They will kill you."

You can drug a bear and study it, of course, "but if things go awry in the field, the bear's going to be shot. And that's not right."

Then came *RoboCop*, a fantasy about an indestructible policeman who is half man and half machine.

"I looked at it and excluded the Hollywood bullshit. I said if I had the money and the time, I could build a protective suit that would allow me to get in close to grizzlies and do this kind of research."

He wanted to know lots of things: Would pepper spray work in the field? Test results were a little sketchy in those days, and if the spray doesn't work, you're in big trouble. How about bear behavior in the den? And all those signs of agitation—jaw popping; the dance on the front feet; slobbering, growling, or moaning, the sounds that biologists describe as "agonistic." Do any of them signify certain attack? Most bear researchers sensibly prefer to analyze such things from afar. Hurtubise wanted to get in close, to try to see things the way a grizzly sees them. So he started working.

The first suit was of leather, and it was a joke. Later versions were of football pads and plastic, with a motorcycle helmet. Those suits were tough. Winch a boxer's heavy bag up into a tall tree, drop it on his face, and Hurtubise would stand up grinning. Place a boot on his butt and shove him over the 150-foot Niagara Escarpment, and he'd just beg you to do it again. But this latest version, the Ursus Mark VI, this was his baby. That's the one that stood up to bullets and log bashings and, of course, bludgeonings by bikers.

Throughout the evolution of the suit, people had been mocking Hurtubise, who often invited his normal-size friends to whack on him with boards and bats. That's when his dad suggested finding some really big bikers. Video footage of a normal, 180-pound guy hitting him in the head with a bat wouldn't silence scoffers, his dad said. He needed somebody who could "almost simulate the swat of a grizzly bear." A four-hundred-pound biker with a splitting maul ought to do the trick.

⚊ ⚊

In a way it's surprising that Hurtubise ever got that far. It cost him $150,000 and ten years, and that's a lot from a man without a history of patience. While still in college, he invited a group of Russian bear researchers to Canada, bypassing diplomatic channels, and the Russians accepted the invitation, or at least tried to. When officials took offense at this breach of diplomacy, he thumbed his nose at them in the newspapers. That queered all but the smallest chances of any sort of government or university job in Canada. Getting paid for a life in the bush, becoming a conservation officer, had become an incredibly remote possibility. So when he got out of college, he went into the scrap metal business in North Bay, Ontario; married his sweetheart, Lori; and kept plugging away on the suit. Conventional researchers shied away from him, so he assembled his own team. His brother, his uncle John, a sharpshooting friend who used to play dangerous hand-grenade games in Vietnam, a few others.

Then the movies called.

Hurtubise had actively courted media attention, and he got quite a bit of it. It didn't hurt that he spent a couple of nights a week at a local dump, trying without success to goad black bears into attacking him. Peter Lynch, a respected Canadian documentary maker, heard about the project. He went to the Canadian Film Board, the government agency that finances movies in Canada, and the documentary *Project Grizzly* was born. Lynch calls it a "gonzo nature film," a "Northern" that is to Canadian archetypes what Westerns are to the United States.

It's a good movie, too. It was a big hit at the 1996 Toronto Film Festival, and reviewers around the country raved about it. Audiences went nuts when that three-hundred-pound log smashed Hurtubise in the chest, when he ricocheted off the truck bumper, when he bounced down the cliff face.

"Grizzly Adams meets Timothy Leary," gushed one reviewer. "A must-see."

Hurtubise wasn't nearly as impressed. The critics were talking about cinema. They talked about "the shadow of millennial doom," archetypes and layers of meaning in the movie. Hurtubise wanted to talk about grizzly bears. The film portrayed him as some kind of vengeful nut who wanted to go wrestle wild grizzlies, he complains.

"People look at it and say because he was attacked he built this suit," Hurtubise laments. "One hundred and fifty thousand dollars later and ten years of his life to go track down a grizzly and wrestle it. It's just absurd. Stupidity. I thought the movie was going to go a lot more on the science. They've made great acclaim, and they've made millions off it. That's great. But it doesn't give me much credibility."

The final edit of the movie wasn't the only credibility problem, though. The suit was strong. That much the bikers and logs and pickup trucks had made clear. But what good was it? It looked like some sort of creature from *Deep Space Nine*. What would a grizzly do if it saw such an apparition lumbering toward it? Nobody knew. But Hurtubise wanted to find out, and the answer would be on film for all the world to see.

In late September of 1995, Hurtubise and his crew of seven friends and relatives packed up the suit and headed west to the Canadian Rockies near Banff National Park. The big film crew came along for the ride. In Alberta a helicopter was waiting, along with a hunting outfitter with horses and tents. It was a bad year for bear attacks in Canada, but it was getting late in the season to find a grizzly, and Hurtubise was edgy about the timing. On the drive west the radio told him about an attack at Lake Louise that sent six campers to the hospital, and his optimism soared.

Parks Canada was gunning for the bear, but Hurtubise wanted to find her first.

"If they don't shoot her, we'll meet her," he told the cameraman riding in the truck with him. "No doubt about that."

⌁

No such thing occurred, of course. Two days after the vast assemblage of cameramen, grips, guides, gaffers, and horse wranglers made camp, a grizzly was spotted feeding on a carcass. Two men lifted Hurtubise so he could wiggle into the suit, while a third held it steady. They closed all the joints at neck and waist and armpit, turning the five foot eight–inch, 150-pound Hurtubise into a seven foot two–inch, three-hundred-pound prop from a science-fiction movie, a creature whose view of the world came on the video screen inside his helmet.

He took two steps, tripped on a sagebrush, and fell flat on his face.

He was immobile, helpless as a child. If his crew hadn't been there to disassemble the suit, he would have stayed there until the ants ate him.

"Well, I blew that," he said, once the crew had put him on his feet. "I'm like a fish out of water in this thing up here. I need a meadow. I need flat ground. It's the only way it's going to happen, boys."

All this was in the movie, making him look incredibly inept, like a guy who spent ten years on a bear suit that could only be used on asphalt.

It didn't have to be that way, Hurtubise maintains. He had tried to get his hired outfitter to get him to a bear on flat ground. But the grizzlies weren't interested. Bait it in with a carcass, he urged, a big, rancid hunk of meat.

"All I needed was a level playing field, a flat meadow where I could walk up to a baited grizzly. At fifty feet he would charge. I would raise my right arm, blow him with the bear-deterrent spray that's on the market."

Not that he has any faith in red pepper bear spray. He's convinced it doesn't work, and he wants to prove it.

"He would come through the deterrent spray, obviously, because we know it doesn't work. Then he would maul me until he felt the threat was over. He'd go unharmed. I'd go unharmed. And we'd repeat the test."

But there was a problem with Troy's plan. It's illegal to bait bears in Alberta, and wildlife managers were unwilling to bend the rules for the sake of this ursine Quixote, this Ahab of the Rockies. The bears wouldn't cooperate, either. The crew finally found a grizzly, but that was on the last day of the expedition, and the suit was ten miles away. Hurtubise grew bitter.

Two months later, he filed bankruptcy papers back in North Bay. He had quit working for four months and emptied his savings account to help make the movie, which made a lot of money for the Canadian Film Board but didn't pay him anything and portrayed him as a charming eccentric,

Troy Hurtubise and the Ursus Mark VI, the suit that cost him everything.

which may not be too far off the mark. The Ursus Mark VI sat in a trustee's office, to be auctioned off to whoever would take it, the proceeds earmarked for his creditors.

But Hurtubise remains undaunted. The Mark VI obviously was a failure, but he's got blueprints for the next version, the Mark VII, locked in a safety deposit box. All he needs is for somebody to give him about five hundred thousand dollars so he can build it.

The Mark VII will be smaller, lighter, and just as strong. It will be fireproof and bulletproof and will let a man survive a thirty-foot free fall unscathed. Like the Mark VI it will have an "endoskeleton" of airbags to shield him from the shock the outer suit has to take. Its binocular-vision cameras will peer through smoke and darkness. It will contain an hour's worth of air and seven blends of titanium alloy. And it will be flexible. The wearer will be able to climb stairs and roll over. He will even be able to get in and out of the suit, by himself, in sixty seconds. To all of this Troy Hurtubise swears. All will be proven as soon as he can find half a million bucks.

The idea may not be as far-fetched as it seems, according to Dr. Stephen Herrero, a University of Calgary bear researcher who wrote the book—literally—on bear encounters. His volume, *Bear Attacks: Their Causes and Avoidance,* is accepted around the continent by professors, bear managers, and outdoor enthusiasts as the definitive book on the topic. He's known Hurtubise for years and considers him eccentric but by no means a nut. And if a practical suit could be developed, it would have plenty of uses.

"It could have good potential scientific purpose," Herrero says. "Though I'm not sure Troy is the man to apply the science."

The suit would have to be flexible and safe and look at least somewhat "humanoid" if any good science were to be done with it. Its wearer could test how human submission or aggression—and which type of aggression—affects a charging grizzly. Different types of bear spray could be evaluated as well.

"If I had the suit, I could think of a million things to do with it," Herrero says.

Could the experiments be done with wild bears?

"With the ideal suit, you could," Herrero says.

⎯ ⁓ ⎯

Since the movie came out, fire departments, police departments, and bomb squads around the world have called, Hurtubise says. A car manufacturer is interested in the suit's implications for crash tests. A tiger researcher from India was intrigued. But so far nobody has offered any cash.

Hurtubise can talk at great length about the value of grizzly bears. "They are an extension of God," he says, and he advocates setting aside vast tracts of wilderness for exclusive use of the bear, letting nobody in there except a few wardens to keep the poachers out. Imagine, he says, the value to the space program of the "trigger hormone" that sends bears into semi-hibernation. Astronauts could sleep for months while their ship cruises on.

"Nothing less than a Nobel Prize will come to the individual who can break through to the trigger hormone," he predicts, and once the Mark VII is complete, Hurtubise will be glad to help researchers get what they need from the bear. "If it's the grizzly that's going to give science that breakthrough, you're going to need the suit to get in to do the study."

But it is the earthly practicality of the suit that Hurtubise hopes will allow him to continue his research.

"A cop can jump out of the truck with one of these suits on, tear gas coming out of each arm. He gets knocked down and has fifty people jumping on him, and he can't get hurt. He's eating a sandwich inside the suit. A fireman drops through three floors? Big deal. It's not going to hurt him."

A lot of Canadians disparage him, he says. He's stepped on too many toes in his own country. So he's been courting the Japanese, hoping to find an investor with enough foresight to see the future the way Hurtubise sees it.

So far, no luck.

"I can't understand the moguls," he laments. "Half a million? To the big boys? That's coffee and doughnuts."

If he could just get the suit built and demonstrate it, he says, then he could keep the prototype, sell the patent, and have enough money to do grizzly research.

He knows that a lot of people laugh at him. But others have been laughed at, too.

People snickered at the Australian couple who made sharkproof diving suits of chain mail, suits now used around the world by divers and underwater photographers. And they laughed at Jacques Cousteau when he was working on his most famous invention, the scuba tank that lets people breathe underwater. Cousteau did a lot for life under the sea, studying it and bringing problems to the surface for human perusal. Hurtubise says he wants to do something along the same lines for grizzly bears, and he's willing to endure scorn and poverty, a biker with an ax, and the Canadian Film Board, if that's what it takes.

"I'd like to be a little Cousteau, not a big Cousteau. Here's a man who had the foresight to invent the underwater breathing apparatus. And with the money he was able to do all the research he wanted wherever he wanted."

Peter Lynch, the director of the movie, says he, like Hurtubise, grew up watching Cousteau specials and lots of Westerns. And he understands the nature of a quest.

"Who wouldn't want to leave an imprint?" he asks. "Accomplish something extraordinary, go up against insurmountable odds and win? Troy and his buddies are looking for a kind of greatness that most of us can't get from our day jobs."

Hurtubise says his pursuit—the years, the expense, the bankruptcy—is simpler than that.

"The minute things become monotonous," he says, "when things become average, I'm done as a human being. I've got to be doing something that keeps me up there."

POSTSCRIPT

Troy Hurtubise isn't the type to give up, but he does get a little discouraged.

He's improved his bearproof suit, though bears aren't his prime focus any more. These days he wants to protect soldiers from roadside bombs in Iraq and Afghanistan. He calls the latest model the Trojan.

"I'm keeping at it," he said in April 2011.

But he's no longer giving interviews, he says, finally picking up a phone in Edmonton, Alberta, where he was taking a break from his life in Ontario. He says he gets thirty to fifty calls a month, all from people wanting a little of his time, and he's not granting it without payment.

"Everybody wants something," he says. "Nobody wants to pay."

End of conversation.

You can't blame Hurtubise for his frustration. He's become something of an Internet sensation—one YouTube video of him has gathered 724,000 views. He works hard. And he's got no shortage of imagination.

In the videos the Trojan seems like a vast improvement over the Mark VI: It weighs about fifty pounds, is flexible enough that he can bust a dance move in it, and has all kinds of gadgets, ranging from a morphine capsule to a knife sheath to a flip-out watch in the codpiece. It has a laser pointer for pinpointing a sniper's hiding place, and there's even a fan in the helmet.

"It's so air-conditioned in there it's unreal," he says in one video. Also, the suit's right arm dispenses pepper spray at three times the level required by the Environmental Protection Agency for bear spray, "something that can knock out twenty or thirty people."

"I'm twenty years ahead of any military in the world," he says on camera.

Still, the suit hasn't sold. Neither have his other inventions: not the fire paste that he says protects from heat nor the Angel Light that lets him see through solid objects nor the God Light that he says will "revolutionize physics" and cure serious illnesses.

According to his hometown paper, the *Hamilton Spectator*, he'd gone broke and been separated from his wife, Lori, three times by the time he was forty-seven. Life with Troy isn't easy, Lori said in a YouTube video, but she loves the guy. "That's the answer."

His life has been made public, people have had a lot of laughs at his expense, and he never made a dime from any of it.

So he's taken up the pen and written an autobiography called *Bear Man*, published by Raven House Publishing of Maine. Don't expect any giggles in this project, he warns.

"It's an absolute trip to hell with no return ticket," he says. "If you're looking for a happy ending, this ain't it."

11

Good Luck in Low Country

KYLE SCHOEPF GOT UP SUNDAY MORNING AND TURNED ON THE TV, trying to find something interesting. No luck. News shows. Cartoons. Football sucked. It was October 20, 1996, and the Montana pheasant season was only a week old, so Kyle thought he'd run down to Ninepipe and see if he couldn't scare up a bird or two.

Since his regular hunting partner wasn't available, the twenty-six-year-old father of two called his mother. She liked to walk and was recently divorced. Maybe she'd like some company?

Mom didn't want to go. That was Kyle's first lucky break.

Then he asked his eight-year-old daughter if she wanted to go. Sure, said the tyke, she liked to walk the fields, liked to hang out with Dad. Then, just as they were going out the door, the phone rang. One of Caitlin's friends had a better offer.

"She decided she'd rather go play than go hunting with me," Kyle recalls.

It's the kind of thing that can prick at a father, especially a young family man like Kyle. He didn't know it then, but Caitlin's decision was his second big break in what would turn out to be a lucky, lucky day.

❦

So it was just Kyle and Charley, his German shorthair, driving to the Ninepipe National Wildlife Refuge on the Flathead Indian Reservation, about ninety minutes south of their home in Kalispell, Montana.

With a couple of big reservoirs and all sorts of potholes, Ninepipe is bird heaven, although it needed a little help to get that way. The federal government manages parts of it for waterfowl; the Montana

Department of Fish, Wildlife and Parks runs other parts for upland birds such as pheasant and grouse; and there are lots of private inholdings where people focus mostly on trying to squeeze a living from a small acreage in big country.

No hunting is allowed on the twenty-five hundred acres of federal land and much of the private land is closed, too, but the thirty-five hundred acres of state land is open. It is there that the pheasants have been nurtured, with wheat and barley and sunflowers planted in the boggy ground but left for the birds to harvest. Thick windbreaks of hawthorn, buffalo berry, and apple and plum trees line the ditches and roads and twist across the flat pastures.

Pheasants love it here, and so do hunters. It's one of only a few places west of the Continental Divide in Montana where pheasants live in any substantial numbers. It's also the kind of place where you need to know the lay of the land, know where the boundaries are and how to get to the open properties. Kyle had hunted the refuge several times, and he got there a little after noon that day. He hunted one patch, but Charley flushed only hens, which are illegal to shoot, so they moved down the road to try another section.

Winter was coming early to Montana that year, and it would dump record amounts of snow. So far there were only a few slushy patches on the valley floor, but there was plenty in the Mission Mountains to the east, looming vast and blue and white over the fertile valley. And there was more of it coming down: Big sloppy globs the size of a quarter flopped to the ground as Kyle tried to figure out what the heck was making his dog so goofy.

"He normally stays pretty close, but he started getting out too far," Kyle says. "He was running without any pattern, and I thought for a while he might be chasing a running rooster. Sometimes he'd be backtracking, working behind me. And he never backtracks. He always stays in front of me."

The grass was thigh high and thick, and there were rows of brush and trees on either side. Kyle and Charley hunted the area for about twenty-five minutes, crisscrossing, working it up and down, and never put up a bird. A strong wind pushed the slushy snowflakes into an angle as Kyle crossed between a couple of rows of trees with Charley about thirty yards away, still goofy.

That's when Kyle heard the funny noise behind him.

When he turned his head, a 370-pound grizzly bear was about twenty feet away and coming hard in a low, bowlegged charge, her snout just inches from the ground, her long claws tearing into the soft earth, chugging out little huffs and grunts of exertion as she ran. Her head was huge.

Kyle said a dirty word and swung his old pump-action Model 12 Winchester, shoving the safety off as he spun and taking the only shot he would get, shooting from the hip. The gun went off, blood blew back on his face, and then the bear was on him, her head at his feet but her big body somersaulting, slamming onto his, crushing him into the soft ground as she contorted and twisted, the life gushing from the hole in her neck.

Looking back, he couldn't believe how quickly the world turned to chaos. One second he was hunting pheasants, working on a dog problem, close enough to a major highway to hear the trucks whizzing by, and the next second he was on his back with a wounded grizzly bear mashing him. The bear was yelling and bleeding and waving all four legs, all twenty claws, reminding Kyle of a blender. She was incredibly heavy, and she covered him with mud and gore and hair. She bellowed and roared and screamed. She sounded, sadly, like a pig in torture.

Kyle's load of No. 6 steel shot had hit the bear in the side of the neck, ripping away the jugular vein and probably deafening and blinding her with the muzzle blast. The shot would kill the bear soon, but it did not stop her in her tracks; she had hit his shotgun first with her head and shoulders, driving the barrel into the mud before flopping onto Kyle's body.

The bear's weightiest parts, her madly writhing belly and hips, pinned Kyle's wiry frame as he tried to get away. He did not know the bear was dying but he knew she was wounded and crazy with pain and he knew he had to get away. He shoved hard into her mass, the ass in his face, the stink of rotten meat and dirty wet fur seeming as heavy as her body.

The bear's legs were whirling, trying to get some purchase in the air as she squirmed and screamed, and somehow Kyle slid from beneath her. He took off, running as he had never run before, and didn't look back until he topped a small rise about 150 yards away. The bear was still rolling, roaring out her pain. She'd stand and then flop on her back. She'd swat at her head, trying to crush whatever mystery had changed her world to darkness and agony.

No decent person likes to see an animal suffer like this, and Kyle Schoepf is a decent man. But the scene did not fill him with the dread it would have caused if he had seen it beside a highway or through the scope of a rifle. The bear was preoccupied, and for Kyle, at that moment, that meant good news. He took off running for his truck about four hundred yards away. Charley came from somewhere and ran beside him. Everybody in that meadow had had all they wanted from each other.

—— ∙∙∙ ——

"The luckiest man alive that day," is the way Rick Schoening describes Kyle Schoepf. Schoening is the Montana game warden who investigated the scene. Grizzlies are a threatened species in the lower forty-eight states, and when somebody reports that they've shot one, people with guns and badges tend to show up pretty fast, even on a soggy Sunday, with supper warming at home. Schoening is one of those lawmen. He likes bears, and he defends them. It's both his job and his choice. He gets upset when somebody kills a grizzly bear for no good reason. He likes to see people punished when that happens.

But Schoening called for no punishment, no criminal charges against Kyle Schoepf. The filth and hair and blood all over Kyle made his story convincing, but the real clincher came when Schoening found the shotgun where Kyle had left it: The charging grizzly had hit the gun so hard that she bent the hardened steel barrel about fifteen degrees to the left. It looked like it had been run over with a truck.

Kyle was lucky in a lot of ways: He trains racehorses for a living and shoots birds for a hobby, a combination that makes for some fast reflexes; his mother wasn't there; and best of all, his eight-year-old daughter had found somebody else to play with that day. Also, he survived a close-range attack by a grizzly bear and walked away without a scratch.

"All he got on him was bear shit," Schoening quips.

After the attack, Kyle drove to a nearby farmhouse and called the sheriff's office. Then he waited, cleaning some of the mess from his face. Schoening was the first to arrive, and he wanted to see the scene. When they got there, they found the bear just a few yards from where she had been shot, lying dead and silent by then. But the two men also got a big surprise. There by the carcass were two more bears, big ones, mostly grown cubs capable of major damage. Kyle couldn't believe it.

"All of this happened, and I had never seen or heard those other two bears," he says, the recollection making him shake his head. He hadn't seen a track or any scat. He'd heard nothing, smelled nothing. He'd been hunting hard. He thought he was paying attention, and a game warden had told him earlier that day that somebody had reported seeing a bear in the general area, so the idea was at least somewhere in the back of his mind. But out here in the flats and bogs, a dozen miles from the mountains, separated from them by the busy highway, he hadn't been concentrating on grizzlies the way he always does while hunting elk in the forest.

"I'd gone back and forth through that area three or four times, thinking there was a bird in there. It just makes me sick, thinking there were probably three bears in there just watching me the whole time."

One bear sat on the carcass while the other one circled it. They were probably her two-year-old or three-year-old cubs. Kyle and Schoening backed off and watched them through a spotting scope. By the time more wardens showed up with a bear trap, the two young bears had run away. The last time anybody saw them they were climbing into the Mission Mountains Wilderness, toward a long winter's sleep.

Schoening used a winch to load the dead bear into his pickup truck. Later, when the bear was examined at a laboratory in Bozeman, the almost weightless plastic wad from the shotgun shell would be found about two inches under the 370-pound sow's skin, proving that she was close and moving fast when Kyle pulled the trigger.

The bear was just over six feet long and measured fifty-eight inches around the chest. She was ten years old, carried two inches of fat along her back, and had a two-inch-wide hole in the side of her neck.

"It was just a big old barrel of a bear," says former Montana Department of Fish, Wildlife and Parks laboratory manager Keith Aune, who examined the bear and had been studying grizzlies for many years. "If he hadn't hit the jugular, he would have hurt the bear, but he wouldn't have killed it."

"It certainly wasn't any bluff charge," adds Dale Becker, wildlife manager for the Flathead Reservation, which includes the Ninepipe area. "There was no doubt in our minds that she was serious."

❦

Any kind of hunting poses hazards. You can get lost. You can shoot your foot off. Somebody could shoot you. You could fall in a hole, tumble from a tree, or freeze to death in a blizzard. Hunters understand these things, and most of them take precautions.

But very few pheasant hunters consider grizzly bears a risky part of their sport. Think about pheasant hunting, and you think about wheat fields and dried cornstalks, trained dogs and fine shotguns, a little brandy afterward. Talk to people who hunt bighorn sheep or elk, even blue grouse in the Rockies, and you will find some bear stories. But pheasant hunters? A more common hazard is stepping on a rattlesnake or getting bit by a dog.

But in parts of Montana, that is changing.

In the Ninepipe area there have been at least nine run-ins between grizzly bears and pheasant hunters over the years, according to Jamie Jonkel, a bear management specialist with the Montana Department of Fish, Wildlife and Parks and the son of Chuck Jonkel, the veteran bear researcher.

And on the east side of the mountains, where the prairies that stretch all the way from Chicago collide with Montana's Rocky Mountain Front, where grizzlies are reclaiming ground where they'd been absent for decades, more and more pheasant hunters are running into bears.

Following brushy river bottoms, grizzlies had been spotted 165 miles from the mountains by 2009, according to Mike Madel, another bear specialist for the state of Montana. They've been spotted near Fort Benton, Montana, and the hamlet of Loma, places where grizzlies so badly rattled the Lewis and Clark Expedition that its members tried to kill almost every one they encountered. And they encountered a lot of them.

"These bear being so hard to die reather intimidates us all," Captain Meriwether Lewis wrote in his journal on May 11, 1805. "I must confess I do not like the gentlemen and had reather fight two Indians than one bear."

In those days grizzlies favored the banks of rivers such as the Missouri because they offered a vast feast of drowned bison carcasses. There are no wild bison in that part of the world any more, but the river and creek bottoms still offer enough food and cover for a growing number of bears. Roaming mostly at night, they break open beaver lodges and eat the inhabitants, scarf bushels of berries, and tear into a dead cow when they find one. In the daytime they generally find a thick copse and hole up, sleeping and digesting.

That's where Brian Grand found a bear late in October 2007, along the banks of Depuyer Creek, about fifteen miles from the mountains that until recent years had been the last refuge of the grizzly.

With two companions and three dogs, Grand had hunted all day. About 1:30 in the afternoon, he was walking a direct line, alongside a thick, sinuous strand of red willow bushes, hoping the dogs would put up a bird. Open fields, the crops long since harvested, stretched into the distance on both sides of the drainage, only about a hundred yards wide at that point.

"We'd hunted there for years," Grand says of that day. He knew that grizzlies pass through on occasion but didn't give it a lot of thought. "If you'd told me I was going to see one, I'd have said you were full of it."

Besides, the hunters were on their second pass through that spot. The dogs wore bells, and the men weren't being particularly quiet, firing off shots now and then. A reasonable man could assume that anything hiding in the bushes had plenty of warning.

And that's probably true. The grizzly bedded in those willows likely had kept a nervous eye on the hunters for some time, Madel said. And when they returned, the bear's disquiet magnified. Grant didn't know it, but he was walking directly toward the bear's bed. When he came within thirty feet, the bear erupted in full charge. That's when Grand first saw him. He veered off the line he'd been walking, but the bear kept coming.

"By the time I did that, it literally just took me out," he says.

Without even thinking about it, he curled into a fetal position. The bear rolled him three or four times, leaving thirty inches of open wounds. The bear hit the back of his head and his chin; it bit down hard on both elbows and laid his left forearm open to the bone. At some point during the ruckus—he doesn't really remember when—Grand's 20-gauge shotgun went off. All of this lasted just a few seconds; then the bear took off at a dead run, skedaddling across the wheat fields. Grand's companions heard the commotion but never saw a thing.

Grand believes the grizzly, a subadult male, had lain in wait for him, had calculated an opportunity.

"He had picked this spot and was more or less defending it from an intruder," he says. "You can't tell me he was surprised."

Madel agrees that the bear wasn't surprised. But he doesn't see it as a calculated attack. Rather, he believes the bear was trying to flee a perceived threat.

In open country like that, where vast distances separate the places where a bear can hide, a grizzly has few options when it sees a man coming. In forested country it can slip away in a number of directions, hiding behind brush and trees. On the prairies that's hard to do. Bears in that environment see people all the time, Madel says, and they know that leaving cover in the daylight puts them at risk. When the men and dogs returned for a second pass, with Grand directly approaching the bear, something clicked in its mind.

"The hunter was there, an immediate threat," Madel says. "So it attacked. And then it was gone."

The grizzly could also have been chasing one of the hunting dogs. Grand remembers seeing one dog take off, "hauling ass, with his tail tucked between his legs."

When he investigated the scene later, Madel found "really loose" bear scat near the day bed, indicating stress. He also found a cow carcass a few hundred yards away and signs that the bear had been feeding on it, explaining why he had lingered in that area.

Bear spray might have helped Grand avoid injury, says Madel, who has used it three times to repel an attack. Grand says he's not so sure. It all happened so fast. And though the attack ended quickly, his stay in the hospital dragged on for six days.

Was he lucky to have survived? Or was he unlucky to have run into the bear at all?

Grand pauses to think that over.

"Lucky, I guess," he says.

But he didn't sound happy.

Deviled by hunters and traps and pavement and plows, grizzlies have been chased from most of their original habitat in the lower forty-eight states. For the past century we've left them only the timbered mountains and sagebrush bowls of the high country in Montana, Wyoming, and bits of Idaho and Washington. That's where, if we're wise, we move more cautiously because we know we are in the bear's home.

But most of the western United States once held grizzlies. In only a few low-elevation flat spots, such as Montana's Mission Valley, where Schoepf was attacked, have they managed to hang on. Now, as grizzly populations continue to recover, the great bears are prodding eastward into the prairie, their ancestral homeland.

"It seems like they go on these exploratory routes and just keep going," says Madel, who has managed and studied grizzlies on Montana's Rocky Mountain Front for twenty-five years. "It amazes me. I never expected to see grizzly bear expansion spread out this quickly."

Bears tend to use the prairies in the spring and summer, when most food in the mountains lies buried in deep snow. But Madel says it's probably just a matter of time before a few grizzlies start using the prairies year-round. That means denning, breeding, and the establishment of permanent home range.

While a Montana prairie can look pretty empty to the casual viewer, it holds a lot of sustenance for a grizzly bear. Chokecherries and serviceberries clog the creek bottoms. There are roots to dig and anthills to demolish and devour. The bison are gone, of course, but deer and antelope and elk abound. So do cattle and sheep and poultry, powerful temptations to a grizzly bear. And grizzly survival on the prairies could hinge on the great bear's ability to ignore those treats.

The lone bear that reached Loma in 2009 just couldn't say no. He killed some sheep, which earned him a capture, an ear tag, a radio collar, and a ride to the North Fork of the Flathead River, 250 air miles away on the opposite side of the Continental Divide. Somehow, he made it back to the prairie. When he raided a chicken coop, game wardens euthanized him.

That news saddened and outraged a number of grizzly bear advocates, people who had been rooting for the bear to keep heading east, to reach the Charles M. Russell National Wildlife Refuge, a place of great wildness and isolation, one that teems with wildlife and has hardly any people.

Madel said the decision to kill the bear arose because that's what bear management guidelines call for after repeated attacks on livestock. Such behavior is seldom unlearned.

Along the Rocky Mountain Front, in the foothills and steep canyons, ranchers and grizzly bears have achieved a teetering balance. Most ranchers have changed how they do things: Nowadays, most people are more likely to grab a telephone than a rifle when they see a grizzly. And ranchers have changed how they dispose of livestock carcasses. Madel and his crew haul those reeking items to isolated places where grizzlies can feed on them safely. When they have to, they trap and move bears. They track them with radio collars, and sometimes, they put down a bear that refuses to stay away from livestock. It's a constant dance, but so far it's working.

People have better tolerance for bears, and as a result the population is growing by about 3 percent a year.

For now, the bears in the lower forty-eight states are protected by the Endangered Species Act. But the law has limited reach. Every year people poach grizzlies despite the possibility of huge fines. Rarely does anybody catch them. Madel worries that, if government doesn't kill troublesome bears now and then, life will become riskier for bears trying to avoid people. More people might start opening up on bears if they think government is refusing to help.

"If we don't stick to the rules, we could lose our existing support," Madel says. And when it comes to bears occupying new habitat, "I think we're in a learning curve, along with the bears."

Bird hunters, too, might have to change how they do things. Madel recommends they carry bear spray and watch closely for bear sign: Scat, crushed berry bushes, uprooted anthills, the presence of a carcass can all be messages telling you to hunt someplace else that day. Avoid poking through the thickest of brush, even if you suspect it harbors pheasants.

Encounters in pheasant country generally end the way they do in elk or bighorn sheep or mountain grouse country, with both hunter and bear going away intact.

"People are hunting right by them, and they don't even know it," Madel says.

But sometimes, as Grand learned, the bear takes things into its own hands.

—～—

West of the mountains, in the Mission Valley where Schoepf was attacked, bears usually behave in much the same way, Schoening says. They just hunker down and wait for people to pass. Or else they run away.

"The grizzly bears are damned well behaved in that area, and whenever we have an encounter, it's almost always because of some asshole" poaching or making bad decisions, Schoening says.

That wasn't the case with Kyle Schoepf. Kyle did nothing wrong that Schoening could see. There is "no question" the attack happened just as he explained it, he says. The bear that attacked Kyle had been spotted earlier that morning, but nobody was sure at the time if it was a grizzly or a black bear. A tribal game warden had checked Kyle's license sometime before the attack and mentioned that a farmer had seen a couple of black bears in the area. There is some disagreement over what was said, how strongly it was put. Dale Becker, the reservation's wildlife program manager, says Kyle had been warned there was a bear in the area, possibly a big one. Schoening says Kyle had been told the bear was a mile away. Kyle says the warden mentioned somebody seeing bears in the area, but he never got the impression he was being warned.

"I thought he was just making conversation while he was checking my license," Kyle says. "He seemed more interested in how I was hunting."

Becker led the investigation into Schoepf's case. He says the bear probably charged from fifty or sixty feet away, got within twenty feet when Kyle first saw her, and a lot closer than that when the birdshot ripped her throat. A bear at full charge can run forty-four feet per second, and that means Kyle had a split second, literally, to turn and hit the bear in about the only place he could have killed it.

Schoening blames Charley the dog for the attack.

The scent of grizzly bear in the area probably caused the dog's goofy behavior, which had been so puzzling to Kyle just before the attack. The dog knew he was onto something unusual, but at only two years old, he had never seen a bear and didn't know what to make of the strange odor.

Schoening says his more experienced Labradors would have raised hell at the first whiff of a bear, and everybody probably could have backed off safely.

But Charley and Kyle didn't know they needed to back off. They stayed in the area and kept working it, looking for a bird until they found a bear.

"I think she felt threatened," Schoening says. "She was a good old wild bear" with no history of raiding garbage or being aggressive around people. But her tolerance had limits. And Kyle Schoepf, hunting in relatively open country, pushed her safety envelope too hard. When he turned his back, she saw a chance and charged.

"When I got out in the open, she probably could see me a little better and decided I didn't look too bad. She was probably just sick of me bugging her," Kyle says.

"If that bear had got him down, he'd have been gone," Schoening adds.

⤙⋯⤚

Everybody talks about how lucky Kyle was, the good fortune that kept his mother and daughter safe at home, that let him walk away merely filthy.

The attack was not without scars, though. Periodically, Kyle's wife awakens to find him thrashing and shouting in bed, and she knows where he has gone: back to Ninepipe and the bear. She always wakes him up just before the bear attacks, and the dreams leave Kyle puzzled about himself.

"You'd think I'd lighten up, but I don't."

But was it good luck or bad, being rolled by a grizzly bear? Being left with no physical wounds, but with dreams that don't want to go away, with a wife who must worry now when you're a little late, with a nagging fear that makes you think twice about teaching your children to hunt? Left with the onus of having killed a grizzly bear, a breeding-age female, a rare member of a magnificent species, an animal that is so much like us?

"I was definitely lucky that I got out of it alive, without even getting hurt. It was unlucky for the bear. I respect them and don't want to have to kill them. I really don't want to. But what's a guy to do? It was either me or the bear."

12

The Cost of Curiosity

DALE BAGLEY IS A CURIOUS GUY, SOMETIMES MORE CURIOUS THAN PRUDENT.
The twenty-nine-year-old lifelong Alaskan was managing cafeterias for a living for oil field workers on Alaska's North Slope, and that makes for a long, dark winter. But by late April he was back home in the relatively balmy climate of the Kenai Peninsula, and the spring fever was gnawing on him pretty hard.

April 26, 1993, was a nice day, sunny and warm without too much wind, and Bagley decided to check out some moose country along the Killey River. There are moose everywhere in that part of Alaska, but this was a new area for Bagley and he wanted to take a look at it, to see if it would be possible, come moose season in the fall, to pack out a carcass from there with a canoe or a four-wheeler. It was also open season for black bear hunting. The season for grizzlies wouldn't open for some time.

"If I saw a black bear I was going to shoot it. But that was kind of secondary to what I was doing, which was looking for a place to go moose hunting."

He had spent the better part of the morning looking at the country, crossing channels of the small, winding river and looking at "whatever grabbed my interest."

Then, while approaching a brushy patch, he heard a bunch of ravens and magpies squabbling. That grabbed his interest real fast. He thought the scavenger birds might lead him to a black bear feeding on a carcass. So he walked into the brush. Then he took another think.

"I was standing there thinking, 'I'm in thick brush, and there's a kill in here. This could be a black bear, but more likely it's a brown bear that brought down a moose. And I'm thinking, I'm not liking this, in the brush, as thick as it is. So I started to detour around it."

He said later he probably should have gone straight back, but instead he started to cut around the birds in a big circle. He didn't get far.

A grizzly bear, a fully grown animal he estimated at eight hundred pounds, had moved a few yards from the moose it had killed and was sleeping off its meal in the brush. Bagley walked right up on it, not seeing the bear until he was less than sixty feet away.

"I woke it up. It sat up and turned its head and looked at me. That's when I knew this wasn't going to be good."

Bagley had come, so to speak, armed for bear. He carried a semiautomatic .30-06 loaded with 220-grain slugs. On his hip rode a .44 Magnum revolver.

It wasn't open season for grizzly bears, called browns in that part of the state near the ocean, or he would have opened fire on the animal immediately, he says.

"I couldn't start shooting. He looked at me, and I looked at him. I really didn't know what to do. I didn't know whether to keep backing away. So I started yelling at the bear."

In some cases yelling at a bear is a good thing to do. It lets the animal know what you are, and many people tell of making a charging grizzly halt in its tracks just by yelling, "Stop, bear." The bear doesn't understand the words, of course, but there is no other animal that yells at bears. Yelling can make a bear stop and think for a minute, give it a chance to change its mind.

But this bear showed no reaction. It just stayed in a sitting position, its massive body broadside to Bagley, and looked at him.

Bagley kept the .30-06 in his left hand, pulled the .44 with his right hand, and fired a shot in the air. Gunshots, too, often make bears turn tail. But this one only made the bear stand up.

"He got to all fours and turned to face me," Bagley says. If the bear woofed or rattled its teeth, if it shook its head, danced on its paws, or showed any other signs of agitation, Bagley doesn't remember any of it now. "I put the .44 back in the holster, and that's when he started coming at me. And it was fast."

He had disengaged the safety on his rifle as soon as he saw the bear. When it started to charge, he threw it to his shoulder and fired. He didn't even try to use the scope.

"At forty feet and closing fast, you'd just see individual hairs. You're supposed to shoot for a shoulder when they're coming at you, but I didn't even want to try. I just fired right up the middle."

The bear stopped "like he hit a brick wall," Bagley says, but he didn't stop for long. Instantly, he was charging again, and Bagley tried to squeeze off another shot.

"Nothing happened. Just nothing happened. The gun didn't even click." He tried squeezing again, as his Marine Corps instructors had taught him to do with a misfire. Again, nothing happened.

He dropped the rifle and started to pull the .44, but he could see he didn't have time. "Because he was there, coming that fast."

A small spruce tree stood just to Bagley's left and he tried to duck behind it. That bought him enough time to get the gun out of the holster, turn, and fire into the bear.

"I don't know whether I hit it or not. It wasn't even ten feet away. Then he was leaping at me and I was falling backwards."

With the first bite, the bear clamped its teeth around Bagley's jaws and bit down hard. Then he chewed some more. Bagley's entire face was in the bear's mouth.

"He bites once, he bites twice, and he bites three times. And while he's biting, the weight of his body is on me, trapping my arms in front of me. I could feel bones popping and breaking in my head, but I didn't feel any pain."

Bagley still had the powerful pistol in his right hand, but with his arms pressed against his abdomen by eight hundred pounds of angry, thrashing, wounded grizzly bear, he was afraid he would blow his own arm off if he tried another shot.

"Believe it or not, my head was in his mouth, and I'm thinking about that. I wanted to push far enough into him that I would miss my arm."

So he shoved the pistol as hard as he could into the bear's belly. He couldn't move the gun much, but he had to try. He pulled the trigger, leaving powder burns all up and down his left arm, but the shot hit the bear hard enough to move him.

"The shot was probably along the ribs. Not a life-threatening shot, but it got him to move."

The first bite broke Bagley's jaw. The second crushed his cheekbones and separated the row of upper teeth from the rest of his head. One of the bear's canine teeth gouged a hole behind his right eye socket.

Bagley squared the pistol into the bear's stomach just as the third bite sank long teeth into the top of his head and the bear started tugging on his skull.

"He pulled me out from underneath him, and as he did that, I fired my last three shots, as fast as I could pull the trigger, right up his belly and chest as he was pulling me up."

On the last shot the bear dropped him.

"He had pulled me out from underneath him and was starting to shake his head, trying to break my neck like they do. That's when the last shot hit him, or the effect of the last shot anyway, and he dropped me and ran off."

His entire head torn and bleeding, his face and jaw crushed, Bagley still had the presence of mind to reload. He had a speedloader on his left hip that let him put six new bullets into the pistol in an instant. But the bear was gone.

"The whole thing, from the moment he sat up and looked at me until he ran off . . . it seemed like a long time, but I bet it wasn't even fifteen seconds."

Bagley said only two words during the entire attack: "Oh shit," when his rifle jammed.

His eyeglasses were lost and blood was running over both eyes. One of them wasn't working right. The broken bones in his skull behind the eye had forced it into an odd position, not dangling but bulging, not where it was supposed to be. Pieces of flesh were hanging from his head and he had no idea where the bear had gone. He left the rifle where it lay, tucked the loose flesh under his baseball cap and started walking toward the road. He hoped the hat would slow the bleeding. He feared the bear might follow the blood trail he was leaving. He thought he might have brain damage. He thought he might die, even if he made it to a hospital. He knew he didn't want to stay there.

"I wanted out of there regardless of what might happen to me."

He could see well enough to keep from running into trees, but with his glasses gone and his eye damaged, he couldn't see any distance. He kept walking, stumbling, looking for the road and his truck, wondering where that bear had gone. It took an hour or more in the bush, wandering across a half-mile of muskeg, before he found the truck. Then he had to navigate the thing, more blind than not, before he could find help.

Luckily, help came pretty fast. Bagley had decided to drive straight down the center of the gravel road for two reasons: He was trying to stay out of the ditch, and if he met an oncoming vehicle, he wanted to make sure it stopped.

"He pretty much had to stop," Bagley says of the driver he finally encountered. The man in the other truck parked his own vehicle, Bagley slid over on his blood-soaked seats, and the man drove him to the closest hospital, in Soldotna.

With most of the bones broken, Bagley's face had nearly collapsed. Dripping blood and filthy, his appearance shocked even the doctors and nurses in the emergency room.

"It was kind of funny when I walked into that emergency room. Everyone ran in different directions at once, kind of leaving me standing there. Everybody was running to get somebody, I suppose. One girl came up and kind of showed me where to go."

Forty-five minutes later he was on a jet to Anchorage, where he underwent ten hours of surgery. It took five doctors to put him back together. With his jaws wired shut and breathing through a tracheotomy hole, he could tell his family what happened only by writing notes.

When the plastic surgeon was called in, his family, relieved that he was alive, gathered movie magazines and started culling pictures of Hollywood stars. Which one would he like to look like? they joked.

❧

"By the time we saw him, his faced looked like a basketball, with just a little bit of nose sticking out," recalls Bagley's father, Nathan. "It was just round and taut and yellow. The doctor grabbed his nose and just pushed it all around his face. With all the broken bones, it wasn't attached to anything."

The surgeons did remarkable work. Within a couple of years after the attack, Bagley still looked like himself. Usually, with a broken jaw, surgeons wire the jaw to the cheekbones to hold it in place. But Bagley's cheekbones were crushed, too, so they had to run the wires under the skin and around his eyes, loop them over screws drilled into his forehead—there's a metal plate up there, too—and stretch the wires back to the jaw.

Removing that wire took three people, Bagley says: two to hold him down and one to pull the wires from the healing, adhesive flesh. Normally voluble and outgoing, he has no words to describe that pain.

Doctors had worried at first about brain damage, fearing that the fang that sank behind his eye had entered the brain. But the wound wasn't as bad as it looked, and as the bones healed around the eye, it gradually returned to its normal orbit, and Bagley's vision cleared up. A few small pieces of bone are still missing, and he can't open his mouth quite as wide as before, but a small divot below his temple is the only visible reminder of the attack.

After ten days in the hospital, Bagley returned to the Kenai, then to his family's remote cabin on Kachemak Bay near Homer. He wanted to get away from the constant stream of visitors, from all the questions he couldn't answer because his jaws were still wired shut. One evening Nathan spotted a black bear on a nearby beach. Did Dale want to go get it?

"He mumbled through the wires that he wanted to go," Nathan recalls. So they grabbed their guns and hopped in the boat.

By the time they got to the beach where the black bear had been grazing on grasses, the animal had disappeared into an alder thicket.

"I asked him, since he had experience in these kinds of things, if he wanted to go in and chase that bear out of there so I could shoot it," Nathan says. "He figured he didn't want to go after this one. We turned around and went back to the cabin."

The bear hunting wasn't over, though. Less than a week later, Dale and his father set out to track down the bear that had mauled him. He felt it owed him something. He wanted a piece of it.

Returning to the area "affected me a little but not much. I wanted that bear. I wanted that bear skull and the claws and a bit of the hide. Anything that was salvageable."

Bagley had pinpointed the scene of the attack on a map while he was still in the hospital, and Alaska Department of Fish and Game biologists had tried without luck to find the bear. With one .30-06 shell and four .44 Magnum slugs in it, they were, of course, looking for a carcass, and they focused on groups of ravens, the same birds that had aroused Bagley's curiosity, that had led him to near death. But Bagley and his father went farther. There were all sorts of bear tracks in the area, but the ones they wanted had blood in them. When they found them, they led steadily away from the attack scene, with spots or smears of blood still stuck to roots and branches on the trail.

The bear was hurt badly, crippled so severely that it abandoned the moose carcass it had defended with jealous rage, leaving the megadose of protein that was so necessary after a long winter in a foodless den, seeking something, anything, to ease the pain. The two Bagleys followed the trail for more than a mile, until it entered a swamp. Then they circled the swamp, trying to find a place where the bear had come out. They searched the sky for scavenger birds, hoping this time they would lead to a dead bear instead of an angry one.

The Bagleys have a long history in the Alaska bush. A Fish and Game biologist described Nathan as "the kind of guy you could drop off in the woods in the winter with nothing, and when you came back to get him in the spring, he'd be fat." Dale grew up hunting and fishing and trapping alongside his father.

But they couldn't find that bear.

Both Bagleys have had a lot of experience with bears. Dale spent some summers counting salmon in streams with brown bears all around. He worked in Alaska's Brooks Range, where grizzlies are hungrier than their coastal cousins and sometimes run for miles toward anything that moves, just to see if it might be food. He'd been charged before by a black bear, running in a stream: He and a friend fired rifle shots ahead of it, kicking up water. That time, gunfire halted a charge instead of igniting one.

Many others have diverted bear charges with a warning shot. But in this case Nathan Bagley maintains his son made a mistake.

If a bear is charging, it knows where you are and, in most cases, what you are. In Dale Bagley's case he had awakened a bear sleeping off a huge meal of meat. The sound of his movement had awakened the groggy animal, but since he didn't rise to all four feet right away, there's a good chance he didn't know what kind of creature woke him up. Still half asleep, he may not have been able to see Bagley yet. The shout told the bear what Bagley was and the gunshot "told the bear exactly where Dale was," Nathan says.

Dale maintains that when he was attacked it was the bear's decision to charge. It could just as easily have run the other way.

"While I was yelling and shooting the one shot, he was deciding what to do, I guess. It really wasn't that long a time from when he looked at me until he got to his feet. I think he was going to get up anyway. He was just getting his wits about him and deciding what to do. Then he decided to do it. If he had allowed me time, I would have quartered away. But I would never have turned my back."

Could it have been a bluff charge?

"At forty feet and coming fast, I'd be foolish to assume that."

Did he consider playing dead?

"Not as long as I had a round in my .44."

———

Bagley says that in hindsight he doesn't think he would have done anything differently, with one major exception: bring a different rifle.

The rifle he carried was a new one, a Remington semiautomatic that had only been fired about twenty times.

"The year before I'd given up a .30-06 pump action that I'd had all my life. My uncle had left Alaska and left it here. Then he came back, and I gave him his .30-06 back. So I decided to go out and buy a new .30-06 with a scope, because I had never owned a nice new gun like that."

That's the rifle that jammed. When the gun was retrieved, a bullet was in the chamber, and it was ready to fire. But a closer inspection showed a worn spot along the top of the magazine. The rifle's action had been pressing against the bullets in the magazine.

"When I'd been firing the twenty rounds the year before, it did jam once, but I didn't think too much of it."

When Dale tested the gun after the attack, it jammed again, with the bullet only halfway into the chamber.

"When I dropped it during the attack, hitting the ground like that was enough to make it chamber the rest of the way."

He's rid himself of that rifle and returned to a pump-action gun with no scope. In Alaska's thick brush country, long shots are a rarity anyway, and Bagley's old rifle had never misfired. Not once.

He doesn't blame the manufacturer for the gun jamming. "It's my fault for being out there with a new rifle is how I look at it. It never had all the bugs worked out of it."

Being attacked didn't even surprise him all that much, he says, and it hasn't changed his attitude about bears. Brushy patches in Alaska are too numerous to avoid, and many people who spend a lot of time in the bush are always half-expecting a bear attack. That's why so many of them are so heavily armed.

Lots of people like bigger guns, but Bagley says the .30-06 is plenty of rifle for him. If his hadn't had a scope, he might have made a close-range shoulder shot and disabled the bear before it got him.

"It's not what gun you use but where you shoot."

Once they got over the initial shock, his family wasn't that surprised that he had been attacked by a bear, he says.

"My brother and I are always doing something to keep them worried. So they pretty much take it as being par for the course. It's not the first time I've been in the hospital."

Could it happen again?

Perhaps, although it's unlikely.

Dr. James Scully is an avid bear hunter himself and the surgeon who put Bagley back together. Since bear attacks are so rare, he is one of a handful of doctors in the world with experience. He's sewn two people back together, and that puts him in uncommon medical company. He compares bear attacks to lightning strikes. The odds of getting hit once are so small, he notes. What are the odds of getting hit twice?

That depends on what you do.

"Some of these guys have more guts than brains," Scully says.

If he had known there was a brown bear in the brush, Bagley says, he would have avoided it.

Should he have known? He agrees he probably should have suspected. He was in brown bear country and moose habitat. He knew that black bears, his designated prey, rarely kill moose. He knew there probably was a carcass nearby, and it was probably a moose. But he thought all this through just a few seconds too late.

―〜⌣〜―

Other people make bigger mistakes, indulge a larger curiosity, and suffer less for it. At least Bagley was trying to get away before he surprised the bear.

Almost exactly three years earlier, in April 1990, two brothers and their father, all from Anchorage, went snowmobiling in the Alaska Range. Grizzly bear hunting was on their minds, but it wasn't the main focus. They were having fun on the machines.

Then they spotted a bear den high on a slope. Soil stained the spring snow and there were bear tracks all over the slope. The den was too high on the slope for the snow machines, but the brothers decided to climb up on foot and take a look at it. They were curious. They wondered what the inside of a bear den looked like.

That's when the scene started looking like a Gary Larson cartoon, a darkly comic fable in which bears lure the unwitting into their den and make a meal of them. Brian Dixon asked his brother Doug a question, "You think I ought to go down in there?" Then they heard a noise deep in the hole, the bear charged, and the brothers started running.

Their father, Jim, was nearby and had a rifle at hand. As his sons ran down the mountain in a rolling, tumbling flight for life, a boar grizzly on their heels, Jim started shooting. He put four slugs from a .300 Magnum into the bear as it chased his boys. The bear died. His sons lived.

Curiosity led Dale Bagley into the thicket, and it nearly cost him his life. He knows that, but he's still a curious guy.

"I guess I always thought something like this was going to happen. I just didn't figure my rifle was going to jam."

He still hunts alone ("It's hard to find someone to go hunting with you") and returned to the Killey River that fall and killed a bull moose there with his new rifle.

Nathan Bagley says he doesn't worry too much about his son going in the woods by himself. It's part of a deal the two men made.

"He lets me go out in the woods, and I let him go out in the woods."

POSTSCRIPT

Dale Bagley has become a politician. After building a successful career in commercial real estate, in 1998 he ran successfully for mayor of the borough of Kenai, which includes all of the vast Kenai Peninsula. He served two terms, returned to his real estate career, and, as of 2011, was seeking another term office.

He said the only physical reminder of the bear attack is an inability to open his mouth fully, because of damage to muscles that run from his jaw to the top of his head.

But that's not a disadvantage in politics, he says.

"They can't call me a bigmouth."

13

Warm Spell

JOE HEIMER HAD THE SOW GRIZZLY'S UPPER LIP CLENCHED IN HIS FIST, shoving and squeezing as hard as he could. The bear had knocked him flat on his back in the deep, sticky snow, and she was standing on his mauled legs, trying to shake his hand loose and sink her jagged teeth into his vital organs. Pushing on that bear's face was like trying a one-armed bench press with a three-hundred-pound barbell, one that fought back with teeth and claws, one that wouldn't hold still.

He held her with his right hand—he could feel the side of a fang pressed hard against his palm—and with his left he kept punching and punching, swinging his fist as hard as he could and trying to keep her away from his organs.

So far it was a draw.

"I was holding her," Heimer says. "I think I kept her from biting me as many times as she wanted to. I had my mind set that she was not going to get me. I thought about my guts lying out in the snowbank."

Then, suddenly, the bear took off.

Heimer, a tough cowboy of fifty-two with short gray hair and a bull-rider's physique, the kind of guy who isn't afraid to sweat through his shirt three or four times in a day's work, twisted his head and saw the bear lunging on all fours, kicking up snow as it charged. Then, just past the bear, he saw Sonja Crowley's hands fly up in the air, and he knew she was in trouble, too. Crowley went down with a scream, and the bear went to work on her.

The morning had started out calmly enough. Heimer, a hunting guide with thirty years of backwoods experience under his belt, was working on the Royal Teton Ranch, a majestic, game-filled spread on the northern border of Yellowstone National Park. The day had dawned warm, with just a touch of wind. The thermometer at hunting camp read forty-five degrees on that morning of November 8, 1996, and a foot of snow lay heavy and wet on the ground.

Such days are not uncommon in Montana winters. Chinook winds or air inversions often bring pockets of springlike weather. In Livingston, fifty miles north and fifteen hundred feet lower in elevation, it was forty degrees colder, and it had been just as frigid at the hunting camp a couple of days earlier.

It was a warm day, but it was definitely winter. Though grizzlies often don't enter their dens until late in November, nobody in hunting camp was even thinking about grizzly bears. Not at this time of year.

Crowley, fifty, had come to the ranch from her South Dakota home with her husband, Maurice—they call him Morey—to hunt trophy bull elk. Morey had bagged his bull the night before, and there were more around where that one came from. Sonja was hoping to fill her tag that morning, and Heimer drove the two of them to Beattie Gulch, a small juniper and sagebrush basin on the park border. Another guide had spotted some bulls nearby, but Heimer and his party were the first to get there. It was like coyotes and rabbits, he joked. The closest coyote got the bunny.

He parked his pickup, and he and Sonja got out. It was warm enough that she didn't even pull on her coat. Heimer said it would just slow her down. Maurice stayed behind as his wife and the guide climbed a small rise to overlook the gulch. Walking along a dirt road, trying to move both quickly and quietly, Heimer asked Sonja if she wanted him to carry her 7 mm Magnum rifle so she could move better through the heavy snow. Sonja agreed.

Heimer kept his eyes focused to their right, searching for the elk they knew were nearby. Sonja was right behind him. Then she tapped his shoulder and pointed to their left, a little behind them.

There were bears in the snow.

The grizzly was only about sixty feet away. Another hundred feet past her three cubs ambled, oblivious to the hunters. The mother was well known to bear biologists in Yellowstone and in that part of Montana. They called her No. 79 and considered her a matriarch of the northern Yellowstone ecosystem, valuable to the grizzly recovery effort there because of the numerous cubs she had produced in her twenty-two years. No. 79 had never been aggressive around people, but she did have a few bad habits, practices that led biologists to classify her as a "research/management bear."

In the jargon of bear biology, that means a bear that must be captured and transferred occasionally, preferably before it or a person gets hurt.

No. 79 became a management bear because of her sporadic appetite for unnatural foods, a track record that stretched back to her first capture in 1981.

From that time on, whenever natural food crops failed, such as whitebark pine nuts, she would move into the Gardiner area to feed from apple trees planted along the Yellowstone River or at old homesteads. She wasn't hurting anything, but the apples brought her too close to people, raised too high the odds of a dangerous encounter, so biologists would lure her into a culvert trap and relocate her deep within the park, hoping she would stay there. In the past the strategy had worked: No. 79 always stayed away from settled areas until another bad food year arrived. Until that day in 1996, she had always shunned people and committed no greater sin than swiping a few apples.

It had been a good year for natural foods, with plenty of protein-rich whitebark pine nuts and moth larvae. There were only two maulings in the greater Yellowstone area that year, and the number of close encounters was down sharply. No. 79 had denned for several winters just across the park border from the ranch, and that's probably why she was in the area. She may have already entered her den briefly before encountering Heimer and Crowley. But she was out that day, still on a single-minded autumn quest for a few thousand extra calories before she began her long sleep.

And on that soggy day, No. 79 showed a whole new attitude.

— ~ —

Joe Heimer knows animals, and he knows wild country. During most of the year, he raises and breaks horses and runs pack trips in the backcountry near Yellowstone. In his spare time he runs a fencing business. You don't find him sitting down very often, unless he's on a horse. But for him the best time of year starts in September and runs through November, the season when bull elk bugle and hunters and horses take to the backcountry.

He rattles off the names of high-altitude drainages like most people list city streets in their own neighborhood. And he tells plenty of bear stories. Grizzlies have bluff-charged him several times. They've kept him awake all night before, left him feeding the fire and watching his horses. He's had grizzlies walk through hunting camp and cause no trouble. One time in the Absaroka-Beartooth Wilderness, after unsaddling his horses in the inky darkness, he passed within three feet of a grizzly with cubs. Everybody backed off and nobody got hurt.

"I never had any trouble with grizzlies before," Heimer says.

No. 79 made sure he wouldn't ever say that again.

When Sonja spotted the bear, a powerful dark animal with a characteristic silver gloss on its coat, Heimer quit thinking about elk and focused on the bear, which showed no sign of knowing there were people in the area. She didn't even look in their direction. Together Joe and Sonja walked another fifty feet away from the bear and stepped behind a juniper bush. Then something happened: Maybe a twig snapped or the wind shifted a little, carrying their scent; maybe one of the cubs spotted the people and let out a squeak.

Whatever it was, something excited the bear and she charged.

"She never lifted her head" during the charge, Heimer recalls. As she sprinted, running low to the ground, he shouted at her, trying to make her look at him and back off.

"I've never been around any animal that never picked its head up to acknowledge me. She was swinging her head back and forth and rattling her teeth and hissing."

Sonja remembers none of that. She remembers the way the bear's muscles rippled in the morning sunlight as it ran. She remembers no particular fear. Heimer was there, and he had the gun.

"I wasn't concerned because he had the rifle, and I knew that she was going to be dead. I expected her to fall in front of our feet. But she wasn't a dead bear. She was an angry bear."

The gun was loaded, a powerful round secure in the rifle's chamber, but Heimer held his fire. He was waiting for the bear to stop and turn away. Not until she was on him, with her head no more than eight inches from the rifle's muzzle, did he shoot, aiming for her head.

He missed.

The bullet "might have cut some hair," he says.

Then the bear tackled him. No. 79's snout hit him under the chin, knocking Heimer on his back and sending the rifle flying. His first injuries were minor—a three-inch scratch on his abdomen and some claw marks on his arm.

He kicked and fought, but the bear sank her teeth into the flesh just above his right knee, raking it to the bone. She planted her feet on his, to keep him from kicking, and then went for the left leg, sinking her teeth into the meat and shaking her head.

That's when Joe got hold of her upper lip. One tooth put a small cut on the inside of his middle finger, but he noticed none of this. He flailed at the bear, trying to keep her away from his innards.

Then, as quickly as it started, it stopped.

Sonja had gone for the rifle, and her movement attracted the bear, making her the new target.

Joe was calling for help, and Sonja tried to provide it.

"I tried to look for the gun and couldn't find it fast enough. Before I knew it, she was after me. I did the thing you're not supposed to do. I just took off running. But I didn't get very far."

The bear hit her in the back first. She remembers it as a gentle blow, one that eased her face first into the snow. Then the bear sank its teeth into her head, its top teeth in the back of her skull, just missing the spinal cord, and the bottom teeth deep into the left side of her face, ruining her eye. It shook her, she went limp, and the bear started dragging the 120-pound woman away.

"The bear was shaking that lady from side to side," Heimer says. "Her body was flying around like a whip. I'm trying to get up, and I discover my leg isn't working."

Sonja didn't play dead, but she didn't have to. It wasn't a matter of choice.

"What was I going to do? I just lay there. I didn't struggle. I didn't move. I thought, 'This is a nightmare, and I'm going to wake up.' When she scrunched my head, my thought was, 'They're going to come over the mountain and we're going to be dead.' I could hear all the bones breaking as she bit down. I could hear every bone just go crunch, crunch, crunch, crunch. Then she shook me and started dragging me away. I think she thought she killed me and was dragging me away to bury me. I remember my feet flopping along the ground."

Heimer had struggled to his feet by then and found the rifle in the snow. But he couldn't take a shot, couldn't risk hitting Sonja instead of the bear.

Then, suddenly, the bear ceased its punishment. Perhaps Heimer's movement distracted her. Or maybe she decided the hunters had had enough. She loped back toward her cubs, stopping about fifty feet from the attack.

Heimer limped over to Crowley, who was moaning in the snow, bleeding hard, and he tried to tend to her wounds as he kept an eye on the bear.

"I thought it was over," Heimer says. "I was going to let the bear go. I wasn't going to shoot her just to shoot a bear."

But it wasn't over. The bear charged again, coming just as fast as it had the first time, and Heimer had lost all tolerance. He put a slug from the 7 mm through her shoulders and the bear went down.

Crowley was bleeding from the ear and most of the left side of her face was hanging by a flap of skin, her teeth and mangled jawbone exposed.

"I could look right down her neck," Heimer says.

He picked up the hanging flesh, put it back in place, and put Crowley's hand over it to try to reduce the bleeding.

And still it wasn't over.

Crowley had risen to her feet and could see over Heimer's shoulder as he tended to her. That's when she saw the bear coming for a third time and let out a muffled scream.

Heimer whipped around just as the bear was on him.

He fired a round at point-blank range, exploding the bear's skull. It died between his feet.

❦

Months later, as Heimer recalled the incident, his right leg began to twitch, the result of nerve damage the bear caused. He told stories of bears on trails and in camp, of times there had been nothing but a sheet of canvas between him and a set of grizzly jaws.

"I never thought it would happen, but it did," he says of the attack.

Morey Crowley was only about a hundred yards away when No. 79 attacked. Another guide was pulling up at about the same time. They heard the commotion, and they heard the shouts for help when it was over.

"I could hear Sonja crying out, 'Help me,'" Morey says. But he thought she had an elk down and wanted help field-dressing it. "It wasn't a few seconds later and I saw two bear cubs run across the road. I told the other guide, 'They've got trouble. They've got bears up there.'

"I started the truck and said, 'We're going to run that bear over if it's still alive.' But by the time I turned that corner, it was all over with. Joe was trying to put himself back together, and I saw a brown bunch of fur lying there. My wife was walking around. Joe had taken his shirt off and wrapped it around her head. She was wandering around saying, 'I lost my ear. I lost my ear.'"

The shirt on her head was soaked with blood, so Morey took it off and wrapped his own around her head.

"I told her her ear was still there and laid her down in the snow to try to slow the bleeding."

Guides on the ranch use radios to communicate, and the bad news traveled fast. People started showing up, including one with first-aid equipment and training. He put compresses on Sonja's head, and the men tried to get a National Park Service helicopter from nearby Mammoth Hot Springs to evacuate her. But the helicopter had already been shipped away for the winter, and for a while confusion ruled.

"It was so chaotic," Sonja recalls. "Nobody had ever had it happen before."

She was awake and alert, could feel the blood spurting from her head. There was radio traffic to the headquarters of the ranch, which is owned by a religious sect, to the sheriff, to other guides.

"I could hear them squawking on those radios," Sonja says. "I just wanted to take them and throw them. Back and forth. 'What are we going to do?'"

"The lady at the office was needing more information. The sheriff was wanting more information," Morey recalls. "Finally, we told them what they could do with that stuff. Get some damn help up here and we'll fill out the forms later."

So they fashioned a gurney from a blanket, put Sonja in a truck, and headed down the mountain road, navigating switchbacks and meeting other guides trying to climb the mountain to help.

Meanwhile, Joe stepped behind his vehicle to drop his pants and inspect his own damage. He wrapped his mangled legs with paper towels and electrical tape, the closest thing he had to medical supplies, and a friend drove him to a hospital in Bozeman, Montana, thirty miles beyond the small emergency room in Livingston. That's where a private ambulance had taken Crowley.

"I figured they had all they could handle in Livingston with her," Heimer says.

It took four hours to clean his wounds and stitch him back together. Joe ignored the doctor's advice, went home that night, and was guiding hunters again within a week.

⌐ ⌐

Crowley was in much worse shape.

Doctors in Livingston stabilized her, but it took a team of specialists in Billings eleven hours to put her face back together. She spent eight days in the hospital there. She has lost all but very limited vision in one eye and now has six steel plates under the skin on her face. The pain in her jaw and ear are constant. After her doctor in South Dakota pulled the wire from her crushed jaw, she found she still couldn't open her mouth. It took nine months of physical therapy to get her mouth to open, stacking tongue depressors between her teeth and increasing the gap by a millimeter a week. For months she lived on chicken broth, baby food, things pulverized in a food processor. "Anything I could fit in that I could slurp."

For her mental healing she got counseling and took medication. She's only had two nightmares about the attack, once when she forgot to take her medication one night and once after she talked to Heimer on the phone. She says some things make her jumpy—a dog coming up behind her, for instance.

"I'm not real big buddies with anybody sneaking up behind me," she says.

Still, the doctors did fine work. A year after the attack, her face sags a little on the left side and her smile is a little crooked, but she retains both her good looks and her tenacity.

On November 8, 1997, she and Maurice pulled out of Billings, Montana, where they had stopped to do a little shopping on their way back to the Royal Teton Ranch. It was late in the afternoon, exactly one year, to the hour, after she had arrived in Billings in an ambulance. This time she was headed in the other direction, back to the Yellowstone border, to finish the elk hunt the bear had interrupted.

Maurice wasn't surprised.

"She's no quitter," he says of his wife.

"We said from the very beginning we were going to come back. I especially wanted to come back and see Joe," Sonja says.

He was waiting for them at the ranch.

⁓

Biologists and game wardens who investigated the scene found evidence No. 79 and her cubs had been eating gut piles from elk killed by earlier hunters. Some people speculated that the spell of warm weather had brought her from the den for one last feed. Despite a search, nobody ever saw the cubs again that fall. The orphans faced a lot of dangers: they might have starved to death, or they might have been killed by wolves, coyotes, or another bear. Or they might have returned to the den their mother had probably been working on for a couple of weeks, slept through the winter, and woke up in the spring, hungry but eager to stay away from people.

A pair of orphaned yearlings were seen several times the next year on No. 79's turf. "We suspect they were her offspring," says Kerry Gunther, a bear biologist in the park. "But we don't know for sure. We don't know what happened to the third cub."

But the cause of the attack remains unknown. The hunters never came between her and the cubs, and the immediate area contained no gut piles or other food sources she was trying to protect. Joe says there hadn't been an elk killed within a mile of the attack for several days.

He says he wonders if she was on some kind of "vendetta," if she was so fed up with being captured and moved over the years that her natural fear of humans had been replaced with a seething anger. Morey Crowley wonders the same thing.

"This bear had been moved several times," he says. "It had been labeled a nuisance bear. It had been poked. It had been prodded. They'd taken teeth out of it to study."

If the bear had only been hungry, they wonder, if it had been only focused on a food source and saw the hunters as a threat to that food, then why did it ignore the sick cow elk only a few hundred yards away? That animal was too ill to rise to its feet and would have made an easy meal for the bear and its cubs.

"Why didn't they put the bear away a long time ago?" Morey wonders.

No. 79 hadn't been killed because, until she attacked Heimer and Crowley, she hadn't done anything to warrant a death sentence. Also, she was an incredibly valuable part of the long and expensive efforts to keep a population of grizzly bears alive in the Yellowstone ecosystem. Females are crucial to that effort, and this one had produced several litters of cubs in her twenty-two years. If every bear that left the park to eat apples was killed for that little indiscretion, Yellowstone's grizzly population wouldn't last long.

Gunther, who lives near No. 79's den site, doesn't buy the vendetta theory.

If she was on a vendetta, why did she never attack other people? Gunther asks. She had had plenty of chances but had always tried to avoid people.

Bear behavior experts advise against fighting a bear once it has attacked, that it is better to play dead. Grizzlies are strong enough to kill bull elk and could easily kill a person but rarely do so. Usually, the experts say, bears are trying to teach a lesson rather than kill somebody.

Heimer agrees that the bear probably saw him and Crowley as trespassers.

"I was on her turf, and she didn't like it. She wanted me out of there," Heimer says.

Still, he says that in retrospect the only thing he would have done differently would have been to put another slug in the animal to make sure it stayed down after he dropped it the first time.

Trying to fight a bear usually only makes the attack last longer, experts say, but Heimer believes that fighting back, keeping that death grip on her upper lip, kept him from more serious injury. And he wonders why she left him to attack Crowley. He wonders why she came for him twice.

"She didn't have to attack Sonja. And why did she come back to me a second time?"

As in many bear stories, there are plenty of ifs in this one.

If the Crowleys had grabbed the right rifle that morning, for instance, the attack might have been avoided. They had two matching rifles, one a 7 mm and the other a .30-06. When they left camp that morning, they took along the .30-06 but brought the bullets for the 7 mm, a mistake they didn't notice until they tried to load the gun. Switching guns meant a return to camp, a trip that took only a couple of minutes but one that timed their travels to coincide with that of the bear.

"Probably ten seconds would have made a difference," Sonja says.

Perhaps if neither Crowley nor Heimer had moved, if they had curled into balls and endured, the story would have ended differently, with fewer injuries and the bear still alive and able to nurture her cubs. If Crowley had held her position when the bear was chewing on her guide, if she had not gone for the rifle in an effort to help him, the bear might have ignored her.

But if she had done that, the bear might have got to Heimer's innards. His death grip on the bear's lip could not have held forever.

The Montana Outfitters and Guides Association gave Heimer its Guide of the Year Award for his actions, an event that put him through something almost as excruciating as the attack: standing in front of a banquet hall of people and making a speech.

He says Crowley is the hero.

"That woman saved my life."

If, after the bear dropped Crowley, Heimer had not gone to her, if he had been motionless for a couple of more minutes, the bear might have considered the two adequately chastised and walked away. But Heimer was a professional guide. The safety of his client was his duty, and lying still and silent, doing nothing, while she was injured nearby, did not occur to him.

When Sonja Crowley returned to the Royal Teton Ranch a year later, she was a little nervous. But Joe Heimer would be her guide again, just as she had requested. He didn't give her much time to nurture her edgy feeling.

"People had asked me, 'You're going back with the same guide?'" Sonja recalls. "I said, 'Why would I want to go with anybody else?'"

"He dragged me out of bed every morning at four, and we went hunting," Sonja says of the six-day hunt.

On the first morning Heimer drove her and Morey back to Beattie Gulch. He didn't tell them where they were going. He just drove there.

"It didn't bother me at all," Sonja says. "Even after we got out and walked. Morey was behind me, and Joe was right beside me. I felt a lot more prepared."

They all had guns this time. And they all had bear spray.

There were twelve hunters on the ranch that year, a season with no snow and almost no elk. "A lot of them went home after a few days. It just wasn't good elk hunting."

Not Sonja. She stayed for the duration, and of the twelve hunters she was the only one who got a shot at an elk.

She missed, but she kept hunting.

Finally, out of frustration she settled for one of the abundant buck deer on the ranch.

On the way home she and Morey detoured to Bozeman, where they stopped at the Montana Department of Fish, Wildlife and Parks laboratory and took pictures of No. 79's hide. Sonja may return to the ranch yet again. She'd still like to complete the hunt the bear interrupted.

"You never know," she says. "It may be a continuing story that goes on for years."

—⁓—

Joe and Sonja stayed in touch during her long convalescence. They talked on the phone, and they've got what Sonja calls "a bond." For Sonja, a self-described "wuss" who doesn't like cold weather, who walks six miles a day at home but maintains she can't hike with the men, returning to the hunt is an accomplishment. Nobody would blame her if she stuck to the pavement from now on. But for a man like Heimer, it takes more than a few dozen stitches and a twitchy leg to keep him out of the backcountry.

In his fifties Heimer still works harder than most men half his age. Like holding onto that grizzly's lip, he knows he can't keep it up forever, but he'll do it for as long as he can.

One thing he says he won't give up, however, is the wild country. And despite what happened to him, he's hoping there will still be bears in the woods.

"Maybe in about thirty years," he says with a grin, when it's time to give up the life he loves, he'll take a last trip.

"Maybe then," he says, "it'll be time then to go out looking for a bear."

It's a joke, of course.

Probably.

Postscript

Sonja Crowley and Joe Heimer remain friends, sealed by the events of that warm and terrible morning. Sonja and Morey drove out from South Dakota to surprise him for his birthday one year, and they all took a ride up to Beattie Gulch, where the attack took place.

On another trip they reenacted the attack for an outdoor news show.

Sonja will never regain sight in one eye, and it doesn't blink, so she has to put drops in it frequently. After eighteen months of therapy, her jaw opens a little wider "but not wide enough to eat a Big Mac." The couple travels widely, she hikes, they tend to two grandchildren with special needs. She thinks maybe that's why she survived the attack, so she can provide that help. And Sonja still takes medication every night. It helps her sleep and fends off the nightmares, mostly.

"I still have the occasional nightmare," she says. "But not very often."

She's backed off on hunting but hasn't given up entirely.

"I'm going out with Joe to shoot a buffalo, once he finds me the right one," she says.

Heimer, too, recovered from the attack. He still trains horses and still hunts the backcountry, though he doesn't travel as many miles after dark or before daylight as he used to, either on foot or horseback.

In hindsight he thinks the bear probably thought he and Crowley were "coming at her," and that's why she charged.

When he hunts in grizzly country, he carries bear spray clipped to the strap of his backpack. And he also carries a .45/70 rifle in case the spray doesn't work.

"I'd have the spray in one hand and the rifle in the other," he says. "I'm not going to let anybody else get chewed on. It's just not worth it."

❧

A couple of years after Crowley and Heimer were mauled, the United States Forest Service bought from the Church Universal and Triumphant much of the Beattie Gulch land they hunted that day. That opened up the property to a lot more hunters.

At least three of them have been mauled in the vicinity since then; others have had close calls; and officials periodically shut the area down because there are so many grizzly bears prowling around.

That generally happens in the fall when members of Yellowstone growing grizzly population—now estimated at a minimum of 600 bears—come to Beattie Gulch, attracted by gut piles and wounded elk the hunters leave behind.

"They're moving to a good food source," says Chuck Schwartz, head of the Interagency Grizzly Bear Study Team. "Over the years, they have learned where these hunting areas are, and they go there."

The year 2007 was a particularly bad one. Grizzlies attacked three hunters in the Beattie Gulch area that year. In two cases a mother bear with three cubs passed within arm's reach of bow hunters, clad in camouflage and crouching in the bushes. In both cases the mother bear noticed them after she had passed. Then she turned and attacked. Both men needed trips to the hospital, but their injuries were minor compared to what happened to the third man.

Virgil Massey, fifty-two at the time, was hunting with a rifle on nearby land the church still owns, and he suffered an incredible beating. He lost his left eye and the upper and lower eyelids on the other eye. With one swipe of its paw, the bear crushed his eye sockets, broke his jaw, tore up his sinuses, and shredded his forehead. Massey, who was about five hundred yards from a companion who had just killed an elk, later sued the church, outfitter Edwin Johnson, and guide Sam Bolinger. He said in court papers that the bear "approached and struck him" on an isolated sagebrush knob surrounded by trees.

Massey maintained Johnson and Bolinger should have warned him about grizzlies in the area and trained him how to deal with them. As this book went to print, the case remained unresolved.

In places like Beattie Gulch, with high densities of grizzly bears, people need to be careful, says Heimer, who no longer guides on the Royal Teton Ranch.

"If you're in bear country where it's happened before, you've got to be careful, that's all I've got to say," Heimer says. "It's one of those things in nature that you've just got to live with. If you don't want to live with it, don't go."

14

Last Run at McHugh

Imagine Larry Waldron's thoughts.

He's lying in the brush, badly mauled by a grizzly bear. He will die soon. He doesn't know this, but he must know it's possible.

He doesn't know where the bear went, but he does know that his mother and his nephew are following him up the McHugh Creek trail, moving fast into the same patch of brush that hid the grizzly that tore him up. He cannot move, and he cannot help them or warn them. He will be remembered as a man of great spirit and life and generosity. And there is nothing, absolutely nothing, he can do to help.

———

It was 1995, the summer of bears in Alaska. Binky the polar bear died in the Anchorage zoo, a year after he made international headlines and became a statewide celebrity by chewing a malfeasant tourist. The mayor of the remote village of Iliamna and his buddy, who helped run the airstrip there, started shooting grizzlies because they were getting too bothersome and one had nipped a paying fisherman. Dan Boccia got chewed up just outside of Anchorage.

Scientists convened in Fairbanks, releasing the latest information about bears. A new poll showed that bears fascinate Alaskans and scare them nearly witless at the same time.

"I had a chance last week to publish a front page where all five stories were about bears," former *Anchorage Daily News* editor Howard Weaver wrote late in July. "Looking back, I can't imagine why I didn't."

And then there was McHugh Creek: two people dead, a traumatized teenager, witnesses left in shock, lives changed, and a city in grief.

Alaskans take bear stories with a mixture of glee and the shivers. With as many as forty thousand grizzly bears in the state, the chances of bumping into one are excellent, although most encounters end the same way: with the bear fleeing into the bush, the people sometimes delighted, sometimes shaken, but almost always unharmed. At any given time between April and November, as many as sixty-five grizzly bears roam in and around Anchorage, a bustling, multicultural city of 290,000, much of which consists of untamed parks and brushy lots, threaded with bountiful streams and tinged with the fragrance of garbage and food, an occasionally irresistible magnet to something as sensitive as the nose of a hungry grizzly.

Everybody tells bear stories, and it seems everybody has a theory about them. Many people pack heavy artillery every time they leave the pavement. You see hikers and backpackers with short-barreled shotguns slung across their chests or pistols on their hips with an extra clip or a speedloader handy. Some people walk with their guns ready, fingers on the trigger guard, a Magnum load in the chamber. Others prefer bear spray. Some wear bear bells. People argue about the benefits of bringing a dog along. Will it distract the bear or merely anger it, then return to the protection of its master and cower between your legs, an angry bear on its tail? Some people are so spooked by bears they rarely leave the streets. Still others don't think much about bear safety at all. They jog and ride bicycles through brushy bear habitat. You see hikers with earphones blasting loud music or books on tape, making impossible the alertness that grizzly country demands. Overflowing garbage cans and dumpsters are a common sight. In busy salmon streams, where anglers and grizzlies compete for fish, some people flee in terror at the first sign of a bear. Others put down their tackle and wade into the stream, trying to get close enough for a good picture with a pocket camera. Alaskans know these stories and usually don't get too excited about them.

But the death of Larry Waldron and his mother, Marcie Trent, shocked Alaskans like no other recent bear incident. The news stayed on the front page for a long time and ignited a lengthy public debate over bears and people and the proper place for both. And it left a lot of people bitterly, unspeakably sad.

Larry and Marcie were not faceless tourists. They weren't even unknown locals. They were well-known, popular Alaskans. Marcie Trent, at seventy-seven, was a long-distance runner who held many records for her age class and had spent forty-nine years in Alaska, a tough land that runs a lot of people off, a place where longevity matters to people. She organized Anchorage's first running club and was often called "the mother of Alaska running." Her son, Larry Waldron, forty-five and also a runner, was a popular musician, composer, and music teacher who was born in Alaska. A bell tower at a church and another at Alaska Pacific University are dedicated to members of the Waldron family. Mourners at their joint funeral included runners, elderly ladies, musicians in ponytails, and the governor of Alaska. Larry had played saxophone at the governor's inaugural ball. Larry and Marcie both inspired people. They taught them important things: to be healthy and to laugh and to make music. They did it for strangers, and they did it for friends and family. Their deaths punched a hole in a lot of lives.

One of those left shocked was Craig Medred, then the veteran outdoor editor for the *Anchorage Daily News*. He's a strong distance runner, and he got to know Marcie Trent at races, where she was a fixture on the trail and at the finish line, where she encouraged everybody.

Medred also knows what it's like to be on the ground with an angry bear. When a sow grizzly mauled him in 1992, he became part of a very small club that nobody joins on purpose. And he summed up best the immediate reaction to the news that the mauling victims were Trent and Waldron. He had learned of the deaths only hours after they occurred, while at a barbecue near his home just over the ridge from the mauling. But he didn't yet know who had died.

"Everyone at the barbecue Saturday night was confident the dead at McHugh were tourists," he wrote in a column two days later. "Terrible as this might sound, there is a certain comfort in that thought. To say this happened to some tourist is to say it couldn't happen to one of us. And then we read the Sunday morning newspaper in shock."

<hr />

The news hit the streets on the morning of July 2, less than twenty-four hours after the deaths. Details were sketchy and contradictory at first. Early press accounts said Marcie was attacked first. The first story said a bear killed them. A story the next day said it may have been a moose. The only witness, Marcie's fourteen-year-old grandson, Art Abel, never got a good look at the animal that killed them.

"It was massively confusing," concedes Rick Sinnott, at that time the area biologist for Alaska Fish and Game.

It took a while, but the details finally emerged.

The coroner's report listed the cause of death: "injuries received in a bear attack." Marcie had a broken neck and spine, indicating the bear may have grabbed the diminutive grandmother by the neck and shaken the life from her one-hundred-pound body. Her son's injuries included a broken pelvis, a crushed rib cage, and many deep cuts. There was a lot of blood on the ground where he died.

There had been maulings in the Chugach State Park, a five-hundred-thousand-acre wilderness that butts up against suburban Anchorage, but this was the first time in the twenty-five-year history of the park that a bear killed somebody.

It wasn't until July 23, after Art Abel, accompanied by relatives and family friends, all of them armed, walked the three and a half miles back to the site, along with *Daily News* reporter Natalie Phillips, that the whole story came out.

"Art Abel—the only survivor of the attack—wanted to go back," Phillips wrote. "He needed to make sure he wasn't forgetting any of what happened, that his memories of the day were clear."

The tragedy began with a phone call. It came about half past ten on Saturday morning, the first of July, and Art, a typical teenager, was still in bed. His uncle Larry told him to get ready. They were going for a run on the McHugh Creek trail.

Larry and Marcie were preparing for an upcoming sixteen-mile race in Palmer. People used a variety of terms to describe Marcie, white-haired and barely five feet tall. "A sprite," one friend called her. "A mountain goat," another said. She had set a national marathon record for her age group when she was seventy years old, and she didn't like to run on pavement. She much preferred the trails.

The McHugh Creek trailhead is about fifteen miles south of central Anchorage, and many in the sprawling, diverse city consider the Chugach State Park, a vast roadless area filled with streams and forests and glaciers, their backyard playground. The McHugh Creek trail was a new one, built by volunteers only two years before the attack. It starts out at a large parking lot/picnic area and winds through a spruce forest, where boardwalks keep hikers' feet out of the bog. Then the trail takes you higher and the vegetation changes to spindly aspen, alder, and a profusion of low brush, punctuated by occasional spires of spruce trees. The trio had run the same trail nine days earlier.

Running in grizzly country can be dangerous: It can trigger a chase response in any predator, much like a cat chasing a ball. This information is repeated in bear safety literature all over the country, but trail running remains a popular competitive sport in Alaska. Most of the time it's completely safe. Runners frequently see bears, and in most cases, as in other bear encounters, the bears run away. Just a week prior to her last day, Marcie had spooked two black bears on another trail. A hawk had dive-bombed Larry while he was running, and the scratches on his face were still healing.

Such hazards are part of life—and part of the magic—in Alaska. If you let them bother you too much, you might as well live someplace with more cement and fewer animals.

"We were making jokes," Art told Phillips as they walked the McHugh Creek trail, reliving the attack. "We were talking about what you do if you see a moose—climb a tree. If you see a bear—you run."

Once the trail breaks out of the woods, it offers stunning views in all directions: The Chugach Range looms ahead, and the Turnagain Arm and the distant Kenai Range lie behind you. Art and Marcie stopped early in the run to admire the panorama. Larry ran ahead, eager to do his training. At one point Marcie said she hoped they wouldn't run into a bear.

"I said, 'Oh, we're not going to run into a bear,'" Art recalled.

After a while, Art's stomach started to hurt, so he slowed his pace. Marcie slowed to stay with him.

Not far ahead of them, Larry had already been attacked by the grizzly and lay bleeding, no doubt worried about his injuries but undoubtedly worried even more about his mother and nephew, coming up toward an angry bear.

Nobody will ever know exactly what happened when the bear attacked Larry, but there are some details.

The bear—probably a medium-size grizzly of several hundred pounds, judging by one partial track park officials were able to find—had been feeding on a week-old bull moose carcass in a dense alder thicket skirted by the trail.

Grizzlies will defend such a prize with incredible force. Other bears will take it away, given the chance. So will wolf packs. When Larry approached on the run, the bear probably saw him as a threat and attacked, knocking him off the trail. Or perhaps it met Larry on the trail. The growth is thick in that spot, partially obscuring the trail, and trail runners have an unconscious practice of ratcheting back their vision when the footing is obscured. Larry probably was focusing on the ground fairly close in front of him, not scanning the medium distance for hazards.

He may have moved off the trail when he first saw the bear or when it first attacked. Somehow, whether he tried to run away or whether the bear dragged him there, he wound up about thirty yards downhill from the trail. Around his body there was blood on the grass and brush, which had been trampled in an area fifteen feet across, feeding speculation that Larry may have struggled with the bear.

Whatever happened, the bear delivered mortal wounds. Larry was tangled in the brush below the trail, slowly dying from deep cuts and crushed bones, as the bear moved back toward the moose carcass, uphill from the trail, as Marcie and Art approached.

The alder patch hiding the moose was incredibly thick. Two years after the attack, finding the place where the moose had lain meant crawling on hands and knees. By then the visible reminders were few: some cleanly sawn branches, cut to allow a helicopter sling to lower to the ground and haul the moose carcass away, and a couple of wallows, twenty-inch-deep holes the bear had dug that were rapidly filling with decaying leaves and debris.

But when the bear came through the alder patch again, it did so with incredible speed.

Some minutes after Larry was attacked, Marcie and Art came by. Art was in the lead, and Marcie traveled at his heels, only about three feet behind him.

Art heard the bear coming, saw the brush moving.

"All I could see was the bushes moving," he told Phillips. "It was charging through them. It was grunting and snorting."

The movement was only about twenty feet away, he recounted, when he jumped off the trail. He thought he was being attacked by a moose.

"I just dove off."

Then his grandmother screamed.

"I wasn't sure if she screamed because it grabbed her or because she saw it. I couldn't really see anything at that point or help her because it was so fast. All I could do is hope that she noticed it too and dove as fast as I did."

But Marcie wasn't quick enough, and it's likely the bear killed the tiny woman very quickly. Then it hid her body under some alders about twenty feet off the trail. It would take some time for rescuers to find her there.

Art, terrified and thinking he was still being pursued by an angry moose, slid face first through the alders, down to a tiny creek bed. When he came to a stop, he didn't know what to do. He climbed the other side of the small ravine and called out to Marcie. She didn't answer, but the brush started moving again. Fearing another attack, he ran.

Later, when he was told that his grandmother and uncle were dead, that they had been killed by a bear and not by a moose, he theorized that the bear didn't chase him because it didn't want to get too far from the moose kill.

But at the time, still fearing a moose, he ran until he found a spruce tree stout enough to climb, and he waited for his uncle, who he believed was ahead of him on the trail and would soon return. He stayed in the tree for three hours, he says, his young mind tortured by indecision. Should he stay in the tree and warn Larry? Should he try to help his grandmother? Should he try to bushwhack back to the trailhead and find help?

After he had been in the tree less than an hour, a hiker came by. Art talked to him from the tree, told him Marcie had been attacked by a moose.

The hiker was bold and returned to the trail. Luckily, the bear had disappeared by then. Moments later the hiker heard Larry's faint moans and tried to help. Larry said one word.

"Bear."

Hiker Jim Blees saw that Larry needed more help than he could give him and started jogging down the trail, where he met a group of five hikers. Three of them agreed to stay with Larry, and the others returned to the trailhead with Blees, hoping to find someone with a cellular phone.

"I started praying as soon as I saw him," says Sandra Small, a New Hampshire woman who went to Larry. He couldn't speak and his breathing was shallow. Then his breathing tapered off, Small told Phillips, and he died.

"He wasn't alone when he died," she says.

Small and the other hikers feared the bear would return, and they felt there was nothing else they could do for Larry. So after about twenty minutes, they left.

Blees had found help at the trailhead, and a National Guard helicopter scrambled. There was no good landing spot near the attack, so three rescuers rappelled to the ground. They found Art at about half past four in the afternoon, still in the tree. The rescuers found Larry's body right away, then found the moose carcass. They found Marcie's body lying on a bed of ferns.

The helicopter gave Art a ride back to the trailhead, where there were state troopers and park officials and reporters, a lot of questions. Art didn't know Marcie and Larry were dead, but he heard snatches of information on a police radio and started to put things together.

Then a police chaplain arrived. Larry's wife and Marcie's husband arrived shortly afterward, and the chaplain brought the three of them together to deliver the sad, sad news.

—◆—

Friends poured out their grief in private and public ways. Musicians from all over Alaska got together for a tribute to Larry, a man who had taught many of them to play and inspired many others to play better. There were letters to the editor, and there were news stories.

And for some the grief took the form of anger, anger at bears and anger at the people who manage them.

In the confusion of the days immediately following the attack, mixed signals were sent and there were some screwups.

The helicopter that hauled the moose carcass away developed mechanical problems, so it left the smelly carcass in a dumpster at the trailhead, where there is a developed picnic area. The trail was closed by then, but the prize the bear had killed for was left among the Fourth of July picnickers.

Some members of the Waldron family wanted the bear killed, and they said that Alaska Fish and Game had promised that would happen. Armed officials returned several times to the site but couldn't find the bear. After a while, they quit trying.

There was a lot of pressure to bring in a dead bear, says Rick Sinnott.

"We like to be able to shoot the right bear if we have to shoot a bear," Sinnott says. "We don't want to just shoot any bear and drag it into town and say here it is."

The deaths were a freak occurrence, biologists say. Marcie and Larry died of bad luck more than anything. They ran headlong into one of the most dangerous bear situations that exists—a grizzly protecting its food. Rockslides and dog bites kill more people than grizzly bears do. So do bee stings.

Steve Waldron, Larry's brother, scoffs at the contention that the biologists couldn't find the bear. He says they never really tried.

There were rumors of lawsuits, and there was talk of retribution against bears. Alaska has plenty of grizzlies, and they are not endangered. When a bear kills somebody, many maintain, it must die.

Jan Waldron, who lost her mother and her brother in the attack, whose son Art was lucky to survive, wondered in a letter to the editor if grizzlies should be allowed in Chugach.

"Perhaps a larger debate needs to be initiated," she wrote. "Should brown bears be extirpated from Chugach Park altogether, given that it is a playground for over half the population of the state?"

People who had never packed guns into the woods started doing so after McHugh Creek. Sales of bear bells and bear spray soared. And there were cries for retribution all over Alaska during that summer of bears. People were losing patience.

Since grizzlies in Alaska don't have federal protections, like the bears in the Lower forty-eight, the killing of them is regulated only by state law, which allows what are known as DLP shootings. The acronym stands for "defense of life and property." In some cases DLP shootings are clear-cut: If a bear is mauling you or another person, or trying to break into your home, you have a right to shoot it. Few people argue with that.

Other cases can be fuzzy. State law also allows the killing of bears posing a "threat to property," as long as you didn't chum them in with garbage, a bird feeder, or something similar. In some cases people open up on a bear just for showing up.

"There's always an increase in DLP shootings after a mauling" and the publicity it brings, Sinnott says. "There's always a spike. The tolerance level goes way down."

That's something to think about, for people who believe they risk only their own hide by jogging through grizzly country.

POSTSCRIPT

Trail running is a rapidly growing sport in the United States and Canada, and you can find races in grizzly country every year, from Wyoming to Alaska. Enthusiasts talk about the endorphin rush, being "in the zone" or "blissed out," the satisfaction and sense of accomplishment it gives. In most places it poses no risks beyond sprains and falls and exhaustion. But in grizzly country the dangers blossom.

That's because it's awfully hard to follow the rules of safe travel when you're running, especially if, like many enthusiasts, you're pounding hard.

Moving quickly and quietly can place you inside a grizzly bear's safety envelope before either one of you knows what's going on. Since roots and rocks and other hazards often clog the trails, runners have to focus on the ground a few feet in front of them, minimizing the field of vision, the stretching of the eyeballs that can keep you out of trouble. Hard breathing and a pounding heart rate reduce your hearing. And just the act of moving fast can trigger a chase response from any predator. Even a housecat will ignore a stationary ball of yarn. But give it a shove, and the cat likely will pounce. It works the same way with people in Lycra.

"Running may elicit an attack from otherwise nonaggressive bears," Yellowstone National Park's website warns.

Official warnings such as that can seem like a hassle at best, the meddlesome hand of Big Brother, especially for talented, committed athletes. But sometimes, listening to The Man is a good idea.

On June 5, 2005, Isabelle Dube was running with two other women near Canmore, Alberta, when they surprised a grizzly bear from about twenty-five yards. The friends backed off slowly until they were able to start running again. Dube climbed a tree, but the two-hundred-pound male bear followed her, pulled her from the tree, and killed her.

The trail had been under a "voluntary closure" for months, but the effectiveness of the closure was a matter of disagreement, and Dube, like many other athletes in the area, had used it anyway.

Could Dube have saved herself if the group had stayed together? Perhaps. Grizzlies rarely attack groups of three or more people. And a month earlier the same bear had approached a woman with a small dog, but they were able to escape by backing off slowly.

Dube left a husband, a young daughter, and many friends. Second-guessing her decisions does nothing for their sadness, no more than it did anything for the Trent/Waldron family.

Yet runners still hit the trails in increasing numbers. More attacks seem inevitable.

"Some of these people are not aware of the dangers they put themselves in," said Chris Servheen, head of the Interagency Grizzly Bear Study Team in Missoula, Montana. That holds especially true for long-distance running contests, the endurance feats that last for twenty-four hours or more. "This long-term running, at dawn and dusk, at night with headlamps: These are the specific things we tell people not to do in bear habitat."

He said runners lag only photographers as the backcountry group most likely to wind up in trouble with a wild animal.

In Alaska, with its high numbers of grizzlies, people continue to run the trails. And they continue to run into bears.

"I think it's a bad idea to do things like that in wild areas," says Rick Sinnott, the former biologist for the Anchorage area for the Alaska Department of Fish and Game. In heavily wooded Far North Bicentennial Park, as many as twenty grizzlies gather when the summer runs of salmon fill the stream there. And the park attracts a lot of trail runners as well.

"They're not out there looking for the birds and squirrels," he said. "They're out there for the exercise."

He sees joggers as putting themselves at more risk than hunters moving stealthily through the woods.

"At least hunters aren't moving very fast," he says. "And they've got a gun."

A grizzly mauled Clivia Feliz in the park in 2008, just six weeks after mountain bike racer Petra Davis suffered terrible injuries on the same trail. A sign at the trailhead warned of bears in the area, but when Feliz saw a bicyclist exit the trail, she thought it was probably safe, she told the *Anchorage Daily News*. Then, about eight hundred feet into the run, she saw two cubs just fifty feet away. She turned and ran, but the cubs chased her. Like Dube, she, too, thought about climbing a tree and veered off the trail. The cubs followed her dog, which had chosen another escape route, but the mother bear leapt on Feliz, leaving her with a mangled arm and a punctured lung. But it didn't take her life.

She realized later, talking to reporter Megan Holland from her hospital bed, that she should have paid closer attention to the warning sign.

"It was my fault," she said. "I shouldn't have been on that trail."

—◦—

Tom Hayes teaches mathematics at Montana State University in Bozeman, Montana, on the edge of the greater Yellowstone National Park ecosystem. Grizzly country begins a few miles south of town and Hayes is an avid trail runner. He particularly enjoys the Black Canyon Trail in the park's northern range, where the elevation is a little lower and snowmelt comes a little earlier. He's run it more than twenty times, usually in the spring. He regularly finds carcasses and grizzly tracks, sometimes places where bears have dragged a carcass over his own tracks. He's encountered three grizzlies, but they didn't give him any trouble.

"It's more risky than I want to admit to myself," he says, but he always carries bear spray and makes noise when visibility is low.

He knows what can happen when you surprise a bear, knows that bear spray doesn't always work, but believes the risk is manageable. It's what mathematicians call "conditional probability." Runners may be at more risk than hikers, but the risk isn't vastly greater, he says, and they're probably at less risk than bow hunters, who sneak through the woods. He also believes that a runner's hard footsteps might help alert bears that a person is coming.

For the past several years, he's organized what he calls the Devil's Backbone Race, a grueling fifty-miler along the crest of the Gallatin Mountains south of Bozeman. He recommends that all participants carry pepper spray but acknowledges that few of them do.

"It's borderline stupidity to go out without bear spray," Hayes says.

Many runners, anxious to stay in shape, need to work out every day, says Meghan Hicks, a writer and outdoor educator who spent four years in Yellowstone, which is almost all grizzly country. But she stuck to her training while living there. And trail running has great appeal, she said: the scenery, the testing of one's self, the ability to "bliss out" with the endorphins released by exertion and accomplishment.

"But you can't do that in grizzly country," she says. "Or at least I can't."

She advises people to think carefully before making fast time on the trails in grizzly country. Measure the risk. Think through scenarios. Be ready to change your plan or your route.

"Before you go out, get educated," she says. "Then decide if it's right for you."

While the National Park Service warns against trail running, it hasn't banned it in Yellowstone. It's hard to keep people from putting themselves at risk.

When he was still a state employee, Sinnott argued for closing Bicentennial Park during the summer, when the bears are fishing there. It worked for a while, but a new mayor was elected and put the kibosh on that policy. The mayor maintained that people were capable of weighing risks for themselves.

The debate over eliminating grizzlies from Chugach State Park, which abuts Bicentennial Park, didn't get much traction. Officials again allow grizzly hunting there, but only one has been killed there in the three years prior to 2011.

And Anchorage residents continue to value their open space. Ask Alaskans what they value about their state, and the word "pavement" doesn't make the list. The city has made improvements in garbage handling and sanitation, but the grizzlies remain, holding their own, so far, amidst a growing human population.

Sinnott says he learned after the McHugh Creek tragedy that maulings were likely to happen again on his watch. So he bought a pager, refined his bear-handling policies, and started working with city officials and the local joggers and mountain bikers, trying to encourage them to ply their sports elsewhere.

Some listened. Some didn't.

Even in retirement, he keeps an eye on people and bears, watches how they deal with each other.

"We kind of cross our fingers," he says. "And hope for the best."

In other parts of grizzly country, some runners make extensive efforts to keep themselves safe.

"Getting blissed out is not going to happen," says avid trail runner Leslie Gerein, who lives in Banff National Park. "Traveling in bear country doesn't really give you that luxury."

Dube's death rattled the trail running community there, she says.

"That could have been me," she says.

She selects her running companions carefully and always makes plenty of noise on the trail, enough that she attracts plenty of dirty looks from other hikers and users. She says it's worth enduring the scorn on the trail to live in one of the world's most spectacular places and to reduce dangers to both people and bears.

But the message doesn't always sink in.

She recalls seeing one runner at a race near the park, pushing hard and wearing earbuds.

"He clearly didn't have a clue about traveling in bear country," she said.

15

Bikes and Bears

IF PETRA DAVIS SAW THE BEAR COMING, SHE REMEMBERS NOTHING OF it. She says it's better that way.

"All I remember is crawling out of the bushes," Davis says almost three years after a grizzly bear tore her up. "And I remember I was very, very glad to see Peter."

When the bear attacked, Davis, though only fifteen years old, was pedaling her mountain bike in a twenty-four-hour race. The course looped through the heavily wooded Far North Bicentennial Park along the outskirts of Anchorage, Alaska, and the bear pounced at about 1:30 a.m. on June 29, 2008. It was as dark as it gets at that time of year in Anchorage; not an inky black, but a lingering dimness compounded by thick clouds. In most places that kind of dusk lasts just a moment. In Anchorage, just after the summer solstice, it lasts a couple of hours before it lifts.

Visibility was maybe fifty feet when Peter Basinger, who had been Davis's cross-country ski coach, found her in the near darkness, covered with blood and alone in the woods.

He saw the bike first, in the tall brush alongside the trail, but didn't recognize it. Then he saw Petra, just a few feet away, sitting in the trail with her back turned. He didn't recognize her, either. He thought somebody had taken a spill and he felt no immediate sense of alarm. These things happen in mountain bike racing.

"I wanted to keep going because I was doing a race," he recalls.

But he's not the type of man who could ride away. He laid down his bike and approached the person, and reality began to ratchet up.

"She was covered in blood and mud, with her hair strewn everywhere," Basinger says. "And she whispered. It was raspy and desperate sounding. She said 'bear.'"

She reached out her arms and that's when he saw through the mess and recognized Davis, one of a group of committed, intense, competitive girls he'd coached. She motioned with her head. He thought she was telling him the bear was still around, maybe behind him. Though it made her yelp in pain, Basinger picked her up and carried her about thirty yards, to a spot where the brush didn't push in quite so close to the trail, where he could see a little better. A steady wind whipped the trees, masking sounds, muffling everything.

He had nothing with him but his bike and his clothing. He wondered whether it was best to stay with her or go for help. He decided to stay, cradling the girl while he waited for help, sitting behind her, his right arm around her, resting her head against his chest. He couldn't judge the extent of her injuries, though the copious blood told him they were bad. Then Petra held out a cell phone.

Basinger tried to call for help, but the keypad was locked.

"I'd never had a cell phone at that time," Basinger says. "And it was dark and the phone was covered in blood."

He couldn't figure out how to unlock the keypad. Petra, struggling with her injuries, managed to do it for him.

"She couldn't talk but she was 100 percent with it," Basinger says. He dialed 911, only to hear a recording. "Your call cannot be completed at this time," the automated voice intoned.

He tried again and got another recording, his frustration growing. Then the phone rang in his hand. Basinger didn't know it at the time, but Davis had dialed 911 before he arrived, though her mangled throat meant she couldn't leave a cogent message. So the dispatchers called back. Help was on the way.

Then another racer arrived, another teenager Basinger had coached. He told him to bust ass to the trailhead and find help. And he made another call, to the race director, and told him what had happened. The director grabbed an EMT working the race and sped to the scene. They arrived before the ambulance crew, which had gone to the wrong trailhead in the confusion. The race EMT had a headlamp, and only then did the men began to grasp the extent of Petra's injuries.

"It looked like she had been shredded left and right," Basinger says. "We could see torn flesh through the rips in her clothing."

Carefully, carefully, the men laid her on her side, but Petra began to choke, so Basinger cradled her again. That's when he saw the terrible wound on her neck. The carotid artery was damaged, her larynx crushed by the bear's bite. "Hang on, Petra," he told her. "You're doing fine." And he stayed on the line with the dispatch operator, trying to get the ambulance crew to the right place in the densely wooded park, on the city's east side. When the crew found its bearings, when a police escort armed with shotguns arrived, when the sizable group trundled a gurney to the scene, Basinger's role was done. He'd been with Davis for a little over half an hour.

By then a few other bike racers had gathered. Somebody turned a light on Basinger, illuminated all the blood and mud that had scraped from Petra's body.

"He thought I was the one who'd been mauled," Basinger says.

<hr />

Three years later Petra Davis, by then a freshman at Montana State University, sat in a coffee shop in Bozeman, Montana. She looked up from her bag of books and told what she recalled of the attack.

"I was pushing hard, maybe ten to thirteen miles per hour," she says. She passed through a clearing and entered a spot where the path narrows to a single track and funnels through thick brush, becoming a curving tunnel in the foliage.

That's where Basinger found her bike, at the mouth of the tunnel. And that's where Petra's memory fades out, likely due to the concussion she suffered, one of the least of her injuries.

"My carotid artery was punctured, and I had a punctured lung, what they call a sucking chest wound," she says.

The bear tore muscle from her right arm and broke eight ribs, clawed open one leg, bit hard on her lower left hip and left more than a hundred puncture wounds on her back. Her face is scarred, and she spent three weeks in the hospital, surprising the doctors, who told her to plan on a three-month stay.

Petra Davis is a strong young woman. Smart, too. MSU accepted her in its honors program. And she has family that backs her 100 percent.

"I've had very little post-traumatic stress," she says. "I talked about it with my folks a lot. That really helped. It was really good."

She wonders, sometimes, just what happened. Did she collide with the bear in the deep twilight of the Alaskan night? Were there cubs involved? She doesn't know.

"Part of me is curious," she said. "But a more dominant part of me is glad" that the details disappeared.

She remains passionate about mountain biking and dreams of doing it for a living someday, of snaring a coveted sponsorship. She has a goal and doesn't want those memories interfering.

She considers the attack a freak accident. Plenty of other people were on the trail that night, with a racer passing every few minutes. The way she sees it, it was just bad luck to be the one that met the grizzly.

"It taught me that my family and friends are very important," she says. "I know now that I'm strong enough that something like getting mauled by a bear is not going to keep me from doing something I feel strongly about. I hope I can keep doing it the rest of my life."

Petra Davis doesn't ride alone in her passion for mountain biking. The sport has exploded over the past twenty years. It expanded by 78 percent between 1993 and 2003 and has grown even more since then. Nearly a third of all bicycles sold in the United States fall into the mountain bike category.

While it's impossible to say how many of these impressive machines—with shock absorbers, space-age frames, and sophisticated gears and brakes—gather more dust in a garage than on a trail, anybody who spends time on mountain trails knows the use is growing.

Throughout the United States and Canada, debate simmers over the appropriate place for mountain bikes. In most places the arguments focus on human values, how and whether to share trails with hikers, horseback riders, all-terrain vehicles, and motorcycles.

In grizzly country the issues become more visceral.

Mountain bikes move fast and they're pretty quiet. You know this if you've ever been surprised by one coming up behind you on a hiking trail. It can be startling. And startling a grizzly bear is never a good idea.

Chuck Schwartz, head of the Interagency Grizzly Bear Study Team, headquartered in Bozeman, Montana, says mountain biking in grizzly country is a bad idea because the bikes move so fast and so quietly, which means bears have fewer opportunities to move away.

"The bears are smart," Schwartz says. "They try to avoid us and use their senses to find out if we're there."

Come at them quickly and the bears can feel that they're being attacked, so people need to use their senses as well as their legs. That means eyes, ears, nose, and brain. In grizzly country the best defense—better than bear spray, better than guns—is a good look around. For mountain bikers that's hard to do. Riders need to focus on the trail immediately in front of them, and both hands are full of handlebars. They're trying to go fast and remain upright under often difficult conditions. And encounters can happen fast.

"Boom," says Schwartz. "You're on top of a grizzly bear."

Still, he doesn't expect to see people give up the sport.

"I guess some people need the extra adrenaline rush," he says. "People like it. And it is fun."

He urges mountain bikers to follow the same rules that apply to hikers: Stay in groups, make noise, carry bear spray, and, above all, pay attention to your surroundings.

That's a lesson that Kirk Speckhals learned the hard way.

———

It was a warm summer day in 2004 when Speckhals—people call him Sparky—and two friends decided to tackle a trail in the Absaroka Mountains, east of Jackson, Wyoming, just outside the Teton Wilderness Area, a place with a growing population of grizzly bears. They hauled their bikes over 9,600-foot Togwotee Pass, then started puffing them up a trail. Speckhals had been riding there since the 1980s; he knew the trail well and pulled out ahead of his companions. He was feeling strong that day.

With him was Mark "Big Wally" Wolling, another veteran biker. The third man was Tom Foley, who was fairly new to the sport. A frequent hiker in the bear and moose habitat around Grand Teton National Park, Foley is a firm believer in bear spray. He'd brought a can on an earlier hike with Speckhals.

"I was giving him shit," Speckhals says. "'Do you take it to the grocery store in case an old lady takes something out of your cart?'"

He lived to eat those words.

"It was fate," Speckhals says. "The next day he saved me with the same can."

In fact, Foley brought two cans of bear spray that day. He kept one with him and loaned the other to Wolling, who had brought his bird dog and worried that the energetic canine might attract a bear. But it was Speckhals, the only one without any bear spray, who drew the bear.

"From the moment I first saw him, he was in a full charge, coming at me like he really meant it," Speckhals said of the big grizzly with a silver back, an animal he estimated at five hundred pounds. He first spotted it from about 150 yards out, and it was zeroing in on him from a ninety-degree angle.

Speckhals jumped off his bike and tried to use it as a shield, though one with a lot of holes in it. He yelled "bear" three times, his voice growing louder each time. When the bear got within twenty-five yards, he says, his voice became "a sort of primeval shriek." Foley, behind him, could hear the shouts but couldn't see what was going on, so he started pedaling faster to see if he could help.

For a while, Speckhals held his ground by hollering at the bear and wielding his bicycle. When the bear reached him the first time, it stopped, perhaps confused by the loud man and strange machine before him.

"He hit the brakes. He turned around 180 degrees. He did a pirouette. And then he came at me again."

The bear made several charges, and each time, the bike served as a barrier, until the bear finally snatched it away and started pounding the bike, jumping on it, and biting it.

"I could hear air coming out of the tires," Speckhals says.

Then, with the bear occupied, Speckhals tried to get away, taking a few quick steps. The bear was on him in a flash.

"He took me to the ground. I'm flat on the ground, just waiting for it. And at that moment I felt bear spray in my face. I got the overspray."

Pedaling like a demon, Foley had arrived in the nick of time.

"I saw the last bit of bear falling on Sparky," he says. "He was buried under the bear."

He remembers thinking and moving methodically, going through the steps: remove spray from holster, unlatch safety, move closer, spray the bear. "I was in the zone or something." He unloaded the spray directly in the bear's face from about six feet away.

But the bear didn't bolt. It moved away from Speckhals but focused its attention on Foley. Only about ten feet away, he locked eyes with the bear and kept spraying. The bear didn't huff or shake its head. It just stared, its eyes open wide.

"His head is down, and he's looking at me like he's going to kill me," says Foley, who was running out of spray and started yelling as hard as he could.

Then Wolling's dog showed up, with Wolling not far behind. The dog barked furiously a few times, then took off. Wolling was fumbling with his pack, trying to retrieve his spray. The bear started moving away, then, at thirty to forty feet, appeared to change its mind again. It started lunging, bouncing around.

Until that point Foley had been staring into the bear's eyes. In hindsight he thinks the combination of bear spray and a stance that said, "I'm not attacking you, but I'm not backing down" finally helped the bear decide to leave. It probably didn't hurt to have a third man and a noisy dog on the scene. And once Foley broke eye contact, the bear fled for good.

By then Speckhals had regained his feet.

"I stood up to see if my arms and legs were still attached," Speckhals says. They were. He suffered some scrapes and bruises, plus some grizzly claw marks on his forearm. But they were etched in dirt, not in blood.

"It was pretty scary riding out of there," Speckhals said. Nobody knew where the bear had gone. And his mangled bike tire kept going flat, even with a new inner tube, because the grizzly had torn holes in the tire, letting the tube bulge out and burst. And the wheel was so bent that the brakes wouldn't work, so Speckhals had to walk the bike through steep spots. It was unnerving, but he was unharmed.

All three men and the dog were trembling with adrenaline, Foley said, but they stayed within ten feet of each other until they reached their car.

As a professional ski patrolman, Speckhals lives with calculated risks every day. He'd ridden the same trail for fifteen years before he was attacked.

"I never felt like I was taking excessive risks there," he says.

And he's not sure why the bear attacked.

Dr. Stephen Herrero, a bear attack expert and professor emeritus at the University of Calgary, analyzed mountain biking in grizzly country and defined a "sudden" encounter as one in which a biker surprises a bear within fifty meters. At that distance about half the bears charged and about half of them ran away, Herrero found, and a handful completed the attack. The bear that attacked Speckhals charged from much farther than that.

Speckhals thinks now that maybe Wolling's dog, roving through the woods while his owner chugged up the hill, might have roused the bear from a day bed. Or the bear might have been investigating him as some kind of prey. It might have been protecting a carcass in the area. Nobody will know for sure.

Speckhals returns every summer on his bike to ride the same trail.

"I just don't make the same mistakes I did that time," he said. "I carry bear spray. I make noise. And the group stays together."

Foley doesn't go with him. He said in 2011 that he hasn't mountain biked in grizzly country since the attack. That's partly because his lifestyle shifted with a new job and his interests changed. But the attack played a role, too.

"It definitely made me think," he says. "There's an inherent risk in biking in grizzly country. You can come on them so fast. And your group can get split up so quickly, if one rider stops for just a few seconds. I think you should always put the slowest rider in the lead."

— ⁓ —

Foley isn't the only one to rethink how he rides in the wake of a bear attack. Petra Davis now carries bear spray on her bike and uses a bell to make noise and alert wildlife and other riders. But she's back in the saddle and within a year of her attack had tackled the Rover's Run Trail, where she was attacked, riding with her mother that time. She said she feels no particular fear there.

Basinger, on the other hand, avoids biking in grizzly country now.

"It's completely changed how I ride," he said of the attack on Davis. "I'm just really nervous about bears now."

An avid biker, he likes to go fast, push himself, cover a lot of country. But he doesn't do that kind of riding in Alaska any more. As a teacher with long vacations, most summers he loads up his bike and heads south. There are a lot of good trails in Utah and Colorado. But there aren't any grizzly bears to surprise.

That attitude makes sense for some bear experts.

Rick Sinnott was a biologist for the Alaska Department of Fish and Game when Davis was attacked. He arrived at the scene less than an hour after it was reported, shortly after the ambulance pulled away with Davis.

For sixteen years his job called on him to investigate bear maulings in and around the sprawling municipality of Anchorage, which includes big chunks of wild land. He says a minimum of sixty-five grizzlies live in or near the city. And he says he's seen an upsurge in attacks on mountain bikers and trail runners as those sports grow in popularity.

"I'm sure the bear was surprised at close range, maybe within a few feet," he says. The trail at times comes within a few yards of a productive salmon stream, which draws grizzlies in the summers. On that night the combination of the loud stream and the wind meant a fast-moving bicycle could easily startle a bear, a creature that then decides whether to fight or flee. Unfortunately for Davis, this bear chose to fight.

In the past, mauling victims in the Anchorage area tended to be hunters or anglers, Sinnott says. But in recent years more of them are joggers and bikers, people who take to the woods more for a good workout than to slow down and enjoy nature.

"We're seeing more and more of the heart-rate people than the nature people in the last couple decades," he says. "And we're definitely getting an increase in the number of those people getting hurt."

A few weeks after Davis was mauled, a woman jogging nearby was chewed up by another bear. In 2010 a man bicycling on the same trail was mauled. Though both suffered, their wounds weren't as bad as Davis's.

Sinnott tried to get the trail closed, at least in the summer, but some people still used it. He's posted trail cameras in the park, hoping to build a database of the types of human users there. He's got thousands of photographs of people, most of them biking or running, moving fast in grizzly country at all times of the day and night, many of them wearing ear buds, often alone. The cameras also capture bears using the same trails. Grizzlies mauled three people in Bicentennial Park within three years. Two were bikers. One was a jogger. At least a dozen others have been chased by a bear, he says.

"Every time I go out, my wife asks me if I have my bear spray," says Mathew Schmor, a Calgary, Alberta, mountain biker whose master's thesis Herrero cites in his study. He found that bear bells are "highly suspect" in warning bears of a biker's approach, especially if the biker is moving quickly. He compares mountain biking in grizzly country to swimming in the ocean near Australia. Everybody knows there are sharks around, but they swim anyway, and almost everybody gets home safely.

Though he hasn't compiled new figures since he completed his thesis in 1999, encounters continue, even with Alberta's dwindling bear population.

"Almost every mountain biker I talked to has had an encounter with a bear, some of them quite aggressive," Schmor says. "The biggest thing is they don't hear you coming. And bikes have gotten faster and quieter. The bears usually have no idea you're there until you're right on top of them."

Usually, he said, they scamper away.

But sometimes, as Petra Davis and Kirk Speckhals learned, they don't.

16

Dinner Bells?

It's the kind of picture a lot of hunters would like to take home and hang on the wall. Two men in winter clothes, their arms around each other as they grin at a time-released camera propped on a rock or a stump, a six-point bull elk dead in the snow at their feet. But William Caspell and Shane Fumerton wouldn't take this picture home. In a few moments the two men would begin butchering their kill. Then a grizzly bear would show up, and their brief nightmare would begin.

The two men had pedaled mountain bikes for several miles that morning, then climbed three thousand feet up the slopes of Mount Soderholm in British Columbia, just west of the Alberta border and the Continental Divide, the spine of the continent. They had both elk and mountain goat tags in their pockets, but they found the elk first, catching it as it crossed a steep rockslide. They killed it, took pictures, and dragged it down the hill to a flatter spot. They had just started butchering and boning the animal when the grizzly charged, apparently with little or no warning.

Both men died. The bear claimed the elk carcass as its own.

Caspell was forty, and Fumerton was thirty-two. Fumerton left behind a wife and a seven-week-old baby. They were back in camp, waiting for him in a small trailer. When the hunters didn't show up that evening, October 9, 1995, or the next day, Fumerton's wife called police. Searchers wouldn't find the bodies for four days, hindered by blinding snowstorms that made it too dangerous to fly to the site and a stubborn bear on the ground that made it too dangerous to walk there.

Caspell's body would be found 150 feet downhill from the elk carcass. His head was so mangled he had to be identified by his clothing. Fumerton's body lay four hundred yards from the elk. He, too, had massive injuries to his head. The coroner's report listed the cause of death as "blunt trauma, consistent with grizzly bear mauling." The men may have tried to run, they might have been able to stumble away after the mauling, or the 255-pound bear may have dragged their bodies away from the elk carcass. Or they may have tried to fight, and the battle covered some ground. But investigators believe the men died fairly quickly. There was, at least, that small comfort for the grieving families.

Searchers found their guns as well. One rifle was sixty-five feet above the elk carcass, unloaded and resting against a rock. The second was about fifty feet from Caspell's body. Like him it was downhill from the elk, but there was a live cartridge chambered halfway into the barrel. British Columbia conservation officers suspected he may have been trying to load the gun and shoot the bear when it attacked. If so, it didn't work.

When a helicopter first flew over the site on October 11, two days after the attack, spotters saw a sow grizzly and two cubs feeding on an elk carcass. Despite being buzzed by the chopper, the bears wouldn't back off. Then the downdraft from the rotor blew up some ominous debris: a plastic bag and what looked like a hunting license.

The weather fell apart fast, and a snowstorm dumped three feet of snow on the mountain, frustrating both ground and air crews for another day. On Friday, October 13, the weather cleared, and conservation officers shot the bears from the helicopter door. Ground crews with dogs sifted through the waist-deep powder, putting together what bits of evidence they could find.

Tim Loader, the coroner from nearby Golden, prepared the reports on the case. "I'm not a bear expert by any means," he stresses. "But it looked like the bear pounced on them."

—◆—

Change a few details and you find similar stories wherever grizzlies roam, though few of them end so sadly, with dead men and bears. From Alaska to Wyoming hunters talk about "dinner bell" bears, bruins that hear a gunshot and come running, knowing it's likely to mean a meal. In most cases the bear is content to wait, usually unseen, until the hunters leave. Then it feasts on the gut pile left behind. In some cases it bluffs the people away and steals their kill. In very rare cases it attacks.

Nobody will ever know whether the bear on Mount Soderholm that sad day was attracted by the shots or just wandered by. Either scenario is a possibility. It's also possible the two men shot at the bear or her cubs. There's even been speculation that another large bear did the grim work and then for some reason yielded the carcass to the sow and cubs. But by the time the bodies were recovered, the evidence was cold and buried under all that snow. Nobody will ever be certain what happened that day.

—◆—

Kevin Frey, a bear management specialist from Bozeman, Montana, works in the northern part of the greater Yellowstone National Park ecosystem, handling problem bears, piecing together maulings, trapping bears that misbehave, and investigating when somebody kills a grizzly. He says the idea of dinner bell grizzlies makes some sense to him. And it's not just rifle shots that attract them.

"I called one in with an elk bugle once," he recalls.

During the fall rut, bull elk often fight to exhaustion, trying to gather the largest harem possible and to chase away all challengers. They announce their presence with long, high-pitched cries, punctuated by a series of grunts. A bull's bugle is a beautiful, chilling sound, and it sounds like heaven to many hunters. To grizzlies it sounds like dinner. The bulls move constantly, checking the cows to see if their estrus, their height of fecundity, is fully ripe; keeping them tightly corralled; chasing away younger bulls and locking horns with other big ones; often putting up huge clouds of dust, eyes red and distended, muscles bulging from neck and shoulders and hips. It's a remarkable thing to see. Bulls sometimes get hurt and most get exhausted, making them an easy mark for grizzlies hungry for autumn calories, especially late in the season when the bulls have been at this routine for weeks.

Inexpensive devices allow hunters to imitate the sound of an elk bugle, and a deft user can taunt a bull within reach of an arrow, bringing him in on the run, looking for the audacious challenger. That's what Frey was trying to do. But he bugled in a grizzly looking for a meal instead.

"I bugled that boar out of one canyon and into another one," Frey says. Luckily, the bear turned and fled once he saw the bugler was a human. Others have stories that didn't turn out so well.

—◆—

Steve Chamberlain and David Wood had put in a long day on September 15, 2001, bow-hunting for elk in Montana's spectacular Taylor Fork drainage, a little northwest of Yellowstone National Park. It was nearly dark, and they were done hunting for the day, sitting on the edge of an old logging road and taking in the scenery. Chamberlain gave a squeak on his "cow call," a device that imitates the reedy chirp of a female elk. Then Wood put his bugle to his lips and made it sing. They were a little surprised when they got a reaction: Something was moving in the bushes, at hand. Then the shrubbery parted, and the hunters got an even bigger surprise: a mother grizzly and two cubs in full charge. Both men wore camouflage and had recently doused themselves with descenting chemicals, making it hard to see or smell them.

Wood, who was already sitting, curled his six foot eight–inch frame into a ball, and the bears passed him by. Chamberlain, an orthopedic surgeon from Medford, Oregon, rose to his feet and stepped toward a tree, reaching for the .45-caliber pistol on his hip, enough movement to draw the mother bear's focus, and she nailed him. The first bite broke his fibula, then she chomped his thigh and shoulder on the way to his head as Chamberlain kept trying to escape.

"I said 'Dave, you've got to get her off of me,'" Chamberlain recalls. And Wood sprang into action, bear spray in his hand. The bear turned to him, and Wood unloaded a cloud of pepper into her face, giving himself a good dose in the process. That's when the bear gathered her cubs and split, leaving one man battered and bleeding, the other squirming on the ground, in blinding pain from the pepper spray.

The nearest passable road was an hour's hobble away, and even then Wood had to jog three miles to fetch their vehicle. Chamberlain, with a broken leg and other wounds, had little choice but to huddle under a space blanket, the pistol in one hand and the bear spray in another, and wait for his friend to return.

"That was not a good hour," he says.

Frey says he doesn't think the grizzly even knew she was attacking humans in that incident. Rather, their calling had convinced her that elk were nearby, and she charged. It's a good hunting strategy for a bear, he says, one that gives her a chance to surprise and latch onto a bigger animal, maybe bring it down. Probably surprised and alarmed to find people instead of elk, she delivered some quick bites and took off, no doubt hastened by the pepper spray in her face.

"We were imitating nature" with the elk calls, Chamberlain says. "The bear was doing its thing."

⤙ ⤚

But will bears come charging at the sound of a rifle shot? Frey doubts it.

"I don't think they'll come charging, but they'll damn sure move for them," Frey says of grizzlies and gunshots. Bears are clever animals and can learn when and where food becomes plentiful. "It's no different than a salmon run in Alaska. They're going to utilize it."

He was part of a study team that calculated that hunters leave 370 tons of guts, bones, and unretrieved meat in the greater Yellowstone area every year. The team also put radio collars on nineteen grizzly bears that live inside the park, where hunting isn't allowed. Of those animals fifteen headed for the park borders when Montana and Wyoming hunting seasons opened in September, each of them following its sensitive nose.

"You can't blame them for being able to smell blood and guts several miles away," Frey says.

⤙ ⤚

There isn't much science to back up claims that gunshots attract bears, but outfitters in the grizzly-dense Shoshone National Forest east of Yellowstone swear it happens all the time, says Dave Moody, a predator specialist for the Wyoming Game and Fish Department. You hear the same stories in the moose and caribou country of Alaska and northern Canada, among deer hunters on Alaska's Kodiak Island, and all along the Rockies from Grand Teton National Park to Jasper.

"I don't begrudge anecdotes. You put a bunch of them together, and you might say you've got some systematic information," observes Barrie Gilbert, a bear behavior specialist with thirty-five years of field experience. "But it's hard to tell what's going through a bear's mind. If they know that people walking around can be associated with dead game, they can put that together. It may not be the gunshot itself."

Which is an even more unsettling notion: a grizzly bear following you around, waiting for you to kill something so it can take it away from you.

And sometimes, the bears don't wait.

⤙ ⤚

In the second week of October, 2010, one of outfitter Ron Good's clients shot a mule deer about fifteen miles east of Yellowstone, in the North

Fork drainage of Wyoming's Shoshone River. The men dragged the animal downhill a ways to a relatively flat spot, where they field-dressed it, then removed the quarters and other meat, leaving a rib cage and a pile of guts on the ground. Good was hoisting a canvas pannier full of meat onto his pack mule when one of the hunters started shouting, "Bear! Bear!"

A young grizzly, maybe three or four years old, was tearing down the hill in a full charge, directly atop the blood trail the men had left while dragging the carcass.

"I dropped the pannier and ran around behind my saddle horse," Good says a few months later. "The horses were going ballistic."

The bear grabbed the pannier and tried to take off with it but decided to drop it and attack the nearby gut pile and rib cage instead.

"He ran to the gut pile and started devouring that thing as fast as he could," Good says. He had removed his gun belt, which had a can of bear spray on it along with a pistol, while gutting the deer and left it leaning by a tree. His guide had done the same thing.

"That was a lesson well learned because nothing was handy," Good says.

Meanwhile, the bear kept eating as fast as he could while casting a wary eye on the four men, four horses, and a mule just a few steps away. The two hunters were grabbing for their guns, but Good stayed them.

"Don't shoot!" he yelled. "Don't shoot!"

The men moved away gradually, wondering what to do about the jackets, the backpack, and other gear still on the ground near the bear. After about twenty minutes, the bear finished his meal and sauntered off.

"I've been outfitting up here for thirty-nine years, and I never had anything like that happen," he said. "He didn't literally take it right out of my hand, but it was damn close to that."

Good theorizes that the bear came across the blood trail, perhaps alerted by the rifle shot, and grew more excited as he followed it downhill. "The adrenaline was so strong by then he just couldn't stop himself," Good says.

In addition, the group had seen two large boars in the area, both of them guarding gut piles, and it's unlikely they had shared anything with the young bear that charged Good's party. That could have added stress to his hunger.

He calls the growing grizzly population in and near Yellowstone "quite a success story" and says the bears scare his clients, but none have ever said they won't return because of the fear.

"My two hunters from New Jersey thought it was the greatest thing in the world, once it was all over," Good says. One of them even got pictures of the bear feeding, right next to a skittish horse.

The leavings of hunters "have definitely become part of the food chain" for grizzlies, he says. The big males in particular "seem to have it figured out. They tend to wait and then take the gut piles later. They know when it's hunting season."

But the young bear that charged him didn't want to wait. While he's glad nobody shot the bear and glad that everybody went home safely, Good feels bad that the bear learned he could get a food reward by charging people

"He learned a really bad habit, unfortunately," Good says, and it could mean the end of him someday. "I think that bear will get shot if he does that too many more times."

⚬

Even if the bear waits until hunters leave, it can mean trouble. Hunters sometimes shoot their prey late in the day and field-dress it, but when they come back the next morning to retrieve the meat, they find a grizzly bear has claimed the carcass. Most hunters yield, figuring the bear won this time. Some try to chase the bear away, which usually isn't a good idea. Good says that in the past he's been able to chase bears away from a carcass. But he's lost some, too.

And Frey warns that, while it may be possible to chase a grizzly from a carcass, hunters need to remain wary. "They're not going far, and they're not gone for long," he says.

Grizzly bears have twice claimed elk carcasses from Tim Manley. The first time was in 1995, after the Jackson, Wyoming, resident killed a bull elk with a bow, hunting alone. When he returned in the morning with two friends, he found the animal buried in dirt and parts of the gut pile eaten, the heart and lungs devoured. Manley excavated his kill and took it home.

Two years later, in the same part of the Teton Wilderness, Manley and his brother Jim dropped a big bull about noon with rifles. They'd bugled him in, coming close enough to the bull and his harem that they could smell their musky aroma. As Jim began field-dressing the animal, Tim began the two-and-a-half-hour walk back to camp to fetch pack frames and helpers. He took with him the bull's underbelly skin, a pungent item soaked with urine and other manly fluids that Tim hoped would mask his scent. He was hoping to bag another elk that day. Jim, a Wisconsin native on his first elk-hunting trip, was a little nervous. They'd seen bear sign all morning, and he was whistling, hoping to let the bears know he was there.

"I said, 'Ah, it ain't going to be that bad,'" Tim recalls, and he started walking. Less than 150 yards down the hill, he heard noise in the brush, to his right and behind him, only about twenty yards away. It was a grizzly, dark-colored and with silver tips that made it look almost bluish in sunlight filtered by the thick lodgepole pines and dense brush. It jumped twice, and Tim threw the skin, hoping to distract the bear, which came running, head low and held slightly to the side, jaws gaping but making not a sound.

"He just come charging at me, low to the ground, like a badger with a jet engine. He was on me in an instant. I went backwards, down on my butt, and was going to curl up in a ball, but before I could even start turning over, he grabbed hold of my inner thigh with his teeth. He picked me up and shook me like a rag doll. I never felt anything like that in my life."

Manley's rifle slipped from his left shoulder, and he used it to push at the bear. With his right hand he grabbed the small can of pepper spray on his belt.

"I unloaded the whole thing right in his face. When the pepper spray was gone, he dropped me. I'm still trying to push him off with my rifle. He dropped me and sort of mouthed my knee. Then he just wanted the hell out of there. He bit my gun, then just run right over me and he's gone."

The whole thing, from his first look at the bear until it ran away, took less than ten seconds, Manley guesses.

He jumped immediately to his feet. The pepper spray was empty, and he had only one bullet in his gun. So he loaded the weapon, his hands shaking hard, and shouted for Jim, who hadn't heard a thing. Jim helped his brother hobble back to the trailhead and drove him to the hospital, where Tim got a few stitches in his leg.

Tim had heard about dinner bell grizzlies but isn't sure if that's what happened. The men and the bear may have been hunting the same elk, or Tim may have awakened it, he says. They may have drawn the grizzly's attention with the bugle or with the smell of the fresh kill.

"But he wasn't that far away. We were making noise, and we had shot just a half hour before that. I have a hard time believing that bear didn't know we were there. And I wonder. . . . If I had walked back to camp, if I had left five minutes earlier and walked past that bear, and my brother had his back to him, who knows what would have happened? I wouldn't have been back there for another five hours."

The next morning the brothers and two other friends from Wisconsin, also novice elk hunters, made the high-tension hike back to the kill site. They found the bull, but just barely. It had been completely buried, with only the antlers sticking out. The animal had died in a small depression, and a grizzly had dug from both sides, covering the elk with earth to hide it from other scavengers. But before it did that, it gutted the animal, finishing the job Jim Manley hadn't had time to complete. And it had grabbed Jim's backpack, which was fifteen feet from the carcass, and shoved it down beside the guts, burying it with the rest of the carcass.

Manley says he got the bear pretty good with the spray, dousing his eyes and nose and mouth with the fire-in-a-can.

"I have a hard time believing he'd come after a human again. I got him so good with that spray."

Maybe so. But either the spray wore off and the grizzly returned, or another bear came by and claimed the carcass for its own.

Because the brothers didn't know how long the elk had lain ungutted, they worried that the meat may have spoiled, and they left it for the bear. But they took the antlers.

"That's all he got," Tim Manley says of his brother. "That and the stories."

Hunters who leave game in the field in grizzly country should separate the gut pile from the carcass by as much distance as possible and hope the bear satisfies itself with the innards. Most fish and game agencies recommend hanging a carcass ten feet above the ground, advice often impossible to follow without a lot of gear. It's sometimes possible to place the carcass in an area where you have a clear field of vision the next morning and can approach from upwind. But this isn't always easy either. Elk, moose, and other large game often die in inconvenient places.

Some people claim you can decrease the odds of surprising a bear on your meat the next day by leaving a sweaty T-shirt on the carcass or by urinating nearby, to leave as much human scent as possible. While these approaches will cause no harm, their effectiveness depends on the hunger of the bear.

However you leave a carcass, when you approach the next morning, you should stop a couple of hundred yards away and search the area carefully through binoculars or a rifle scope, making sure to check the nearby shrubbery. Yell or whistle, do something to make a bunch of noise, then check again. The bear may be sleeping, digesting, and preparing for a second meal. You want to wake it up long before you step on it.

Other possibilities include fairly lightweight electric fencing you can erect around a carcass. And Montana bear specialists recommend "critter getters," devices that detect heat and motion. When they spot a critter, they put up a 110-decibel racket and set off bright lights. They cost about fifty dollars.

＊　＊

While it's a matter of debate whether gunshots attract grizzlies, few people disagree that hunting season can concentrate them in areas where there are lots of people.

Bears learn from experience, notes Tim Thier, a wildlife biologist for the Montana Department of Fish, Wildlife and Parks.

"If you've got an area where game populations are plentiful, and starting around November 1 these gut piles start showing up, to a bear it's no different than learning that the huckleberry patches start ripening up at the end of July. But I don't think they're sitting down to listen for a gunshot, and then they take off in that direction. It's just that they know it's an area where they can expect gut piles. They're responding to the smell of blood and guts, and a gut pile is a high-quality chunk of food for a bear right before going into a den."

Whether the bears are responding to gunshots or just using their uncanny sense of smell, the number of disputes between bears and hunters over fresh kills appears to be growing, at least in Montana and Wyoming, where grizzlies are trying to spread out from the national parks there. And that is leading to some calls to reopen the hunting season on grizzlies, even though they are protected in the lower forty-eight states as a threatened species.

There are two basic schools of thought about hunting grizzlies, both of which rely on the intelligence of bears. One says it makes bears more wary. The other says it just kills them.

The first school maintains that hunting bears teaches them to avoid people as dangerous predators. Any experienced hunter knows that elk, deer, and other big game animals grow more wary as the hunting season progresses. Thier believes that concept might have some validity with bears, but only in places where bear numbers are high enough to sustain considerable mortality.

"Someone goes out and shoots a bear," Thier explains. "They take the hide, maybe the whole carcass, and leave the guts. Another bear is going to come along. They're attracted to odors, and they're going to check things out. They know what death is, I'm sure of it. They're going to smell this blood, the guts, and they're going to smell humans right there. When they put the two of them together, that creates the wariness that they devote toward people. That knowledge could probably be passed down for two or three generations."

Rick Sinnott, a retired biologist for Alaska Fish and Game, maintains that hunting grizzlies can alter evolutionary trends. Wary bears that shun people are hard to find and rarely get shot. Bold or curious bears that routinely make themselves visible are much easier prey. Removing them from the gene pool can have an impact on overall bear behavior over time, he says.

The second school of thought, that shooting bears does more killing than teaching, makes strong points as well. Shooting a grizzly might teach it that humans are dangerous, but it's the last lesson they'll ever learn, says Chuck Schwartz, head of the Interagency Grizzly Bear Study Team. And most grizzlies try to avoid people anyway.

Also, an unknown percentage of hunted bears walk away wounded and are never found. Most probably die eventually from their wounds, but until they do, a pain-ridden and therefore incredibly dangerous animal is in the woods.

Watching bears interact with each other also sheds some light. Female grizzlies know that males will kill their cubs. When they meet boars, they do the same thing they do when they meet people: Depending on the circumstances, they run away, they attack, or they content themselves with keeping a wary eye on the boar, in this case one they know without a doubt is a potential killer.

And in British Columbia, where Caspell and Fumerton died, there are approximately ten thousand grizzly bears, a population that is hunted every year. If anybody ever shot at the bear that killed those men, if she ever sniffed the mingling of man scent and bear blood, it didn't teach a lesson that she learned very well.

Thier agrees that bears may be too complicated, too individualistic, for us ever to understand fully. What works with one animal might not work with another one. There are no easy answers.

"One thing I've learned is that just about the time you think you've got things figured out, you find out you're dead wrong, that there's something else going on that you've never really considered before. We always try to explain things. Sometimes I wonder if we should even try."

Postscript

Jamie Jonkel, a bear management specialist in Missoula, Montana, says hunters in grizzly country need to get primal.

Humans have shared landscapes with grizzlies for thousands of years, he says. Native Americans, armed only with primitive weapons, survived amidst a much larger bear population. They did so by staying alert.

Watch for sign. Pay attention to scavenger birds. Think twice before you enter the thick brush. Don't become so focused on your prey that you stumble into a grizzly bear. Carry bear spray, but don't put yourself into a position where you need it. Avoid trouble. Show the bear some respect.

Grizzly populations are growing in the lower forty-eight states. If you hunt among them, consider them one of the many potential hazards hunters must negotiate: storms and bitter cold, getting lost, falling off a cliff. Most people know how to prepare for or avoid those dangers. Add grizzlies to the list.

"And when you shoot, be aware that now you've set the table," Jonkel warns.

17

A Friend in Need

WHO COULD BLAME THE KID FOR STARING? YELLOWSTONE NATIONAL Park is a pretty interesting place, what with the bison and geysers and bears. But this was a whole new attraction. You're riding along with your family one minute, and all of a sudden, sitting next to you in the back seat of the minivan is a cowboy with his head all chewed up by a grizzly bear. He's covered with dried blood, and he's not saying much, but you're a fourteen-year-old boy, and this is the most interesting thing you've seen in a long time. Your mother turns around and tells you not to stare, but that's an awful hard order to follow.

The cowboy's name is Robert O'Connell. At the time he was a thirty-two-year-old power plant operator from Gillette, Wyoming, and his life had just been changed by a grizzly bear and probably saved by his friend, Brian Moore. It was Moore who had chased away the bear, who put O'Connell back on his mule, who brought him down to the highway and flagged down a car so he could go to the hospital.

The boy was pretty wide-eyed, but O'Connell didn't mind. He had to admit it was a pretty interesting situation. He was pretty interested himself.

⌁

The day had started early, a few miles outside Yellowstone's northern entrance near Gardiner, Montana, where O'Connell and Moore had pitched camp after a long day on their tall riding mules in the Blacktail Deer Creek drainage of Yellowstone's northern range.

"It was probably the most spectacular riding I'd ever done," O'Connell remembers of the day.

After catching a night's sleep, the two friends broke camp and drove south through the park to the Hayden Valley, a vast grassy bowl bisected by the Yellowstone River and home to most of what makes Yellowstone so compelling: thermal features, elk and bison herds, grizzly bears. By the time they had their mules saddled, about eleven o'clock, it was already brutally hot and getting hotter. The mercury would rise well above the ninety-degree mark that day, Wednesday, the seventeenth of August, 1994, and the men and mules avoided the trails. Rather, they stuck to the timber whenever they could, trying to find a little shade. It would be the last day of a quick trip to the park most Wyoming residents consider part of their backyard. Jobs and normal life waited back home.

About half past two, the two men took a break, dismounting and downing a tepid soda, kicking around a dry basin and looking at the rocks and other debris they found there.

"Did you hear that?" Moore asked suddenly. He had heard what he thought was a growl coming from a patch of trees. It had to be a loud one to carry a half-mile through all that heat. O'Connell hadn't heard anything. He laughed at his partner, and the two men didn't think much more about it.

When it was time to go, Moore jumped on his mule, but O'Connell decided to walk for a while. He wanted to get a little exercise, and besides, his mule, Jim, was acting a little squirrelly. Jim was always trying to get next to Moore's animal, and O'Connell thought that if he led him for a while it might help break him of the habit. They headed for the trees, the place where Moore thought he had heard the odd noise. The shade looked appealing.

O'Connell entered the timber first, moving about fifty yards into the trees and sidehilling back toward the road, Jim following close on the end of a lead rope. Moore was about twenty yards away, slightly downhill and moving parallel to O'Connell. It was a little cooler in the island of forest, but the mule riders weren't the only ones around. O'Connell was skirting uphill around a little patch of deadfall when he awakened the bear he didn't know was there. It was already in full charge by the time he saw it.

O'Connell dropped the lead rope, shouted, "Bear, bear," and reached for a tree. He got his hands on it, and his right foot was off the ground, but that's all he had time to do before the bear grabbed him by the calf of his left leg and jerked him to the ground.

"The bear was about twenty yards away when I first saw him. I took a step and a half, and he was there. I could not believe how fast that bear got to me."

O'Connell tried to hang on to the tree, but it was no use: The animal pulled him right down, leaving scrapes all over the inside of his arms.

"As soon as I hit the ground, he went directly to my head."

O'Connell had his face in the dirt, and the bear raked his back with its claws and kept biting and biting, a long series of quick chomps he thought would never end.

"It seemed like fifty times. I could feel the teeth on my skull. It seemed like he was crushing my head."

He felt no pain at the time—that would come later—and was screaming for Moore. He wondered if he was on his deathbed, if this was the way he would die. He had a small can of pepper spray on his belt and tried to reach for it. The movement only made the bear bite harder: He could hear the bear's jaws popping as it worked on his head. He moved his forearms up beside his head and neck, and at some point the bear bit off the middle finger on his right hand, leaving it hanging by a flap of skin.

Then Brian Moore charged.

As soon as his partner yelled, Moore saw a light-blond, medium-size grizzly coming on a dead run. He lost sight of O'Connell after the bear knocked him down, but he "could see the bear jumping up and down on something, presumably O'Connell," he told rangers investigating the attack.

Moore knew his friend was in trouble, and though his mule didn't have much enthusiasm for the situation, he goaded it into an attack. The bear lifted its head, and O'Connell reached again for the pepper spray.

"Boom. He was right back on my head again."

Moore's mule was bucking and sidestepping, not liking this business at all, and it took a moment to force it into a second charge, Moore on its back screaming and yelling at the bear.

This time it worked. The bear looked up and stared at him, its muzzle dripping blood, and it took off, planting one massive paw on O'Connell's back as it began its sprint into the woods. The soreness in his back would last for weeks.

"Get up!" Moore shouted. "Get up! We've got to get out of here."

O'Connell couldn't see. There was too much blood in his eyes. It covered his entire head. There was so much of it on him that he scared his own mule after Moore caught it for him. Then came the ride back to the road to find help. O'Connell's left leg—the first thing the bear had grabbed—wasn't working. He couldn't lift it to the stirrup. Moore, who is considerably smaller than his 170-pound friend, just grabbed the bigger man and lifted him into the saddle on a mule that stood sixteen hands high.

"I thought the attack lasted for an hour," O'Connell says. "In reality I don't think it could have lasted more than twenty or thirty seconds."

After he got in the saddle, when he realized he probably wouldn't die, he started to get mad. He looked at his right hand and saw the dangling finger, "the big California howdy finger," and thought briefly about ripping it off and throwing it away. Instead, he reached in his fanny pack for a bandana, wrapped his hand, hooked both his arms around the saddle horn, and pointed Jim downhill, toward the road and help. He could feel blood pooling in his hiking boot.

"It seemed like forever, riding back."

Dick and Julie Lefevre, of Lander, Wyoming, were taking their annual summer trip through Yellowstone, seeing the sights and visiting friends who work in the park. They had just changed drivers, putting Dick behind the wheel, when they noticed the two riders approaching the highway between Lake Village and Canyon Village. They made an awful pretty picture from a distance: two cowboys, bison scattered on the grassy hillsides around them, big mountains in the background. Friendly, too. One of them was waving his cowboy hat at all the cars passing by. The tourists liked that, and most of them were waving back. A couple of them even took pictures.

It was Julie who noticed something wasn't right. "We realized he was flagging people down. He wasn't just waving at people."

She told her husband to pull over, and Moore approached. His friend had just been attacked by a grizzly bear. The man right there. The one slouched over his saddle. Would they take him to the hospital at Lake?

The Lefevres spread out some beach towels in the back seat of the minivan and put O'Connell in one of the captain's chairs.

"He wasn't leaking much blood by the time he got to us," Dick recalls of that day. The blood on his head was baked dry by the heat by then. That may have been why nobody stopped sooner. There was so much of it that he looked as if he was wearing a dark hat or was dark-skinned.

O'Connell was very weak and very quiet. Julie got his name and a relative's phone number in case he passed out on the way to the hospital. She had put her youngest son in the front seat with her and led a family prayer for O'Connell's recovery while the boy in the back seat did more than just stare. He rolled up a towel and put it behind the injured man's head. He loosened his belt, did what he could to make him more comfortable. O'Connell appreciated the help, though he didn't say much at the time. Months later, when he was back at work, his leg out of the cast, his finger reattached, his stitches healed, he wrote to the Lefevres and sent them a box full of gifts, including one with a little irony: a stuffed bear.

Despite the morphine the pain settled in during the ambulance ride to Cody, Wyoming, the location of the closest real hospital. O'Connell remembers his ears being especially painful. They were all chewed up and felt as if they were on fire.

Doctors in Cody put forty-seven inches of stitches in O'Connell, closing twenty-one separate wounds.

This was not the first grizzly the avid outdoorsman had run into, though it is the only one that ever charged. He credits Moore with saving his life.

"Absolutely. Not a question in my mind. I think the bear would have killed me right there. There was no sign of him letting up, even after I finally quit screaming. He wasn't just swatting me around like he wanted to play. Any little movement and he was back at me. Brian did a pretty amazing stunt there. Charging a bear with a mule . . ."

It took a while for him to heal up. O'Connell missed six weeks of work and did his job in a leg cast for quite a while after that. Mental repair took a little longer.

"It was bad that first year," he says. Dreams occasionally made him relive the attack, leaving him drenched in sweat. "I wasn't really comfortable by myself. I was looking over my shoulder all the time."

These days he still hunts and recreates in grizzly country, often going out alone. "I respect bears a lot more now, but I'm not worried about them. I go out in the woods all the time. I sleep out there just fine." But he's careful to keep a clean camp, and he carries bear spray—not a little canister like the one he had the day of the attack but a big one designed to repel a grizzly. And he keeps it handy all the time.

"Even when I'm in the saddle, it's on my finger," he says.

Rangers believe the bear that attacked him was probably a subadult, independent for no more than a year or two, and that he was in the woods that day for the same reason as O'Connell and Moore: seeking a little relief from the oppressive heat. O'Connell agrees. He probably awakened the bear from a midday nap, and the cranky animal saw him as some kind of threat.

In hindsight he believes trying to scamper up a tree was probably a mistake. There just wasn't enough time.

"I think I should have stood my ground, pulled that spray out right away. No matter how much time you have, you don't have half as much as you think."

He's also got a new hunting partner now, a big, well-trained Labrador dog, the kind of animal that will roust birds all day, track a wounded elk, and, O'Connell hopes, help him out in case of another attack.

The Lab sticks close, doesn't chase animals, and "he's the extra set of eyes and ears behind me. If a bear was on me, he'd probably buy me some time."

❧

O'Connell still owns Jim—now called Jumpin' Jim Grizz because of the bear encounter and his disregard for tall fences—and says he wouldn't give him up for the world. He's strong enough to pack out an elk by himself and can walk all day without complaint. And as long as O'Connell is on Jim's back, he probably doesn't have to worry about grizzlies. Bear attack expert Dr. Stephen Herrero maintains that being on horseback is probably the best way to avoid a bear attack. A horse or mule will usually sense a bear's presence long before a person will, and Herrero's extensive research found no incidents in North American national parks of people being mauled by a grizzly while on horseback.

"If safety is a primary concern and you like traveling by horseback, then this is for you," he writes.

Bob Murphy agrees with Herrero. The retired ranger with thirty-four years' experience in national parks, half of them in Yellowstone and Glacier, has had four close encounters with grizzly bears while riding in the backcountry. Grizzlies have often attacked and occasionally killed unmounted horses. But the combination of a rider and a horse makes for a tall profile, an imposing configuration that looms well above even the largest bear. Murphy thinks a mounted horseman intimidates a bear the way neither horse nor man can do alone, as long as both creatures keep their wits. A skittish horse or an inexperienced rider meeting a bear can create an instant rodeo that will bust you up as badly as a bear will.

Grizzly charges have left Murphy's pack strings tangled and his heart racing, but never has a bear attacked him while he's on horseback. They've never even forced him to make a detour.

"I know a lot of guys who've run into grizzlies horseback," he says. "They might have been charged, or sort of charged, but they didn't feel alarmed about it. If they'd been afoot, it would scare the hell out of you."

One incident took place on the west side of Glacier National Park in 1958. Murphy and another ranger, Bill Yenne, were hauling a load of furnishings to a backcountry cabin with a string of four mules when they ran into a mother grizzly with two yearling cubs. The horses and bears and men were all trying to use the same narrow trail through a dense alder thicket, and they all were trying to do it at the same time.

One of the cubs jumped up first, turned tail, and fled. Then came the mother. She didn't run away.

"She immediately took right after us," Murphy recalls, and charged to within sixty feet. "She stopped and put her head down and slobbered and clicked her teeth and moaned a little bit. Then she backed up two or three steps and turned sideways."

Such body language sometimes indicates submission, and the bear may have been more frightened than outraged at the moment. Then the second cub appeared behind her.

"She wheeled around and just jumped on that yearling and knocked it down and chewed on it," he says.

That kind of punishment would probably send a two-hundred-pound man to the hospital for a long stretch. But that sixty-pound cub took off and ran out of sight, the sow chasing behind it.

"She was just out of sight and we were chuckling a little bit, and God, back she came. Man, that time, the hair on her back was standing up, and she had her head down to the ground. She must have been about forty feet away and she wasn't going to go anywhere."

The rangers stayed on their horses, using their spurs to keep their nervous mounts pointed toward the bear. She would act as though she was going to leave, then turn and rush toward them a few steps, an action she repeated several times. Then she gradually moved away, stopping every ten or fifteen feet to glare at the rangers and their animals.

"We remained quiet, and she kept that up until she finally went on down the trail. We never saw her again," Murphy says.

When the bear was at last out of sight, his partner turned to him with a question.

"How would you like to be a backpacker about now, Murph?"

Postscript

Former park ranger Bob Murphy died in 2008 at the age of ninety. His adventurous life included scouting the West Coast for Japanese fire balloons in World War II, helping to catch mass murderer Charles Manson in Death Valley, and spending as much time as possible on horseback. Before he died he published *Bears I Have Known*, a chronicle of his years in Yellowstone and Glacier National Parks.

Robert O'Connell still lives near Gillette, now has two children, and still owns Jim the mule, who at twenty-eight rarely jumps fences any more but still packs a load or a rider into the high country.

O'Connell says the nightmares went away, and he doesn't think about the bear attack much.

"The mind is a powerful thing, but it also forgets," O'Connell says. "The only reminder of it is I can still stick my finger in the hole in the back of my head."

Brian Moore still prefers mountain life to town life, which makes him a hard guy to track down. He likes it that way.

18

You've Got to Wonder

She meant it as a joke both times, though it was an odd one for somebody like Sarah Muller to tell. Out of character. Worse than that, it wasn't even funny.

She was just finishing a shift loading luggage into the belly of an airliner at Bozeman, Montana, when she told it the first time. It wasn't yet noon on a sunny Sunday, and she was looking forward to a couple of days in the backcountry.

"I'll see you guys Wednesday," she told the crew. "Unless I get mauled by a bear."

Then she hopped in her car and drove for three hours to the northeast corner of Yellowstone National Park.

＊

Toting luggage was a new thing for Sarah. She had spent the previous nine summers in the park, most of them working on a trail crew, learning about the sweaty end of a shovel, a Pulaski, and a chain saw. The work was good: camaraderie, fresh air, and it paid pretty well. Besides, she got to hike hundreds of miles of trails in the Yellowstone, a place where most visitors never leave the pavement. But she had just bought a house and thought it was time to get a "real" job, something that lasted all year, that would make the payments and let her start fixing the place up in the evenings. That's why she had spent the morning contorting her wiry, six-foot frame in a cargo hold not quite tall enough to stand up in. Trail crew had been hard work, but this was no piece of cake either. She was anxious to get out and move, to stretch her long legs. And she wanted to see Pete Walsh. He worked for an outfitter and was spending the summer at a camp along Buffalo Creek, just north of the park border in the Absaroka-Beartooth Wilderness Area. She'd met him in the mountains the previous summer, they'd hooked up again on New Year's Eve, and that's when they became a couple.

It was July 26, 1992, and it would be her first trip back into the mountains since she had taken the new job.

The eight-mile walk from the trailhead to Pete's camp was a smooth one. She knew the trail well because she'd spent long days working on it just a year earlier. Anywhere you looked you found a pretty picture, but there wasn't much new to see. A little boring, even. She was looking forward to her destination.

She got to camp that evening, and the three-day weekend was glorious: long horseback rides, being with Pete, just being there, in the middle of the mountains, instead of standing on the tarmac watching them shimmer through the heat waves. It ended too soon. Wednesday morning came, and it was time to head back to town, back to the belly of a Boeing. Pete and Sarah Harvey, the camp cook, were heading out, too. Pete offered his girlfriend a horse to ride, but she turned it down. Twenty miles in the saddle had left her more than a little sore, so she was glad to walk but didn't mind letting Pete strap her backpack to a mule.

Sarah Muller left first, taking a head start so she and the riders, who could move faster than she could, would meet somewhere near the trailhead. Pete asked her if she had everything, and Sarah remembered the car key in her pack. She slipped it into the pocket of her shorts, and Pete asked if she wanted a leather thong or something so she wouldn't lose it on the trail.

"Oh, I won't lose it," she said. "Unless I get mauled by a bear."

———

"I don't know why that came out of my mouth," she says years later, after five surgeries, some long stints of physical therapy, a bunch of scars, and some terrible memories that left her with a head full of questions. "That was twice I said that. In all my years in Yellowstone, I never joked about that. And less than an hour later I was mauled by a bear."

Sarah first saw the bears, a female grizzly with two cubs, from about forty feet away. They were grazing through a meadow filled with brilliant yellow wildflowers and lush, waist-high grasses. It was about 10:20 in the morning, late for a bear to be using a trail on a hot summer day. But there they were, clambering up the south side of a small hill while Sarah strode up the north side on a collision course. They met just before each party reached the peak, and Sarah realized first what was up. She froze, her heart hammered. She didn't know what to do. A pair of spindly spruce trees stood to her left, and she moved toward them, but they offered no refuge. They were too small to climb or to hide behind.

"She was down grubbing plants, and I didn't even see her cubs at the time. I thought, 'Oh shit,' and I started backing up. I thought it was a black bear because I couldn't see a hump on its back and I couldn't see its snout. I was moving backwards, looking for a tree to climb."

Then one of the cubs yelled.

"It was this incredible shrieking sound, like it was alarmed, giving a warning cry to its mom.

"My heart was beating a million miles an hour, my adrenaline was really up. But I still didn't really feel threatened because I thought it was a black bear. I'd come close to them before, on trail crew, and never had any problems."

Then the sow lifted her head, and Sarah saw trouble: Behind the distinctive dished face, the grizzly's beady eyes locked on Sarah's for just a flash. Then she charged. Fast. Faster than you can imagine.

"I jumped off the trail and my natural reflexes were to throw my water bottle down. I was hoping she would go for the bottle and not for me, that it would distract her."

The bear never broke stride. Sarah hoped for an instant that it would be one of the bluff charges she had heard about, that the bear would stop, that it would leave her alone. But it didn't stop. Sarah had a stuff sack in her hand, with nothing in it but toilet paper, a tiny first-aid kit, some lip balm. She raised it, tried to cram it in the bear's mouth, but the animal went right past it and sank its teeth in her pretty face, sending her eyeglasses flying. All of this, from initial charge to first contact, took a second, maybe two. Sarah thought about playing dead, curling up into a ball, but it was too late.

"Before I even had a chance to play dead, she was biting me, mauling me."

Bites broke her left arm and tore open her shoulder and her legs. One crushed seven ribs that will never heal, collapsing a lung. The bear shook her like a terrier does a rat. She heard cracking sounds when the bear bit into her ribs, but the crunching of teeth in her skull, the bear's top teeth in the back of her head, the bottom ones in her eye and forehead, was even louder. She had odd moments of detachment.

"I was thinking, so this is what it's like. This is what I've been fearing so many years. This is what it's like to be mauled by a bear. That was the thought going through my mind. I'm being mauled by a bear."

She remembers flying through the air at some point. She remembers hoping she wouldn't die because there were places she wanted to go.

"I love to travel. That thought came to me, that I hadn't done enough traveling yet. It's weird, the things you think about."

She screamed and screamed, as loud as she could. She screamed for Pete. She knew he was behind her somewhere, and she wanted his help. She screamed out to God for help. Or maybe she only thought about God. She isn't sure, but she knew she wanted help.

Maybe she got it. The bear stopped biting her. The attack started and finished in seconds.

"I don't know why she left. That's the million-dollar question. Did she leave because I was down on the ground and no longer a threat to her cubs? Did she leave because I screamed so loud?"

The former seems the most likely. She had surprised a sow with cubs, it neutralized the threat, and it went away.

Sarah still wasn't sure where the bear was, though. She tried to look, but she couldn't see; there was too much blood in her eyes. Her nose was crushed. One of the bear's canine teeth had sunk through her eye socket and sinus, making a small puncture in her brain cavity.

"I wasn't sure if she was gone, but the excitement was over with."

The danger wasn't.

Sarah was alone, a long way from help. She was bleeding hard from her head wounds, and she couldn't breathe; her left lung was full of blood. Bones jutted from the mangled flesh on her left arm, and one thigh was flayed open. The stuff sack was still on her left wrist, so she reached inside it for the toilet paper, trying to staunch the bleeding on her head, but there was so much blood she wasn't sure where the wounds were. The tissue was saturated in seconds, but she kept it pressed against her eye. She knew Pete and Sarah Harvey were coming up behind her, and she told herself to keep breathing, to stay calm, to stay awake. Rescuers were coming, she kept telling herself, and she wanted to stay awake so she could tell them where she was hurt. She wished the bleeding would stop.

The flies, she recalls, came in swarms.

—◆—

Sarah had fallen in love with Yellowstone as soon as she got there in 1982, even though her first jobs had her selling beer in the Bear Pit Lounge at Old Faithful and cleaning toilets in a campground. Prior to that she'd been a receptionist for a concert promoter in Minneapolis.

"It was a stressful, busy, low-paying receptionist job in downtown Minneapolis," she says. "I was really sick of it."

Aside from one trip to Colorado, she'd never seen real mountains before. But she took to them like a natural. She needed only two seasons to move up from toilet scrubbing to trail maintenance, a coveted, reasonably well-paying job that not everybody—man or woman—is cut out for. In the off-season she skied, worked some odd jobs, and hung out in Bozeman, a rapidly growing college town that was being discovered by swarms of urban refugees. Sarah liked being out on the trails but didn't care much for government work. Even out in the woods she had to deal with the bureaucracy, the paperwork, all the policies. When the crew started working in the spring of 1992, her boss pointed out how obvious her frustration was becoming.

"He said to me, 'You're not happy working for the Park Service.' I said, 'I know.' I had to find something else to do."

Anyway, at thirty-four, the nomadic life was getting harder. For years when the season started in Yellowstone, she could move everything she owned there in one trip in the car. Then it started taking two or three trips, and she still needed a storage locker. Buying a one-hundred-year-old home in Belgrade, a bedroom community for Bozeman, was a logical next step, even though the house needed a lot of work. Then she took the job at the airport, and the combination of work and new house kept her in town a lot. That's why she was so glad to finally get back to the mountains.

She recalls a conversation she had with a friend in Yellowstone, a woman ranger who worked alone in the Bechler River country, some of the most remote in the park and a place filled with grizzlies.

"I asked her, being alone, a female—not that that really matters—with all the bears around here, aren't you ever worried? Don't you get scared?"

"Not really," the friend told her. "One thing you never want to do is let your defenses down. You always want to be aware that they're out there."

⌐ ¬

Sarah had been having a great day until she ran into the bear.

"I was just as happy as can be, kind of half running down the trail. I'd had a great weekend. A new house. A good job with the airline. A semi-new boyfriend that I really liked."

Her happiness that morning illustrates her character. The good weekend left her ebullient, feeling good about the future. A lot of people would have been a little glum, disheartened at the prospect of going back to work.

Her mind on happier thoughts, Sarah let her defenses down. "I wasn't making noise, and you should never do that in bear country. I look at it as a very stupid mistake on my part. If I had been making noise coming up that little hill, the bear would have heard me, and I know she would have taken off. That was my big mistake, not making noise."

For years she had carried bear spray while she worked on the trail crew. She turned in the canister with the rest of her equipment when she quit the job. She meant to get some more but never quite got around to it.

She hadn't thought all this through as she lay bleeding in the trail that morning. She was just glad and a little surprised to still be alive. She'd taken the kind of beating that kills a lot of people.

Pete's horse found her first, rearing and snorting as it caught the smell of blood and bear and fear. Sarah lay in the trail and raised her good arm, moaning two words: Pete's name and "bear." He thought at first it was a joke. Then he saw the torn leg beneath her shorts. He rushed to her and saw the other wounds, the mangled eye socket, all the blood. Sarah told him to have Sarah Harvey ride to the Slough Creek Campground about four miles away and get help. She wanted him to stay with her, but he was the better rider, he had the better horse, and Sarah Harvey had worked at a ski hill. She knew first aid. Nobody had a weapon, and nobody had any idea where the bears had gone. Sarah Harvey would stay and Pete would ride. It made more sense that way.

"Sarah Harvey was worried sick that the bear was going to come back. I was a little worried, too, but I was just lying there happy that I was still alive and wondering if I was going to make it or not."

Pete jumped on his saddle horse and was gone, riding as he had never ridden before. He didn't know if his girlfriend would be alive when he got back, but at least she was conscious and he thought maybe she had a chance if he rode hard enough. There was no question of moving her. She couldn't sit up and could barely breathe, let alone ride or walk. By the time he got to the trailhead and found a ranger with a radio, his horse was lathered and panting. He'd run four miles in record time.

When life is normal, Pete Walsh doesn't treat an animal like that.

Forest Service ranger Larry Sears was the man with the radio. He called for help, and a team assembled fast. Ranger Colette Daigle-Berg, a medic, hopped on a helicopter, and it landed forty yards from Sarah at 11:31 a.m., less than an hour after Sarah Harvey and Pete discovered her.

Sarah Harvey had done what she could with what she had. She checked for spinal injuries, making sure the mauled woman could still move her legs, then slowly rolled her off her mangled left side and onto her back. That's when she discovered the wound in her back, the one where the bear had bitten through to her lung. It was sucking air, and she packed it with the bit of gauze from her small first-aid kit. She didn't think her friend would be able to keep that arm; the bear had nearly torn it off. All the flesh was jammed up around her shoulder, and the forearm was attached only by a strip of skin on the inside of the elbow: Luckily, that's the part of the arm that carries the artery, the life force.

Sarah Harvey really didn't want the bear to come back.

"I remember thinking that she can't take any more. I'm going to have to lie on top of her or something if it comes back."

She quickly tethered her saddle horse and the pack animals nearby, hoping to use their eyes and ears.

"I just kept watching them because I knew that if the bear came back the horses would let me know before I ever saw it."

The pack animals were loaded with dirty laundry. She used a towel and a couple of sticks to splint the mangled arm, tying it off with a pair of dirty purple socks. She talked to Sarah, trying to keep her awake, telling her to keep pressure on the worst head wound, hoping a helicopter would come soon. She spread out a big white tarp so the pilot could find them more easily.

Once the work was done, there wasn't much to do but wait and hope. At one point a hummingbird paid a visit, a piece of beauty flitting among the hordes of flies.

When the chopper landed and Daigle-Berg took over, Sarah Harvey could let down her own defenses. Daigle-Berg sent her on a mission to find a dropped radio, kind of like telling an expecting husband to go boil water.

"That's when I could finally cry," Sarah Harvey says. "It was very shaking. But it didn't really hit me until it wasn't my responsibility anymore."

And she cried for a long time, all the way to the trailhead on horseback, a trip that wouldn't even start for a couple of hours. She had spent years in the backcountry and would spend many more there after the attack, living for weeks at a time in the kind of place where it's no surprise to find grizzly tracks in the snow outside your tent. She's never had any more trouble with a grizzly, except in her dreams.

"I had dreams of riding into camp and everybody's been slaughtered, arms and legs all around. In my dreams the bear always came back."

~ ~

Fifteen minutes after the helicopter landed, Pete and Ranger Sears arrived on horseback. Pete took Sarah's hand.

"He was holding my right hand and comforting me and I said, 'Oh, honey, that hurts.' Here I am, all mangled all over, and I'm complaining about this little baby puncture wound. We couldn't see the hurt because there was all this blood all over."

She would learn later the bear had bitten clear through her hand. With all her other injuries, she hadn't noticed that one.

While the medics worked on her, Sarah had a little time to think, to realize she'd made a mistake, moving fast and quiet and alone through grizzly country. Rangers were asking her to describe the bear, and she did that. The animal was brown and medium size and had two cubs. She knew the National Park Service had killed a lot of bears in past years, some on purpose and some accidentally. She had a request: Leave the bear alone, she asked. It was only trying to protect its children, and who could blame any mother for that?

~ ~

It didn't take long for Daigle-Berg to figure out that Sarah needed a lot more help than she could get in Yellowstone Park. A medevac helicopter was summoned from the trauma center in Idaho Falls, Idaho. It got there fast, and Sarah was in the air by a little after one o'clock. As she made the miserable trip, the vibrations rattling her broken bones, her internal injuries making a sip of water impossible, more rangers and investigators arrived on the scene.

One of them was Kerry Gunther, Yellowstone's bear management specialist. This was a hard one for him. He knew the victim—Sarah was a friend of his.

Rescuers had trampled the immediate area around Sarah, and the rangers would find no bear tracks there. They did find a new trail trampled through the tall grass, however. It led from the scene to nearby Buffalo Creek, then turned north.

"This was a trail of more than one animal and very recent. The duff under the grass had been pushed downslope in a manner that indicated a heavy animal running," the investigators' report says.

The investigators gathered the bear hairs plucked from the ground and from Sarah's body (the hairs would later prove the bear was a grizzly), and they searched the area extensively. They could find no carcass the bear was trying to protect. They found no sign she had been digging the abundant yampa roots in the meadow, no day beds, no scat or tracks on the entire length of the trail.

"It was our conclusion that while this bear with cubs may use this area from time to time she was primarily passing through at the time," the report says. "It was a chance encounter and unlikely to be repeated."

⌐━⌐

Sarah would spend two and a half weeks in the hospital in Idaho Falls, then travel twice to the Mayo Clinic in her native Minnesota for plastic surgery. Her eye sockets were wired to her nose, which had to be rasped back into shape. A piece of bone from her skull props up one eye. A Canadian surgeon with the unlikely name of Dr. U. Bite did outstanding work. Look at her face today and you notice nothing unusual. Just an attractive woman, tall and athletic and friendly, the type of outdoors person who often chooses to make a home in the Rockies.

Her years in Montana and in Yellowstone had built a network of friends who pitched in to help after the attack. So many flowers arrived at the hospital in Idaho Falls that they overflowed the room. Sarah sent them to the bedsides of other patients. Phone calls came from all over. So did letters, including one from Yellowstone superintendent Bob Barbee, who told of how, two days before Sarah was attacked, hikers in the next drainage to the east had come upon a grizzly cub. Then the sow appeared, but she did not attack; she just hustled the cub to safety. They were lucky, Barbee guessed.

News stories focused on her request that the bear be left alone, and strangers wrote to thank her for her attitude, to praise her strength. Friends who knew her sense of humor sent bears: stuffed ones, candy ones, and one printed on a note card with a cartoon balloon hand-drawn on top of it. "I'm sorry, Sarah," the bear is saying.

Her scrapbook of cards and letters is not a thing you can read with a dry eye.

Doctors could fix her face, but her other scars remain. A long jagged one stretches across her arm; the limb still works, though it's tender. Others mark her shoulder and her leg. The ribs will never heal, doctors say, and they bulge some because they float freely in her body. They hurt all the time, and they mean her collection of vintage dresses no longer fits. She can't shoulder a backpack, dancing is tough, and if somebody wants to give her a hug, they have to know how to do it right.

As time goes on, she thinks about the incident less. It's no longer a daily thought. But some things bring it right back: the sound of a helicopter; seeing her border collie, Pelly, take a Frisbee in its teeth and try to shake it to death. Reading about other attack victims is hard. Sometimes she telephones them, offers encouragement and the name of her plastic surgeon.

"It helps me, too," she says.

She sold the house in Belgrade and moved to Paradise Valley, just north of the park, in a place where grizzlies are roaming again after long absences. Finding bear scat on the property makes her nervous. So does hiking. She's usually got a can of bear spray with her.

On a trip to Alaska, she and Pete each carried two big cans of it. Pete had a shotgun, too. When they tried to drive into the Yukon, Canadian customs officials said she couldn't take the spray with her. It wasn't the approved variety in that country.

"I was wearing shorts and I said, 'These are bite marks from a grizzly bear. If you take that spray away, you don't know what you're going to do to me.'"

The border guard let them through.

The attack left a lot of questions, and she's not finding many answers.

Part of her physical therapy called for swimming in a hot spring near Bozeman, wearing a suit that exposed her scars, still red and angry at the time. Children stared and asked innocent questions.

"How did you get that owie?" they asked.

"I didn't know what to tell them. I didn't want to scare them. Sometimes I'd tell them I got in a little fight with a grizzly bear and she did that with her teeth. Sometimes I'd tell them it was a car wreck."

It seemed easier, somehow.

She wonders what the attack means. She'd spent nine years in the park, walked hundreds of miles of backcountry trails, and never seen a grizzly bear except from a car. But then she'd always been with a crew: never alone and always making noise. There is roughly one grizzly for every forty thousand acres in greater Yellowstone. What are the chances of her and the bear meeting in the same place at the same time in broad daylight?

She likes grizzlies and still appreciates the thrill of seeing one in the wild, from a distance. She doesn't regret asking that the bear's life be spared, although it's doubtful the Park Service would have taken any action against a bear with cubs that attacked when surprised. Still, she can't help resenting the animal a little.

"I'll probably carry that resentment the rest of my life. Why did it hit me? I wouldn't hurt it, and there are a lot of people who would."

She wants people to know that bears are out there, that they are incredibly powerful and can be dangerous. She wants people to be careful, to make noise and pay attention. There are more bears in the Yellowstone ecosystem now. They've bounced back from the terrible years of the 1960s and early 1970s after the park dumps were closed and more than two hundred were killed. But the human population is growing, too. She's not optimistic that there will be enough room for everybody.

"More and more people are moving into these areas. I love seeing grizzlies in the wild, but I don't think we have enough space for them and the people. There are going to be more and more encounters and more and more maulings."

The attack means she can't do the physical labor she had done all her life, and her employment options are slimmer. She sews. She cleans houses. She wonders what to do next.

She knows she should have made noise that day, probably shouldn't have hiked alone. But thousands of people do it every day without a problem.

"Sometimes I think I want to forget it ever happened and go on with my life and try to figure out what to do next. It's like being hit by lightning, any natural sort of freak deal. But I always wonder why it happened to me. Did this happen for a reason?"

So far she doesn't have any answers.

"But I keep thinking I'm going to."

POSTSCRIPT

Sarah Muller now owns a small but successful lodging business, the Homestead Cabin, near Chico Hot Springs Resort in Montana. For a few years after the attack, she cooked in a cabin for the hunters that Pete Walsh outfitted. She doesn't mind talking about the attack, but don't ask her to tell the story at night.

"It gives me the heebie-jeebies," she says.

The scars have faded, and she remains a striking woman, tall and strong and lithe, though the ribs still act up, especially if she's under the weather for some reason.

Sarah Harvey, who tended her wounds that awful day, still works the backcountry. She's worked in Antarctica and Greenland and cooked in a hunting camp in Wyoming, in the midst of grizzly country.

Sarah Muller said she's still never found any great answers to the attack and her miraculous survival. Maybe there's nothing metaphysical about it. There was bad luck, meeting the bear, and then good luck, with the rescue.

"I just try to be a good person and help people out," she says, and she's stayed busy building her dream: a comfortable cabin in a beautiful corner of Montana.

But she won't have a bear rug on the floor.

"That's one thing I no longer want."

19

Suffering the Fools

MOST MAULING VICTIMS DO SOMETHING WRONG, MAKE SOME MISTAKE that attracts a grizzly or earns its wrath. They keep a dirty camp, or they try to run when they should curl up into a ball. They feed a bear, they get too close while trying to take pictures, or they simply aren't paying attention when they should be.

Often the mistake is a tiny one, and some of these people suffer horribly for it, enduring hours of surgery and months of therapy trying to stitch life and body together again. Others die on the spot.

Some people make no mistakes at all and still get attacked for reasons that nobody but the bear understands.

And then there are the people who do everything wrong and live to tell the tale, who indulge in incredibly moronic behavior and walk away without a scratch.

That's what happened on June 11, 1997, in Yellowstone National Park when a tourist walked right up to a grizzly cub and touched it on the butt. The cub scampered, its mother came uncorked, and the idiot walked away.

It had been a brutal winter that year and thousands of elk had died in and around the park, but cow elk were trying to make up for it by producing a good crop of calves in the lush bottoms along Obsidian Creek, in the park's northwest corner. Bear No. 264, a six-year-old sow, knew all about those elk calves. She had been preying on them every June, rousting the almost scentless newborns from the brush where their mothers had hidden them and making meals of their tender flesh.

Sometimes she ate the entire animal. Sometimes she just ate her fill, left the rest for the coyotes and the ravens, and found another calf the next day.

No. 264 is a predatory bear, a killer with a taste for fresh meat. Yet she also is remarkably tolerant of people, as one of Yellowstone's most foolish tourists learned that day.

No. 264's spectacular cruelty is part of what makes Yellowstone such a compelling place; the cold primeval relationship between predator and prey and scavenger makes the park's biology tick. Usually, the drama takes place out of sight, away from the roads, but in this case, hundreds, perhaps thousands of people watched the spectacle during the rainy weeks of early summer.

Yellowstone is a vestige of wild America, a conscious attempt to let things work at least partly as they did before Europeans settled the West, driving the great bears from all but a few islands of habitat, where they clutch at survival with the tips of their four-inch claws.

But it is also a tourist mecca, attracting more than three million people every year, almost every one of them anxious to see a grizzly bear.

And that's where the job of the National Park Service gets tough. The agency must balance the needs of all those people with all those animals. And it must do all it can to ensure the safety of both. Idiots can make this a hard chore. Also, if a bear chews on them, they tend to sue. Bear managers do a lot of scrambling in Yellowstone.

This combination of bears and people means that, if bears are to survive in the park, some of them have to get used to people. That's what No. 264 did, and in 1997 she brought to Obsidian Creek two cubs, the first of her life. There she taught her cubs how to find and eat fresh elk meat. And she taught them how to ignore people.

The fact that No. 264 did not maul the ignoramus is all the more remarkable because she had once been taught in an explicit way that people can be easily intimidated, that just walking toward them can provide a tasty reward.

Two years earlier she had killed an elk calf in the same area, buried it, and was taking a nap on top of the carcass, all within sight of the road. Tourists were watching, and a line of photographers, their cameras on tripods, was assembled along the highway. Then the bear woke up and started walking toward them. The photographers did what they were supposed to do: They grabbed their cameras and moved back. But one man left a small backpack on the ground. No. 264 nosed it, then grabbed it and took it back to the elk carcass, where she tore it apart.

"We chased her off and got the pack," Yellowstone bear management specialist Kerry Gunther says. "But she had already eaten his lunch."

A few days later the bear was captured, fitted with a radio collar, and given her number.

"We worried that she had learned to bluff people out of their packs," Gunther explains.

By doing what comes naturally—eating something that smells good—the bear had earned herself a lifetime of close scrutiny.

But the actions were never repeated. For many bears in the greater Yellowstone ecosystem, one meal of human food leads to calamity; they like the taste and they get more and more aggressive in search of it. Sooner or later, the aggression becomes intolerable, and the bear is shot or shipped to a zoo.

But No. 264 didn't turn out that way. She contented herself with elk calves and pine nuts and natural vegetation. Despite the food reward, she kept on ignoring people and showed incredible tolerance of them.

Obsidian Creek carves a narrow valley as it twists through ancient volcanic formations, stones that attracted Indian toolmakers for thousands of years to quarry the obsidian, make tools, and pack the rock away on ancient trade routes that stretched as far as Michigan.

A narrow road winds alongside the creek, bisecting some pockets of the best elk and grizzly habitat in the park. Through the generations, both elk and grizzlies have learned that if they want to use the habitat, they have to tolerate the people. Rangers call such animals "habituated," which means they show no apparent fear of people. But it doesn't mean they aren't dangerous.

Which brings us to the events of June 11, 1997.

No. 264 had been killing an elk calf almost every day, sharing the rich protein with her twin cubs and passing it through her body in the form of milk. Since her hunts often took place within sight of the road, the spectacle created what park managers call "bear jams," dozens of cars and trucks and motor homes lined up on both sides of the road, anxious tourists squealing and pointing, taking pictures and watching through binoculars.

Rangers always try to get on top of these situations, to direct traffic, to keep the rubberneckers from running each other over, and, most of all, to keep the people away from the bears. But a bear jam can form in moments. Even people who don't want to stop often have no choice. A couple of Winnebagos parked on the narrow road means a long snarl of traffic.

On that day no ranger had yet arrived at the bear jam. There was nobody to keep the anxious tourists in line, to protect them from the bears and from each other.

About half past five, things got stupid.

April Varn, a twenty-one-year-old from Augusta, Georgia, had decided to spend her summer in Yellowstone as a volunteer for the Student Conservation Association. She was driving south from Mammoth Hot Springs, where she had been getting some training about noxious weeds. She was looking forward to her job at the park's south entrance when she came to the bear jam.

The bear family was about twenty yards west of the road, and "there were all these people getting out of their cars," she recalled a few days later. "And kids were running everywhere."

Then she saw a tall, pale man about fifty years old leave the road and walk toward the bears, which were foraging rich forbs and grasses growing in a snarl of burned snags left by the wildfires of 1988. One cub, the closest one to the road, was clambering over a downed log, its butt in the air. All three bears were facing away from the road, trying to ignore the clots of people.

"I rolled down the window and yelled at the man," Varn says. "He was just sauntering up the slope. He wasn't in any hurry. He looked like he had just come from the country club."

Meanwhile, several children were running up the slope, trying to approach the other cub. There was movement all around the bears.

So Varn left her car and took off at a run down the roadway, trying to head off disaster. She yelled at the man from the road, but he either ignored her or didn't hear her and moved steadily closer to the cub. She followed him into the old burn, trying to make him stop. But she couldn't catch him, and that's when he did something an intelligent person wouldn't do to a strange dog in a city.

"He just reached out and touched it, like if you were touching an animal in a petting zoo," Varn says.

By that time Varn was only about two feet from the man. She could have touched the cub, too.

The cub took off toward its mother, who immediately went ballistic. She charged the man, scrambling over the deadfall, but halted about three feet away from him. For a long time—Varn estimates almost a minute, which is a lot longer than most people want an angry grizzly in their face—the bear held her ground, swaying her head and huffing. She didn't roar and didn't snap her teeth, but she was clearly agitated. She was on a log, uphill from Varn and the moron, putting her several feet above them.

"She looked huge," Varn says.

At a time like that, the best thing to do is shut up or perhaps speak firmly to the bear. The worst thing you can do is make a lot of noise and movement; it only makes you look more threatening, more deserving of a clout. But that's what the tourist did.

"He was just screaming, waving his arms and screaming," Varn says. "I couldn't believe what was going on. It was your worst nightmare. The bear wasn't doing it vindictively. She was trying to protect her children. He was trying to scare her away, and I didn't know if she would charge again. He was frantic, and I was scared to death."

After what seemed like forever, Varn got the man to shut up and move quietly back toward the road. He rejoined his wife and a younger man, perhaps his son, in a white van.

She asked him if he had read the park newspaper handed out to all visitors at the entrance gate, the one that says everybody must stay at least one hundred yards from all bears. The man seemed badly shaken but said that, since the bears were only about twenty yards from the road, he thought the one-hundred-yard rule no longer applied. In his mind that somehow meant he had the right to walk up and touch a wild grizzly bear.

Then he drove away. Varn identified herself as a worker in the park, but she was not in uniform. Tourists were looking at her with blank expressions, as if to ask what gave her the right to tell people what to do. They didn't understand that she might have just saved a man's life as well as the lives of the children scampering nearby. (A man had sat in his car nearby, reading a map, apparently unconcerned that his children were approaching a family of wild grizzly bears.) If the bear had attacked, people would undoubtedly have started running and screaming, which could have triggered a chase response in the bear. Nobody knows how many people could have been mauled.

Varn had no radio, couldn't make the cellular phone in her car work, and didn't get the man's license plate number. As a volunteer, she had no power to give him a ticket, but she wanted somebody in authority to punish him. So she drove to Norris Hot Springs, looking for a ranger. By then the adrenaline was receding, and her right leg was shaking so badly she had to drive with her left foot on the gas pedal.

Nobody ever found out who the man was, but his behavior didn't make life easier for No. 264, a breeding-age female so valuable to the eventual recovery of the Yellowstone grizzly.

"She's got to be using that roadside corridor for a reason," says Gunther, the bear management specialist.

Bears don't like people and prefer to set up a home range away from them. But they also need to avoid larger bears, which won't tolerate intruders in their own home range and often kill the cubs of other bears. No. 264 had spent her first two or three summers of independence, when she was small and vulnerable, eating elk calves along Obsidian Creek. She knew it as a prime source of high-quality food. The arrival of her cubs made the food even more important but also made her more vulnerable to bigger bears. So she had to choose between two perils: bigger bears or people. She chose the people. In most cases they are easier to ignore.

(A few days after the incident, one of her cubs was found paralyzed, unable to move his rear end, and No. 264 had a slight injury on one of her forepaws. Rangers euthanized the cub and trapped the mother but couldn't catch the surviving cub, so they released the mother the next day, placing the dead cub's corpse nearby so she would realize the baby was dead. The two live bears reunited and moved away from the road, at least for a while. Later, the cub carcass was retrieved, and a necropsy revealed teeth marks that showed, as suspected, that the cub had been crippled by another bear.)

But No. 264 couldn't ignore the fool who touched her cub. While she didn't injure him, what will happen the next time somebody gets too close? There might not be an April Varn around to pull him to safety. If

No. 264 attacks someone, park managers may have to kill her. At the very least, they'll have to capture her and the surviving cub and move them someplace else.

But moving the bears is a disagreeable option, too. There's a good chance it will only bring them closer to death.

If rangers place a habituated bear like No. 264 somewhere else in the park, she probably would return to home range as fast as she could, "wasting our time and her energy," Gunther says.

Most Yellowstone grizzlies, the wary bears who shun roads and people, are seen only as rumps disappearing into the forest. But a habituated bear often doesn't run away from people, so moving her outside the park, farther from her home range, just turns her into poacher bait or sets her up to wander into the camp of an excitable hunter, where she probably would be shot by somebody who saw her as a threat.

"We're going to be seeing more and more of this type of habituation," Gunther says. "In a way it's a mark of the success of the bear program. It shows that bears are filling up the habitat. But we have to come up with some innovative ways of dealing with it. The bears have learned to live with us, and now we've got to learn to live with them."

One idea may be to hire some roving naturalists, people who could patrol areas where habituated bears live, "go to bear jams, give talks, manage traffic, and make sure people don't do anything stupid," Gunther says. Such a system could increase the safety zone for both bears and people, teach visitors how to behave in grizzly country, and still give them the unforgettable experience of watching a grizzly hunt.

But putting people to work, even volunteers, takes money, and Yellowstone has been laying off a steady stream of workers as budget crunches continue.

Without changing things, people like Gunther are left with a "management nightmare that could mean the death of that bear," he says.

Looking back on the incident, Varn says she thinks she did the right thing but probably wouldn't have gotten as close to the man who touched the cub—and therefore the mother grizzly—if there hadn't been so many children running around. She worried about the kids more than she did about the fool.

"I'm not a brave person," she says. "I'm just a regular little old Southern girl."

Gunther agrees that Varn probably did the right thing, even though he wonders if saving somebody like the cub toucher was worth the risk.

"She risked her life to save that guy's," Gunther says. "In a case where somebody's doing something really stupid, that may not make sense."

Varn got the man away from the bear, but what really saved him may have been the large number of people only twenty yards behind him, which the bear may have also seen as a potential threat.

The man is not alone in his imbecility.

Wayne Brewster, a park scientist for many years, says he has seen similar things a number of times. People think the park is a zoo, that the animals are tame because they don't all run away immediately.

Unlike Varn, Brewster doesn't get in the middle of such situations. He keeps his distance and shouts: "You are very close to dying. Now back up slowly."

So far it's worked every time, he says.

Someday it won't. And the result will be an injured or dead person and possibly a dead bear.

The man who touched the cub was never located, so his motives will never be known. Perhaps he thought he was being clever or brave. If so, he should heed the comments of retired general H. Norman Schwarzkopf, who was in Yellowstone at the time as part of his new job as a national spokesman for grizzly bear recovery.

Schwarzkopf is a war hero, an international celebrity known all over the world for his brains and his bravery. His assessment of the situation?

"Sometimes," the general observes, "stupidity is its own reward."

POSTSCRIPT

Bear No. 264 continued living in the Obsidian Creek area, and she retained her tolerance of humans, becoming one of the most photographed wild bears in the world. When she did something particularly interesting, such as finding a bison carcass in a roadside creek, a chunk of meat that kept her and her two cubs busy for several days in May of 2002, word flew through the grapevine, and people drove hundreds of miles to watch and photograph her.

A big blond stripe around her middle made her easy to recognize.

Then on June 14, 2003, she darted from a patch of dog-hair timber and was struck by a car. Park officials anesthetized her, made her as comfortable as possible, and took her to a veterinarian in Bozeman, Montana.

But the injuries were too severe, and she had to be euthanized. Bears die in Yellowstone all the time. But this one was a little different.

"Rest in Peace Bear 264," the sign at the Super 8 Motel in nearby Gardiner, Montana, said for several weeks. "You will be missed."

She had chased off her last two cubs in 2002. A few years later two other females began using her territory, hunting elk calves. One of them produced two cubs in 2010, the other a remarkable four cubs, making her another sensation for photographers. By November of that year, they were last seen heading to the high country, seeking a den before winter's harshness swept in.

Bear manager Kerry Gunther found some money to hire extra people to man the park's "bear jams," to keep both people and bears safely separated. In 2010 there were 994 bear jams in Yellowstone. Nobody got hurt at any of them.

But budgets remain an issue and patrolling bear jams "will likely only get more costly as visitation continues to grow," Gunther says.

20

The Honeymooners

THE HONEYMOON WAS NOT WITHOUT SOME RAGGED EDGES, BUT JOEL and Jane Larson were doing their best to build a marriage and a life in Alaska's stunning Matanuska Valley. Laboring together, they were building a home near one of the many small lakes in the area, putting their sweat and their shoulders into it.

It wasn't easy. Both of them had demanding steady jobs—Joel did construction work all over that vast state, and Jane was a guard at a nearby state prison for men—and it took every available minute to turn a pile of boards and wires and pipes into a home. Both Larsons worked hard, but nerves got a little frayed. There were arguments. Finally, there came a time when the best idea was to take a weekend off. Married just six months, the Larsons decided to do a little camping and hiking in the crisp October sunshine, to take advantage of what Alaska had to offer before the snows came for the long subarctic winter.

"The only way we could relax was to get away from the house," Jane recalls. "If we stayed here, we would have just worked."

So they headed northeast from their home in the hamlet of Chick-aloon, up the Glenn Highway that skirts the Matanuska River and passes dozens of unnamed peaks, the kind of road that offers a new vista at every curve.

The Glenn Highway puts on elevation fast, and the Larsons quickly left autumn behind and found winter. Joel hadn't yet put snow tires on the car, and the roads were getting snotty, so the couple turned around. But the weekend wasn't spoiled. It was still early in the day, and they drove right past their turnoff and turned north, heading into unfamiliar country toward Denali National Park. Maybe, with a little luck, the weather would cooperate and they'd get a good look at Mount McKinley. The continent's tallest mountain often plays shy games with viewers, hiding its face in the clouds for weeks at a time.

"We thought we'd go up toward Fairbanks and just stop wherever," Joel recounts. "We took our time and got to Byers Lake and pitched our tent and spent the night. We thought we'd go for a little walk in the morning."

It was cold that night, October 13, 1984, and in the morning there was ice in camp.

"We didn't know the area at all," says Joel, a strapping former North Dakotan who stands six feet eight inches tall and, at the time, tipped the scales at 240 pounds. But the couple wanted to explore so they broke camp and took off in the car in search of a trail.

"The first trail we came to was Little Troublesome Creek," Joel says.

—❦—

Little Troublesome Creek isn't much of a stream, as Alaskan waters go. After a few miles of rocky tumbling, it drops into the Chulitna River. But the trailhead there is the start of an extensive trail system that twists and loops into millions of acres of roadless land. And every summer the creek attracts spawning salmon to its shallow waters. Plus, there are berries everywhere. All of that translates into prime grizzly bear habitat.

This is no secret. Almost all of Alaska supports black or grizzly or polar bears and often more than one species. Little Troublesome Creek is a particularly productive spot for bear food, and that's why the trail is closed to people during the summer, when the fish are running and the berries are ripe. But the trail closure signs had come down six weeks before the Larsons began their hike.

"We're talking late in the year," Joel notes. "The fish are gone, and the berries are gone. The leaves are down. It was the last weekend before the snow."

—❦—

Little Troublesome Creek is a beautiful spot, with its clear waters tumbling through stands of dense alder and groves of mossy spruce trees, and the Larsons were enjoying their morning hike. There wasn't another car in the parking lot, and they had the place to themselves. Joel left his .44 Magnum pistol in the trunk of his car. Thirteen years later, he still wonders if he did the right thing. When the Larsons met the bear later that day, the repeated attacks were so close and came so fast that the pistol might have saved them. But it might have done more harm than good.

They walked a couple of miles up the gentle, well-maintained trail—at one spot someone had even fashioned a handrail from a spruce limb—and stayed close together, talking almost constantly and dissolving some tensions. They talked about Hawaii, maybe squeezing the time and money from their busy schedules to take a real honeymoon.

"We thought maybe we could do it," Joel recalls.

The idea of warm breezes and sandy beaches must have been a pleasant one, with winter on the way. Though it was sunny, the day was brisk. Joel was walking with his hands in the pockets of his new canvas Carhartt jacket, a garment still so stiff it was hard to get the buttons in the holes. Jane was bundled up in a heavy chamois shirt, a thick sweater, and a down vest.

The Larsons were on their way back to their car, no more than a quarter-mile from the parking lot, when they saw the bears. The trail had been following the noisy, tumbling water for some time and was just turning away from it, climbing a small rise. Joel was in the lead and saw the bears first.

"I looked up, and there was a sow with cubs on the trail," Joel says. That's what he thought at first, anyway. Later, he wasn't sure. There was definitely one sow and one cub that started bawling as soon as it saw Joel, and there was a third bear, not as big as the sow. Perhaps a three- or four-year-old, still following its mother around. Perhaps another sow. Nobody would ever find out.

He turned to Jane, close enough that they could have touched if both had stretched out their arms.

"I looked back at Jane and said, 'We've got to get the hell out of here.'"

"But I couldn't hear what he was saying because the creek was real noisy," Jane explains. "You couldn't hear anything because of the creek."

Then she looked past him, over his shoulder, and saw the bears, no more than thirty feet away.

The cub scrambled away, and the sow was swinging her head back and forth, perhaps trying to catch a good whiff of the people and identify them, perhaps signaling her agitation to the people or to the other bears, perhaps still trying to decide what to do about this new surprise.

Then the sow charged.

Jane remembers the beauty of the bear, the way its muscles rippled, the way its toffee-colored fur glistened in the sun. But that thought didn't last long. When the bear came at them, the Larsons turned and ran, too, but they only made it a few steps.

"I wonder where that bear is right now," Joel said to himself as he tried to flee. "I'm not running fast enough. Then bam! She's right on top of me."

Joel turned as he went down and threw up his left arm to protect his face. The bear's open mouth was right there, and her teeth ripped into his forearm. "With her face coming down and me pushing back, her teeth slipped around the bone. It scratched the bone but didn't break it."

For a second Joel couldn't think of what to do. He's a big man and a strong one, a man accustomed to applying his muscle.

"I remember thinking, 'How come I'm lying here? How come I'm just lying here like this?' It wasn't like me. I wasn't moving at all. I reached up and grabbed a thick handful of hair. Then I let it go and opened my eyes. She was standing on my head, with her claws across my face, and my arm was in her mouth."

The bear moved her foot, hooking his eyeglasses with a claw and tearing them off his face.

Then Jane attacked.

"I saw Jane coming with a stick. She took it and whipped the bear right on the back. Just like that, it let go of my arm."

The sow roared and reared on her hind legs for a better look around. Then she lunged at Jane, knocking her to the ground and sinking her teeth into her back, ripping a wide hole, one deep enough to expose the movements of Jane's shoulder blade and the muscles around it.

Jane, who is five feet ten inches tall and strong, says she doesn't remember attacking the bear. She remembers it coming after them, she remembers running, and she remembers that, suddenly, the bear wasn't there anymore. She remembers telling herself, "I can get away, I can get away.

"Then I could hear Joel yelling, 'God help me, God help me.' And I thought, if I go now, he dies. I can get away, but he dies. I don't remember picking up that stick or any of that. I just remember that moment."

When Joel saw the bear chewing on his wife, he told himself he had to do something, anything, to help.

"Gotta move that bear," he repeated to himself. "Gotta move that bear gotta move that bear gotta move that bear."

So he grabbed a stout stick and clobbered the bear as hard as he could. It was, he says, a blow that would have crushed a man. It didn't slow the grizzly a bit, but at least it got the animal off Jane. The bear turned and leapt at Joel, springing at his chest like a huge and unruly dog, and a claw ripped a jagged gash across the right side of his jaw.

"The next thing I knew, she was going after Jane again. I honestly thought of jumping on her back. I'm glad I didn't do that.

"Suddenly, I can't hardly explain it, an anger came over me . . . that this bear was after Jane. It was almost like a jealousy anger."

As the fear left, a "clarity" of thought came over him.

"Everything was right there. I looked off into the trees and saw there were no trees with limbs low enough to climb without that bear getting us. She was after Jane, and I took after the bear with another stick. I let her have one, and she turned around, lunged, and hit me in the chest with her front paws."

The new canvas jacket probably saved his chest from a clawing, but Joel still flew, slamming the ground on his back and hitting hard.

Then the bear turned to Jane again, and Joel told himself he was going to have to do a lot better.

"It was like there was someone right there, like a wrestling coach, telling me what to do."

"You've got to keep your feet," the voice said. "You're falling down. You've got to keep your feet."

Again he clobbered the bear with a stick, and again the bear knocked him down before turning to Jane for the third time.

Much later, the Larsons figured they had successfully confused the bear, teaching it that it couldn't keep its back to either of them without being attacked. But at the time they focused only on survival. When Joel got to his feet again, the bear was chasing Jane around a big cottonwood tree, one that had split into two trunks. Jane would take a couple of steps one way, and the bear would lunge toward her. When she moved the other way, the bear took after her in that direction.

The bear was a big one. Jane remembers its head being almost level with hers, which was bent as she tried to avoid being treated like a tether ball. She thought at the time the bear was standing on its hind legs, its head was so high, but realized later that was impossible. The bear couldn't have moved that fast on only two feet. She remembers thinking they were going to die, wondering when it would end. This was bad trouble. This was real.

Then she fell. Joel remembers Jane making a "woof" sound, and the bear was on her. With a claw it ripped off a large piece of one ear (she would later need fifty-two stitches to rebuild it), and its face was at her neck. Joel saw his wife's blood on the bear's face and he attacked yet again.

The bear's mouth was only inches from Jane's neck, and Joel was afraid he would miss the bear and hit his wife, so he grabbed a four-inch-thick stick with both hands and punched the bear in the skull with the end of it.

"She came around that tree so fast I could hardly believe it. She hit me in the leg with her paw, and I flew sideways in the air. Before my feet touched the ground, she hit me in the hip with the other paw, and I stood straight up with both feet on the ground. The next thing I knew, my left hand was on her throat and my right hand was in her mouth. She bit down right between the bones on my hand."

Then she lifted him by the hand, slammed him to the ground. The effort split Joel's hand, separating the first and second fingers with a ragged, inch-and-a-half gash.

"When my hand was in her mouth, my feet were off the ground," he says.

Then the bear turned again to Jane, biting her chest, ripping a hole through the sweater, the shirt, and the down vest but not leaving a scratch on her body, and turned to Joel, who thought he was ready this time. Feet spread, dancing like a boxer, he was pumped and set, but the bear just knocked his massive frame to the ground as if he were nothing, grabbed his leg in her mouth, and started dragging him away. Joel lashed out with his fists, hitting and hitting and hitting. Finally, the bear dropped him and went after Jane again. Once more, Joel grabbed a stout log, holding it like a staff. He clouted the bear with one end of it, then again with the other end. The bear lunged at him, mouth open, and Joel jammed the log in its mouth sideways. Her teeth clamped down on it and started working. The four-inch log broke as if it were a twig.

"So I was just standing there with a stub in my hand."

The bear backed off for a moment, then came again, and Joel brought the log down hard on top of her head. It was the only time he fazed her.

"I remember her eyes closing and her going down a little bit, just for a split second. Then she came back up, missed my hand but grabbed that stub, knocked me down, and just tore the stick to shreds, roaring."

That's when Joel, too, thought it was the end.

"This ain't a dream. This is it. I'm not going to get away from this."

A few feet away the second large bear was sitting with its paws up, watching over the brush, and Joel was hoping against hope that the second bear wouldn't jump in. He knew they didn't stand a chance if it did.

During the scuffle, the Larsons had gotten separated by about thirty feet, and the sow was running toward Jane. Joel got back to his feet and the bear halted, turned to him, and charged. Joel braced himself, but the bear stopped just inches away and ran after Jane. Then it turned again and stopped about halfway between them, panting, out of breath and confused. Jane moved to Troublesome Creek and started wading across.

"I wanted to get something between us and the bear," she recalls. "If we could just get something between us. I knew there was a cub, and I wanted her to know we weren't after the cub. I started yelling for Joel. 'Get in the water! Get in the water!'"

Joel wasn't listening.

"I was pumped up and dazed and didn't know nothing."

The bear started running away but kept watching Joel over its shoulder.

"And just for a split second, our eyes locked."

The bear flipped around and came back at full speed. Joel thought he was set, ready for an attack, but the next thing he knew he was lying on the ground again, the bear roaring in his face.

He called out to God for help: "I need help and I need help now."

And the bear jumped. She flew sideways, like a dog, using all four feet. Then she did it again. Then she turned and ran like hell.

Jane was still yelling for Joel to cross the stream, but he wasn't sure why. He went toward her, and when he was knee deep, he looked back and saw the other large bear, still watching him from ten feet away. Then he lost his footing and went tumbling down the fast waters of Little Troublesome Creek. But he washed up on the other shore, scrambled up the bank, and tried to embrace his wife.

It wasn't until then that he noticed all the blood pouring from his wounds.

The two struggled through the brush to the highway, a quarter-mile away, watching constantly for the bears. Joel tried to flag down the first vehicle to come by, a pickup with elaborate lights all over it. The driver veered into the far lane and punched the gas.

The second car stopped. A businesswoman urged the sodden, bloody pair into her immaculate car and took them up the road to their own vehicle, where Joel insisted he could drive. And he did it, too. They went to a nearby roadhouse, where the owner laid them on the floor and called for help.

As often happens in rural Alaska, a place that isn't always as empty as it looks, EMTs and paramedics "came out of the woodwork" and started dressing their wounds. Both were lying on gurneys, ready to be put in an ambulance, when Jane noticed the large picture window.

"Look out the window," she told Joel. "There's Mount McKinley."

Wardens investigated the attack, determined it was a chance surprise encounter, and took no action against the bears.

The bite on Jane's back was two inches from her spine, and she could easily have been paralyzed. One bite on Joel's inner thigh narrowly missed both the femoral artery and his testicles. But the doctors at the hospital in Palmer stitched the Larsons where necessary, packed the deeper wounds with gauze, and sent them home after a few days with detailed instructions on how to clean each other's wounds for the next several weeks.

Thirteen years later, sitting in the comfortable living room of their long-since-completed home, surrounded by three growing children, Joel still has a pink scar on his jaw, but he usually covers it with a beard. He's got more scars on his hand, his arm, his leg. One finger is still a little numb where the bear split his hand apart. Jane's arm and shoulder work fine now. She gave herself physical therapy by extending her arm and pushing a small magnet up the side of the refrigerator with her fingertips. She still remembers finally reaching the top. That was a milestone.

Both Larsons feel they were lucky. If the bear had wanted to kill them, she could have done so easily. They walked away with all their body parts still working, and the experience brought them closer.

"It made us closer to each other and to our God," Jane says.

"It's a real emotional situation. I felt the same thing that hostages do, when you feel real grateful that they didn't kill you. When we came out of there, I was amazed that we could even walk. I was even more amazed that all our parts were there."

Joel says he thinks the attack probably lasted seven to ten minutes but agrees it could have been a lot less than that. He knows it lasted a lot longer than he wanted it to.

The mental shock still endures, though it's easier to talk about the attack now. For years, it was wrenching. Joel dreamed about it every night. In the dream they crossed Troublesome Creek only to find two or three more bears waiting for them. Jane slept with her car keys in her sock so that, when a bear broke into the house, she could climb out a window and drive away. All that winter, as she drove to work, she worried about bears attacking the car, an idea that now makes her nine-year-old son giggle.

"Bears hibernate in the winter," he tells his mother.

"I know, honey," she explains. "It's like the bogeyman. The bogeyman never sleeps."

Even today, the sound of a noisy stream sets something off in her.

"Hiking is still fun, but it's scary," she says. "There are certain places where the panic will come and you just have to leave."

Joel didn't hunt for a couple of years after the attack, but he carried a .45/70 rifle around his property for protection. At night "there was a bear behind every stump and tree," and he'd start sweating.

One evening they went to a nearby lodge for a beer. A friend was there, a good friend. He started a little innocent horseplay and snapped a towel at Jane.

"There was something about the way he turned his head and the way he was smiling," Joel says. "And I slipped right back into the woods. The next thing I knew, I had him by the throat."

Jane understood.

"No, Joel," she said in the lodge, soothing him. "Come on, we're at home. We're at home."

He apologized to his friend. "I'm sorry, man. For a split second you weren't you. You were that bear."

Both Larsons say they still aren't sure if they did the right thing or not, fighting the bear. Like all Alaskans they've heard plenty of bear stories. They know about bluff charges, and they know about playing dead. They had left their daypacks in the car because they knew the packs smelled of food, and they didn't want to attract bears. They made plenty of noise on purpose, talking and snapping branches, but the creek drowned it all out. Leaving the pistol in the car might have been a good idea or a bad one. Joel says there was one moment—the time when the bear was attacking Jane and he thought about jumping on its back—when he probably could have stuck the .44 in its ear and killed it. Any other time he would have risked merely wounding the bear or accidentally shooting his wife.

They're both skeptical about giving anybody advice. Fighting the bear like they did might have just angered it more, but it might have saved their lives, too. Joel says he would have played dead if he could have known that Jane would play dead, too. But he didn't know that, and neither did she.

Running probably wasn't a good idea, they say, but standing still isn't easy, either.

"Maybe I shouldn't have run," Joel says. But that's hindsight, which is always perfect. "You tell your story, and you run into a lot of 'professional' bear fighters, bear hunters. But if you've got yourself with a seven-hundred-pound to one-thousand-pound bear running at you, at a distance of about thirty feet, I'd like to see you just stand there. I'd like to see that."

POSTSCRIPT

In September 2008 one of the worst kinds of trouble landed in the home the Larsons built, the kind of thing that can overshadow even a bear attack.

By 2006 Joel had taken a job as a corrections officer. And he was denying a young girl's claims he had sexually molested her. But the girl persisted and even wore a police wire to record a conversation with him. By 2008 he was facing six charges of sexual abuse. In 2009 he pleaded guilty to one consolidated count of sexual abuse.

The judge gave him nine years.

According to his hometown newspaper, the *Frontiersman*, the judge "considers Larson to have a potential to re-offend but doesn't consider him beyond rehabilitation."

She urged him to take advantage of the support offered by his family and his church.

"For his part, Larson had very little to say except that he was sorry," the paper reported.

21

The Bear's Story

You're in a dense thicket of lodgepole pine, a place where spindly trees grow as thick as the hair on a dog's back. The deadfall, too, is everywhere, logs and branches scattered all over the place, and sometimes you have to get down on your hands and knees just to move any farther and you can't see even when the light is strong but now it's getting dark and somewhere in this mess is a grizzly bear, hurt and probably angry. It is your job to find this bear and you hope and hope you do not have to kill it because you did not take this job to kill bears and you want instead to help but you will shoot if you have to and you cannot see and the bear is in there and it is making not a sound. You stay and search until the darkness is complete, and then you leave, careful and feeling bad and breathing maybe a little easier because you can come back and finish this job in the daylight.

Only a hundred feet from the place where you turn around lies the bear, knowing these woods like you never can know them, watching you and your companions and wondering what you will do and what harm you intend. She is feeling the pain in her foot and the weight and confusion of the trap that holds her and she is unable to move much at all. Snagged, caught, chained to a root or a snag. For the first time in her life, she has no choices. She cannot run away or fight or charge. She can only try to hide and if she had a choice she would find a place even better than this dense wood where people cannot see.

For a long time she is stuck. She is stuck after the glow in the western sky is gone, stuck and confused after the stars turn bright. And then another bear comes into the wood, looking for her like you did, and again she cannot flee or charge or fight. He is a big male and this is mating season and he smells her fecund heat. She is in trouble now and tries to fight, but the trap and chain on her front foot will not yield and the male is a creature of much power. He swats and bites and grows angry. In his rage he sinks his teeth again and again into her face and her throat and with his powerful paws he crushes the ribs on the right side, the same side where the trap pins her front foot, ripping her open and collapsing eight of the thick rib bones, forcing the jagged ends into her liver and heart and lungs. After a while, she is dead.

And that's how you and your companions find things in the morning.

It was June 1, 1996, and the trio of Glacier National Park rangers on Dutch Creek that morning were not at all happy with what they found. The female grizzly had stepped in one of several toehold traps set for wolves. Researchers from the University of Montana had placed them as part of a study on the relationships between ungulates and the big canids, which had migrated to the park only a few years earlier after being exterminated early in the century. They hoped to catch a wolf, weigh and measure and take blood from the animal, put a radio collar around its neck, and turn it loose, a little groggy and suffering from some sore toes but with no serious damage done. They had set seven or eight traps along an abandoned road near the North Fork of the Flathead River on the park's western border. The traps were close enough to the road that the researchers could reach out from a vehicle and bait them with stinky offal, with wolf urine gathered the previous winter as yellow snow. They didn't have to step from the vehicle that way, didn't leave much of their own scent on the ground. Each set consisted of a toehold trap and a six-foot length of chain that ends in a grappling hook. It's a design meant to allow a trapped animal to move a short way into cover before the hook fastens to something immobile. It's meant to capture a wolf with the least possible trauma. It's not meant to capture a grizzly bear.

The one that stepped in the trap the night before, a 250-pound, fifteen-year-old female, carried the trap well into the woods, moving a lot farther than a wolf could have gone. It didn't take long for the wolf team to figure out what had happened when they checked the trap line that evening: The set was gone, and they could hear the bear out in the woods and the deadfall, moving around and growling if they tried to approach.

The same thing had happened two years earlier, in the same place. They immediately called rangers.

The first time a bear had been caught there she was anesthetized, the trap was removed, and she wandered away. When rangers arrived that evening, they hoped to do the same thing. A three-person team led by subdistrict ranger Scott Emmerich went after the bear. A rifle that shoots tranquilizer darts was the weapon of choice, but they had a can of bear spray and two shotguns loaded with slugs as backup. They talked over contingency plans. They talked about what to do if the bear charged, how close they would let her come before they would use the shotguns. But mostly they talked about being careful, about avoiding any situation that would make the guns necessary. When darkness fell, it was just too dangerous to follow the bear any farther, and everybody but the bear went home.

"She wasn't moving, we didn't know where she was, and it was dark," Emmerich recalls of that night.

"In the morning two of the researchers who were on the wolf project had tears flowing out of their eyes," he says. "They felt so godawful bad. This is your life, protecting these animals. The worst possible thing that could happen for the animal had just happened there."

In hindsight, Emmerich says, he should have left somebody on the scene all night in a patrol vehicle.

"We didn't sit on her all night long. In the future if we ever have a bear caught in a trap and we have to leave it out overnight, we'll put a pickup truck as close as we possibly can, with somebody there. And if they hear a fight, then they could use the lights and the siren, something that could scare away the other bear."

＊

But why did the bear attack? Grizzlies kill each other in fights over food, over breeding rights, to protect cubs. But this case was unusual: a temporarily helpless though otherwise healthy female killed by a male nobody even saw. Rangers could tell he was a big one: They measured his tracks at eleven and a half inches by five and a half inches, and that's a big bear. Breeding season might be what started the fight. Male grizzlies are sexually active longer than females are, or at least they try to be. She may not have been in full estrus and therefore not responsive. In a normal situation she would have fought him off or run away if she wasn't ready to breed.

Grizzly courtship can be rough. But she couldn't do that with three toes held fast in a trap, the chain taut. Even if she was in full estrus, the trap undoubtedly did nothing for her mood. If her heat was full, the male may have become enraged at her reluctance, not stopping with his lusty insistence until the object of his ardor was dead. Nobody could tell if the bears bred that night. The boar left without feeding on her body.

Or it may have been something harder to define that triggered his rage. He may have simply sensed something was wrong, that the sow was vulnerable, and taken advantage. Animals often single out the oddball or the weakling for abuse. Horses do it, and so do dogs, though not as often as people do.

"With predators especially, they key in when things aren't normal, either with prey animals or with other predators," says Tim Thier, a wildlife biologist with the Montana Department of Fish, Wildlife and Parks who has twenty years' experience with grizzly bears, mostly in northwest Montana. "There's some kind of instinctive reaction that goes on there. I don't know how best to explain it."

But he's seen it.

He tells of bugling in a spike bull elk one day, of "playing with" the sexually aroused adolescent animal and making it run back and forth. Then, out of the clear blue sky, a golden eagle attacked the four-hundred-pound elk. Killing such a target is an impossible goal but one the eagle felt compelled to reach for, probably because the elk's behavior was so odd. Thier was reluctant to tell the story at first because he didn't think anyone would believe him.

He tells of a black bear that killed a goat crippled by a mule kick. Some theorize that once a bear gets a taste of livestock, it's hooked. But Thier also has a theory about why the bear attacked. He thought the goat's injury had drawn the bear's attention, so he captured, collared, and released the bear. It lived near the same farm for three years after that "and never once attacked a goat or anything else."

Grizzlies are solitary most of their lives, but when they do come together they display such personality traits as pride, common sense, joy, and anger. They often pick fights with each other, but they also know when to back off. And they get frisky sometimes, playing and roughhousing for hours at a time even after reaching adulthood. Captive bears have been known to tease and torment one another. And they can display incredible rage, using their awesome speed and strength to take what they want, whether it be food or sex or a chance at safety.

Most bear fights occur during the early summer breeding season, and many bears carry abundant scars. Males fight each other for the right to breed females. Bears of both sexes fight to establish dominance and pecking order. Sows will fight to the death to protect their cubs, which boars often try to kill, sometimes as a food source and perhaps to increase their own chances of breeding. In Yellowstone, Glacier, Canada, and Alaska, bear researchers report finding carcasses of bears they believe were killed by other bears. Sometimes grizzlies eat the fallen. Sometimes they don't.

Bear research can also contribute to such deaths. Bears coming out of drug-induced stupors occasionally fall victim to other bears, lending credence to Thier's theory about bears that attack the weak or the odd.

Cubs are a particular target. In some populations as many as 50 percent of cubs die before reaching three years old, a large number of them killed by boars. Some biologists theorize that they kill the cubs to encourage the sow to come into estrus again, increasing a male's chance of breeding again soon. But that theory doesn't apply for cubs killed after July, when there isn't much chance of estrus, cubs or no cubs. And boars kill cubs at any time of year. They sometimes kill mothers trying to defend them.

Folklore tells us that males will kill and eat their own offspring. Thier isn't so sure if that's true.

"I believe that bears are smart enough that males know which females they've bred. And I believe that's why females will breed a number of different males, given the opportunity. By being promiscuous she can better ensure the survival of her cubs."

According to his theory, a female grizzly with hot pants protects her cubs from a larger number of males than does a female that breeds with only one mate.

"It's been shown that males will kill cubs, but I don't know where it's been verified that they kill their own cubs. There's no doubt in my mind that bears are smart enough that they know who's who out there."

If males are killing their own cubs as often as they do those sired by some other bear, it remains to be proven, Thier says.

"I just don't think the data's out there to show that. We're delving into the area of biology where there just isn't a lot of information, and there probably never will be."

But hunger sometimes outweighs sentiment or any biological imperative to continue one's own family tree. Mother grizzlies occasionally kill and eat their own young, and cubs have been reported feeding on the carcass of their mother only hours after she died, which may explain why grizzlies on rare occasions eat people they have killed in defensive actions. At some level meat is meat.

There are few other creatures on earth that could kill a fully grown grizzly bear, acting alone. Gary Brown's *Great Bear Almanac* describes some fights between grizzlies and other animals staged for the macabre amusement of humans. A California grizzly killed an African lion in Monterrey, Mexico, "so quickly that the big audience hardly knew how it was done," Brown records. That happened in the 1920s. Bison have killed grizzlies on occasion, although bears usually avoid the big bulls, and moose have been known to chase grizzlies away. The infamous bull and bear fights that appealed to a sick sense of entertainment in nineteenth-century California usually wound up with a dead bull and a badly injured bear.

One of the most lethal four-legged enemies of a grizzly bear is a small one, the porcupine. Bears hapless enough to try to eat one often wind up with a mouth full of quills and a bad infection, sometimes starving. There may be an obvious natural selection process working in such cases.

But the only animal that kills grizzly bears with regularity—with the notable exception of man, their greatest foe—is another grizzly bear. And if grizzlies wanted to prey on people, to treat them like food, they could do so easily.

"They're way more tolerant of people than they're given credit for," Thier points out. "If they wanted to, they could be an incredibly efficient predator on people. And the fact that they don't speaks a lot for them."

In July 1997 a case of bear-versus-bear predation showed in no uncertain terms the power of grizzly bears, both large and small. It happened early in the morning of July 14 on the Brooks River in Alaska's Katmai National Park. A pair of rangers at an observation platform captured the whole thing on videotape.

Two male bears met in the middle of the stream, a place where dozens of grizzlies gather every summer and where the bears establish their own pecking order, usually with more bluff and bravado than bloodshed. The biggest, most dominant males get the best fishing sites, where the salmon gather at the foot of a small waterfall. Then come smaller males, then females with cubs, and subadult bears get what's left. One of the bears that summer was a big one but not huge by Alaska standards, perhaps seven hundred or eight hundred pounds. The other was a subadult, maybe three hundred or four hundred pounds. By the time the camera started rolling, the larger male was holding the smaller one with his front claws, standing behind him and sinking his teeth between his shoulder blades again and again, tearing strips of flesh from his back, chewing and eating them as the smaller bear struggled, as helpless as a doll in the grip of the larger bear.

At one point he escaped, splashing only a few steps before the larger bear grabbed him again, ripping away more flesh and turning the water red with the smaller bear's blood. Finally, weakened by the loss of blood, the smaller bear went submissive as the bigger one exposed more and more of the bone along his spine.

Finally, he turned his victim over and gutted him with a swipe of one paw.

The smaller bear, an animal that could easily kill the strongest of humans with a shake of the head, stood up to the punishment for twenty minutes. The body lay in the river for several days, and despite the rich run of salmon, other bears occasionally fed on the carcass.

But most of the bears in the river kept their distance and only watched.

Sometimes, even bears have bear stories.

22

Bears Are Important

BARRIE GILBERT WAS LOOKING AT A BEAR TURD, WHICH IS NOT AN
UNUSUAL thing to find on a gravelly beach in Alaska's Katmai National
Park. Katmai contains what is probably the world's highest concentration
of grizzly bears, and the bears there get huge, gorging every summer on
the natural abundance of salmon and plant life. This bear had been eating
berries, lots of them. The scat made that obvious. Gilbert calculated there
were about four thousand seeds in the turd.

Then he did a little more math, curious about how many berries a grizzly can eat in a day. He studies bears for a living, you see, and such calcula-
tions intrigue him. The number he came up with was a stunner. His math
showed that a big bear can pass four hundred thousand berries through its
body in a day, leaving behind it a trail of seeds encased in rich fertilizer.
Gilbert looked up at the mountains and forests beyond the beach, and he
wondered about bears: They can easily travel thirty or forty miles in a day.
What else are they spreading around? Did a bear scat that was a salmon
yesterday fertilize a tree somewhere today? Did the bear hasten the process
that transforms moose blood from hemoglobin to nitrogen to chlorophyll?
Did the shrubbery that held the chlorophyll filter the water that fed the
stream that spawned the salmon that fueled the bear that ate the berries?
These are big questions and would not be answered on the beach that day.

Then he took a picture of the scat and went back to work, watching
bears and trying to document how they live with people and with each
other. The photograph would wind up on his desk back at Utah State
University, where he was a professor of animal behavior and wildlife management. The bear's digestive process would provide something to chew
on for a long time.

"If you've got a high density of bears eating a lot of berries and distributing a lot of seeds and dung over the landscape, this is a service in terms of maintaining the diversity of an area, helping out after fires or clear-cuts or avalanches or blowdowns," Gilbert says later, the photo in his hand. "We know that bears distribute seeds over huge areas and that they spread nutrients. They have a clear ecosystem function in carrying nutrients, like from salmon, up into the mountains. What we don't know is how important that is."

Simply not knowing such things, not knowing how important bears are to trees and water and fish, is a good enough reason to keep the bears around, Gilbert maintains. Once they are gone, the answer may become clear. But then it's too late.

"People say you can get rid of grizzly bears, that they don't have any real dominant role in the ecosystem function. But we don't know that. We hear about these new ideas every day."

Gilbert has spent his professional life studying bears. In Alaska and in Yosemite, in British Columbia and in Yellowstone, he has focused on bears, how they interact with people, what they need to survive. Most of that work he did as a contract researcher, when he wasn't teaching students about conservation biology, about the interconnectedness of things. On his own time he worked with environmental groups and native peoples who want to keep bears alive. This is not such a unique position. A number of people do similar work, laboring tirelessly on behalf of the great bear and the wild ecosystems it needs to survive. The fire in Gilbert's belly is shared by many. But Gilbert is unique in other ways. Unique because he has spent so much time so close to so many grizzly bears. Unique because, years before he ever began that work, the first wild grizzly bear he ever saw almost took his head off.

It was June 27, 1977, and Gilbert had just started a contract in Yellowstone National Park. Officials there had closed the last of the garbage dumps just six years earlier, shutting the park's grizzlies off from a huge source of nutrition and leaving a lot of hungry bears wandering around. This had caused problems, and the Park Service wanted to know more about how grizzlies and people interact in the wild. How often did bears run away when they heard someone coming? If they ran, how far did they go? Would they just back off for a few minutes, then return to whatever they had been doing? Or would they abandon the entire drainage? Would they attack or bluff-charge a human trespasser? If so, what seemed to trigger the attack?

Gilbert and Bruce Hastings, a graduate student at the time, were hoping to learn something about all of this. They paddled a canoe along the shores of Lake Yellowstone, looking for good vantage points to set up their optics and settle down to observe. They had no luck. They found no bears and they couldn't find the right spot, so they moved to the west side of the park, shouldering their gear to the top of Bighorn Pass, a 9,200-foot saddle in the Gallatin Range that overlooks the lake and the river that carry the same name. They knew it was bear country and took some precautions. Their tent was pitched against a cliff, and Gilbert gathered dead trees, branches, and bits of wood to make a rough fence around the camp. He had no illusions about its keeping a bear away but figured it would make noise if a grizzly came through the structure, giving the men a brief notice, a moment to decide what to do.

The next morning they found bears: five of them, down in a valley on the west side of the pass. A sow and three cubs were grazing on the tender vegetation of late spring, turning over boulders, digging up and eating what they could find. There was a lone bear there, too, probably a boar, that approached the family group a couple of times, forcing the mother to charge him, to warn him, to make him back off. She was on her toes that morning. A few patches of snow remained in the high country, and there were elk around, grazing on the green shoots that emerged from the edges of the melting snowbanks. After a while, the bear family wandered into the trees, out of sight.

The men wanted to watch them some more, so they took off, cutting a wide circle around the bears and heading for a long spur that jutted from a landmark known as Crowfoot Ridge.

They bushwhacked up the steep slope, and near the nine-thousand-foot top Hastings had to stop to relieve himself. Gilbert said he would continue ahead a short way, over the top of a nearby knob. He was a little impatient.

It was alpine country, just shrubs and grasses and stunted trees, twisted by the nearly constant wind, the wind that was whipping so hard that morning. Gilbert was walking fast into the gale, but he moved carefully over the top of the glaciated granite outcrop, keeping low so he wouldn't make a silhouette against the skyline.

"I didn't want to have some elk bark at us after seeing movement up high. I cleared the skyline and dropped down, moving fast."

That's when the bear spotted him.

"I heard this mighty roar, and when I looked up, I saw this bear clawing at the rock, trying to get to me. Full speed out, low, with its ears laid back sleek. It looked like a lion. Just your ultimate nightmare. This was not a bluff charge, and I would have done anything to get out of there. I clearly remember seeing the claws digging into the rock as it tried to accelerate toward me."

He isn't sure, but he believes the grizzly was forty or fifty yards away when she began her charge.

"Way too close," he describes it. "She launched toward me when I looked up. I've often said to people, if you have only a second and the bear isn't doing something, then you might get your act together. But if you look up and see the bear in full charge toward you, your mind just goes berserk.

"All I could think of was, 'I've just got to put some distance between us. I'll be dead if I stay right where I am.' So I turned and ran as fast as I could. Which didn't change the charge.

"I don't think I made two or three steps before the bear was on me. It grabbed my leg, or I went down anyway, and it tore the back of my scalp off with one great big bite. It left a groove you could set a fountain pen in, right in the top of my head. It was like a pickax coming down on my skull. Doctors spent a lot of time pulling bone chips out of it."

Running from a bear is never a good idea; it often triggers a chase response. Gilbert knows that now, but this was his first grizzly project and he was only one week into it. He was trained as an herbivore biologist. He had studied pronghorn antelope in the park before, and his graduate studies had focused on deer. Grizzly bears in the field were a new thing for him, and now one of them was all over him with teeth and claws.

"Right at that moment my mind said fight this thing off. So I rolled over and jammed my arms in its mouth, which got me a few bites there. Then it just dropped its teeth and pulled away the side of my face. I could feel the cheekbone breaking off. I figured I was dying."

One canine tooth punched through his left eye, destroying it forever and opening up the sinus cavity, gouging deep enough to touch his brain. One bite peeled the skin from his forehead. His right eye, the one that he would keep, was hanging slightly out of the socket. His nose was torn away; so were his ears. There were rips and holes all over his chest, abdomen, and arms.

Hastings was just finishing his business in the woods when, despite the violent wind, he heard something odd. The sound was indefinable, but it rattled him. "Some noises just don't sound right," he told rangers later that afternoon.

"I heard something, but the wind was blowing very, very hard, so I couldn't be sure what it was, and then I realized that something was wrong and pulled out my knife, for whatever good that would do. I couldn't tell exactly what the noises were, but they just didn't sound right."

He moved to his backpack, just a few paces uphill, feeling edgier all the time. He took a few more steps, and then he saw the bear, a chocolate-colored grizzly, the same female they had seen earlier that morning from a mile away. Now it was close, too close, less than twenty yards away, and it was working.

"I couldn't see Barrie, but I could see the grizzly was mauling him. I wasn't quite sure what to do."

He remembered reading somewhere that low, deep sounds might scare away a bear. Standing behind a small tree, he tried it: He yelled "Ha!" as low and as loud as he could, bringing the single syllable up from his belly and his chest.

It was enough. The bear lifted its head. Hastings stepped further into his sparse cover. When he looked again, the bear was bolting for the horizon.

Gilbert was lying in a pool of his own blood, but he was conscious and coherent. His down jacket was tied around his waist and Hastings took it off, then covered him with it. Hastings put a shirt over Gilbert's mangled, almost fleshless face. Gilbert was cold and knew he had lost a lot of blood. He worried about hypothermia and shock. Luckily, the men carried a handheld radio, and Hastings called park headquarters at Mammoth Hot Springs for help. Gilbert said a mental goodbye to all the people he loved, his wife and young children. Then, speaking with his throat and teeth because his lips were gone, he tried to get Hastings to climb a tree and wait. He didn't want the bear to come back and attack Hastings, too.

"I knew he was my lifeline to survival."

Hastings did everything he could to stem the bleeding. He stayed on the ground and kept up radio contact with Mammoth.

Luckily, the chopper was in Mammoth, and it was ready, only a few air miles away. Hastings's call came in at 10:50 a.m. The chopper left the ground at 11:27, with the pilot and a ranger who had some first-aid training on board. The pilot spotted Gilbert and Hastings seventeen minutes later.

— ⌣ —

Ranger Tom Black had a stiff hike ahead of him before he could help Gilbert. The winds on the ridgetop were too much for the small helicopter, and pilot Jim Thompson was having a devil of a time. He tried to put the Bell helicopter—similar to the bubble-topped ships used in old M*A*S*H episodes—on the ground close to Gilbert, but the wind was just too much.

"And right in the middle of all this, the turbocharger flubbed out on me," Thompson says.

After "too many dangerous attempts," he was able to land three hundred yards away and four hundred feet downhill. Black was out of the helicopter "before I could shut the thing down," Thompson said. He grabbed all the medical gear in the chopper and started puffing up the hill, but not before he gave Thompson a 12-gauge shotgun and a Stokes litter.

"I did two tours in Vietnam, but I didn't have any idea what to do with a shotgun," Thompson says.

But both men rushed to help. Climbing that much in that distance is not an easy job, and Thompson, unaccustomed to the altitude, found it particularly hard. He soon began to taste blood in his mouth, and a doctor told him later the alveoli in his lungs had begun to rupture. It happens, when lowlanders exert themselves at altitude.

The two men quickly realized they were going to need more help, so a crew of smoke jumpers was summoned, and they tossed supplies and then themselves from a fixed-wing plane, despite the treacherous winds. They brought more medical supplies and skills, then helped carry Gilbert's litter to the helicopter. Thompson, apologizing for his inability to land his ship closer, took Gilbert's camera and started snapping pictures. He got the plane coming in, the parachute drop, Gilbert being bandaged.

"It's almost surrealistic to see your own accident like that," Gilbert says, twenty years later.

But getting Gilbert to the helicopter didn't end the problems. Because the turbocharger had "gone south," Thompson had a miserable time trying to fly the thing, especially since Gilbert's extra weight—he was on a litter strapped to the chopper's skids—threw it way off balance.

Tom Black "had to almost sit on my lap," to offset Gilbert's weight and every time he slid over to check on Gilbert the chopper "rolled into an uncommanded right-hand turn. Then when he returned to my lap, we were able to fly straight and level again."

Gilbert was forty years old at the time and had just landed the job at Utah State. "It was a hell of a way to start a career."

❦

Gilbert never blamed the bear for the attack that cost him an eye, that drained 40 percent of his blood and left him in the same damn room in a Salt Lake City hospital for six weeks. The initial repair job alone required a team of surgeons, eleven hours, and 990 stitches in his head. Afterwards came repeated plastic surgeries. All that, and he still carries the scars. All that, and he never blamed the bear.

He and Hastings had tried to circle around the bears and climb well above them for observation. Instead, they walked right into them, the wind masking their approach. Then Gilbert came in low and fast, moving like a carnivore. Though they never saw the cubs, both men believe the bear was the sow they had watched that morning.

"The thing that I misjudged, of course, was that the bears would go up that high," he says. Investigators would find the bear's day bed later, not far from the attack.

Because he was moving fast and coming closer, he probably startled the bear, an animal already left on edge by a morning spent protecting her cubs from the nearby boar.

"A female may have been well primed to hit anything" at a time like that, says veteran Yellowstone biologist Mary Meagher, who had hired Gilbert and helped investigate the incident.

Gilbert has a unique way of seeing things from the bear's point of view.

"I think I just scared the hell out of it," he says. "I interpret it to be a defensive attack. I had come too close, and it treated me the way it would treat a bear."

The bear bit him on the head and face "because she wanted to neutralize my weapons. She thought I had big teeth."

Gilbert did get angry once on the mountain. Somebody—one of the smoke jumpers, maybe—said the Park Service had killed a lot of bears recently, had destroyed a number of the animals trying to find a substitute for the closed dumps.

"He was trying to make me feel good by telling me how many bears they had killed. I said, 'I don't care. I don't want you to kill that bear.' I told the Park Service not to go after the bear and kill it. I said that on the mountaintop."

❧

The history of the grizzly bear in the lower forty-eight states is a history of white people going after it. There once were more than fifty thousand of them, maybe as many as one hundred thousand. Now there are perhaps fifteen hundred, and the future of those animals remains questionable. Their demise started with Lewis and Clark on their Voyage of Discovery across the newly American territory of the Louisiana Purchase.

The men on the expedition were understandably terrified of the great bears: They'd never seen such a critter. And ever since the men returned in 1806, historians and editors have repeated tales of marauding grizzlies stalking the hapless explorers. But the men of letters got it wrong, according to Gilbert. Apply a biologist's perspective, and you find a different story altogether.

"Encounters with the bears were almost all initiated by the expedition members," says Gilbert, who went to the original writings of the explorers and analyzed what happened. "It was a willful choice to go after the bear. The bear was not coming after the people."

An example:

Captain Meriwether Lewis shot a bison one day. He talked about the blood spitting out of its nostrils as it died. But he neglected to reload his weapon, and a bear showed up as the bison took its last breaths. The bear was about twenty yards away, Lewis tells us, and the explorer hotfooted it eighty yards to a river and waded in. He tells of how the bear chased him. But he also says that, when he reached the river, the bear was still twenty feet away.

"There's no way" that constituted an attack, Gilbert says. Either Lewis embellished the story or his interpreters did, most likely the latter. A grizzly that wanted to could easily run a man down in eighty yards, especially over rough terrain. And once Lewis turned to face the bear, it went away.

"My interpretation of this incident is that the bear was curious. And when he ran, the bear followed him, a little faster. But it did not charge. Read the actual words. It covers about a page. There's no way you could conclude that it was a charge. In fact, the bear bugs off as soon as Lewis turns to face it."

Gilbert went on to look at three dozen other interactions in the journals.

"And I made a matrix of who charged whom, who started the interaction, and who ended up dying. In the vast majority of cases, the bear was being harassed and killed by people, a willful choice by humans to close the distance and shoot the bear."

Pop culture has told us that Lewis and Clark faced two kinds of trouble, Indians and grizzly bears.

"Sorry," Gilbert says. "The journals don't say that. The journals say they had a lot of trouble with cold water and hard work."

In actuality the Indians provided food and shelter and horses. And the expedition's hunters pursued grizzly bears because they provided fat, a food with three times the energy value of carbohydrates or sugar, which was important to cold men doing hard work. "Grizzlies were the biggest packets of fat around." One big male bear produced five gallons of rendered fat, and that was a prize, out on the prairie.

"Besides," he adds. "It's good for frying other sorts of things."

Nevertheless, when Lewis and Clark and their men returned to the settled parts of America, their tales of grizzly bears grew more hair and longer teeth the more often they were told. Followers came armed. When a bear approached, guns went off. But guns weren't very good in those days, and bears don't die easy even with powerful modern weapons. That meant a wounded bear and a weapon that took a long time to reload.

"I don't disagree that they had some nasty encounters with bears," Gilbert says. "So would you and I if we shot a bear and only wounded it and it tried to tear us to pieces. But who started the fight? That's the big question."

North Americans are still picking fights with the grizzly. Its reputation as a marauder is almost unmatched in the world. Other creatures formerly reviled and feared now enjoy new reputations.

"You wouldn't get the same view of the mountain gorilla among reasonably literate people," Gilbert notes.

Killer whales? Despite their ominous name, people swim with them in pools.

Even sharks, creatures that, like grizzlies, on rare occasions attack and eat people, are going through a transformation in the public eye as their numbers dwindle.

"But the grizzly hasn't had that treatment. We're still promoting it for its fear value instead of something else."

But what about the native people? Tribes and nations all over the northern hemisphere venerated the bear, but they feared it, too. They held special ceremonies when they hunted it and when they ate it. Some believed bears could read human thoughts. Some saw the bear as a guide to other worlds. The constellation Ursa Minor contains the North Star, the guide to the seasons, the pole around which the cosmos revolves. The ancients of Greece, Siberia, and Scandinavia all honored it with the name of bear.

All true, Gilbert agrees. But neither the ancients nor the more contemporary native people demonized the bear. Much of their mythology was built around trying to live with it.

"I think those people had a lot more personal experience. I have a lot more empathy with those people, with my own experience. They had to live day to day without very good weapons. So they tend to tell stories that would be very important on how to deal with these creatures."

Some native cultures taught that looking a bear in the eyes was taboo. The same rule applies today but with a different rationale: Bears see that gesture as a threat and often attack in response.

"I'm a believer that whatever the mythology, whatever the tale is, it has a natural selection value. If you put your dead up on platforms and let the crows and eagles carry them off, we say they've been carried to heaven, but what we've really done is stop bears from eating them so the bears won't eat us.

"I think life in North America, with the grizzly bear, and the short-faced bear before that, was a constant struggle to have grizzlies learn to not carry away you or your food. I suspect that a lot of the mythology was based on how to deal with grizzly bears in a practical way. Because they're a major impediment to your survival under certain conditions. So you try to find out, culturally, what the conditions are to get along with them."

Gilbert has spent a lot of time figuring out how to get along with grizzlies. Since 1983 he has spent many summers at Brooks River in Katmai, possibly the ideal place for such a study. For thousands of years, bears have arrived there by the dozens to feed on the summer and fall runs of spawning salmon. In recent years the same fish have drawn lots of anglers, who share the waters with the bears. More recently, planeloads of tourists have been crowding in to watch the bears. Tourists and bears routinely come within a few yards of each other, and both species have learned how to get along, although both have needed some training—more for the people than for the bears. There have been some close calls over the years—a man napping in his tent was nipped on the foot once, and an eight-year-old boy was bowled over in 1997 by one bear trying to escape another one—but there's never been a mauling along the river. Indeed, some bears have learned that people can be helpful. Females with cubs, ever wary of large males looking to eat their children, occasionally leave their young on the bank within a few feet of people, taking advantage of the free babysitter, knowing that the boars tend to avoid the human zone.

Gilbert and his graduate students spent long hours on the river, carefully recording the numbers of bears and how long they stay. More importantly, they recorded how the bears react to varying numbers of people.

"There were a lot of human-bear interactions, hundreds of them," Gilbert says. Most of them consisted of a bear moving away, maybe growling a little. But he also found that, as the number of people in the area increases, the fewer hours bears will spend on the stream, especially females with cubs and especially in the fall, when bears need the calories the most.

"We have some very clear-cut data," Gilbert says. "The bear hours declined precipitously. It was something like 92 percent for females with cubs."

Those kinds of numbers got the attention of the National Park Service. Between 1987 and 1997 the number of visitors soared by 900 percent, rising to about fourteen thousand people a year at Brooks River. That works out to about 250 people a day, fishing or just watching bears, as many as sixty of them. The whole conglomeration is bunched up along the same half-mile stretch of river beneath Brooks Falls, where the salmon gather. Traffic problems become severe.

In recent years park rangers have started acting like maître d's in a restaurant, taking names of visitors and calling them when a space becomes available at the viewing platform nearest the falls, where the bears are the most photogenic.

"'We have a table of six waiting,'" former Katmai superintendent Bill Pierce says, imitating his rangers who shuttle people to the platform. "Literally. They'll wait two or three hours before they can actually get their spot. Then they'll walk up to the falls and spend their one hour on the platform. When it's real busy, we'll knock it back to forty-five minutes."

Pierce says the river is at its "saturation point" and has proposed capping visitor numbers. He wanted to impose limits by 1998, an idea that really irked former Alaska Senator Ted Stevens, a Republican.

During the last days of Congress in 1997, Stevens attached a "rider" to the bill that would fund national parks for the next year. Riders are an especially insidious way of making law. If a single politician has an agenda or a favor to repay, he writes a rider and attaches it to an important or popular bill. That way Congress avoids the unpleasant task of voting for or against a pet project being pushed by a member of the club, a measure that often benefits some special interest at the expense of the general public.

Or in this case of grizzly bears.

The Stevens rider banned the implementation of any limits on the number of visitors at Katmai. It also put a halt to National Park Service plans to move the busy lodge, which straddles the main thoroughfare bears use to get to and from the river, to a piece of benchland a thousand yards away. Such plans could impede commerce, cut into the sales of meals and airplane tickets and hotel rooms. Science said it was a good idea, that it was good for the bears and for human safety, but Stevens didn't like it, so he made the idea go away, at least for a while.

"That's the power of the special interests," Gilbert says. "I was really upset about the whole thing. They're just trying to increase the cash flow there at the expense of bears and the aesthetic environment. You've got a couple hundred people there, stepping off aircraft from Tokyo or Paris. They have no idea what a grizzly bear is about. It's a marvelous place, but it's being chewed up by too many people."

As of spring 2011 no caps had been placed on the numbers of visitors. And the lodge remains where it was.

Gilbert loves Katmai, but building that affection was not an easy job.

"The first couple days there I thought I'd made the biggest mistake of my life, signing on to something like this."

He first arrived at Katmai six years after the mauling, and his life had moved on. He was teaching, doing research, and he thought the attack was behind him. Then he got to Katmai, where grizzly bears surrounded him.

"I didn't realize it, but I still had a deep-seated fear."

The first night, sleeping in a big tent, he made it a point to pull his feet away from the canvas wall.

"I had this very clear fantasy of a bear dragging my butt into the woods and tearing me to pieces. I would not go into the woods by myself. I waited for other people to go with me, or I hung around for the biologist I was working with. I thought, 'Jesus, if I have to go through these woods for a mile and a half and climb a tree to observe bears, I'm going to need a Valium. And I'm going to be up to the armpits with shotguns.'"

The fear passed, however, and Gilbert, who carries constant reminders of the danger a grizzly bear can pose, grew accustomed to the bears, occasionally guiding back to camp people who had stayed out too late and found themselves in a dark wood full of grizzlies.

"It was just a matter of time until my mind said these are animals that are looking around for fish. They don't want to screw around with you, and you don't want to screw around with them."

In Katmai bears and people have learned to live with each other, as long as people adhere to the rules. Because it's a national park, human movement is regulated, and people must yield to bears in all circumstances. If you have a salmon on your line and a bear grabs it—a common occurrence—you must break the line and let the bear have the fish. If you don't move quickly enough, you could be bluff-charged. Although there are up to two hundred "interactions" in a year, there have been no major injuries so far.

How it will play out in the future depends on what the Park Service and Alaska's prodevelopment politicians can work out. Some people criticize Katmai, maintaining it has been converted into a zoo. Others complain about possible restrictions, worrying about lost opportunities to make money. Former superintendent Pierce wonders if he isn't looking at a collision course of too many bears and too many people, if the world's most celebrated example of how bear and man can learn to live with each other won't be destroyed by its own success. Many are outraged that Alaska allows hunters just outside the park to gun down bears that have spent the summer cheek by jowl with crowds of tourists and don't understand the dangers that people can pose.

Barrie Gilbert looks at Katmai and wonders if the lessons learned there can't be applied in other places where grizzlies live.

Gilbert maintains that people can live with bears if they are willing to make the effort. It works in Alaska, a state with a grizzly bear for every fifteen or twenty human residents, and it works in British Columbia, the Yukon, and Siberia. He realizes that on occasion bears are going to hurt people. But being a scientist, he points to statistics.

"You want animals attacking little children?" he asks. Look at man's best friend. Domestic dogs have killed and maimed more people than bears ever will.

Lightning strikes kill more people than bears do, often on golf courses. People without the sense to come in out of the rain must take their chances.

Car wrecks? It's not even worth making a comparison. Yet people continue to drink and drive, to speed, to pass on curves.

"What we're talking about here is public perception of how danger-ous it would be with grizzlies around. People have what is almost a fan-tasy of the threat of danger. It's not reality based."

Coming from Gilbert, that's a loud message. He tries to avoid talk about his injuries, to point out that both he and the bear would have preferred to be someplace else on that day in 1977. He'd rather focus on his science, look you straight in the face with his one eye, and say give the bears a break. But if he had lost that eye in a car wreck, you wouldn't pay as much attention. His scars add weight to his words.

People who see grizzlies as a threat to their pocketbooks or merely an inconvenience often fight hard to keep them out of the neighborhood. What good are they? they ask.

Gilbert knows the value of bears. He knows their value as a measur-ing stick for the health of an ecosystem, their role in telling us something important about ourselves. And what they tell us is not very good.

"It's crushingly depressing to see how little we do for the bears. In less than two hundred years, we've been able to almost blink them out. Why is that?"

He holds back no thunder when talking about government policies that turn bear habitat into golf courses, that let cattle graze berry bushes down to the stem, that turn wildlife refuges into parking lots for Winnebagos.

"The perception that we've set aside national parks for wildlife is a joke in a lot of cases. We're using them as national recreation grounds."

He wants hunters to be more careful in the woods, to use their eyes and brains instead of their guns. He wants the cattle out of the grizzly recovery zones. He wants big chunks of wild land set aside for grizzlies and salmon and other creatures, the more of it the better. He wants to make sure that nobody, nowhere, feeds a grizzly bear. Not on purpose. Not by accident. If you give a bear food, you make it dangerous, and somebody will probably have to kill it sooner or later. Carry bear spray when hiking in grizzly country. It could keep you and the bear alive. Pay attention.

"He loves this animal," says Doug Peacock, who is himself a powerful writer and an activist who works with Gilbert to preserve grizzly habitat in British Columbia. "That is not lost on people. It's certainly not lost on me. He has as much scientific credibility as anybody working with bears, he guards his independence, and he's been on the ground with a dangerous grizzly. He knows like few people know that the bear can kill whenever it wants, but it chooses not to. It makes him incredibly effective. I think he's much more powerful than he even knows."

Still, Gilbert is not optimistic. Saving the grizzly bear, especially in the lower forty-eight states, will require a "societal change," he says. But if it means things like losing a favorite campsite or fishing hole, handling your cattle differently, and changing how and where people hunt, society may balk.

"We're an atavistic society that wants it all. American society has no respect for native people and no respect for native animals."

It saddens him to see the chain broken, to see the vast clear-cuts and the overgrazing, to see disrupted the links between bears and forests, berries, and salmon.

"Are we so impoverished of spirit that with all our wealth we are willing to create deserts? Relatively speaking, that's what you do when you extinguish a species. Most conservation biologists don't like to use religious arguments, but God gave us these beautiful productive systems. Salmon streams and bears and ocean fisheries. By what right do we disgrace God by destroying them and creating deserts on Earth?"

And if Barrie Gilbert can say that, talking with lips that still don't work quite right, with an eye gone, with half his face covered with scars, it's time to listen.

POSTSCRIPT

Barrie Gilbert retired from Utah State University in 2001 and built himself a home on a river island in his native Ontario, "where I misspent my youth." But he hasn't retired from advocating on behalf of bears or showing people how to get along with them.

In the summers he helps crew a seventy-foot sailboat for a tour company and leads small groups onto the shores of British Columbia to watch bears, film them, and hike bear trails. And he stays in touch with pilot Jim Thompson, who describes his rescue flight as "the toughest, most fatiguing flying day I have ever experienced. That includes two helicopter flying tours in Vietnam."

Gilbert worries particularly about the grizzlies of Yellowstone, whether they can find foods to replace the nuts of the whitebark pine tree, which is dying rapidly. He'd like to see more land protected for them, so they can have more options. And he'd like to see people behave themselves in bear country.

On one of his annual trips to Yellowstone, he came across a magnificent grizzly, "the biggest I've ever seen in Yellowstone" and one that was trying to ignore the crowd of tourists watching it cross a road.

Then a woman darted from the crowd and approached within ten feet to snap a picture.

"I totally lost it," Gilbert says. "I really chewed her out."

The woman stood still and took the scolding, fixing her eyes on the road. Gilbert gave a command.

"Look at me," he said. And she lifted her eyes.

"You could end up like me. I've been there."

He hopes she listened.

23

A Rare and Ghastly Night

DEB FREELE WOKE WITH A FLUTTER OF UNEASINESS. SOMETHING WASN'T right. Then, before she could even open her eyes, the bear chomped into her upper left arm. It didn't chew. It didn't shake its head. It didn't growl. It just kept pushing her into the ground, squeezing its jaws ever tighter, carving a furrow of flesh you could roll a golf ball through. She heard something crack. It was loud.

She thought it was a bone breaking. Later she would learn the grizzly had snapped off one of its own teeth.

"It was like a vise," she said of the grizzly's grip. "Getting tighter and tighter and tighter."

Freele screamed. She called out for help. "It's a bear," she yelled. "I'm being attacked by a bear."

But no help came, not for a long time. It was July 28, 2010, and she was alone in her one-man tent, her thirteenth night in the Soda Butte Campground a few miles from the northeast entrance to Yellowstone National Park, near the mountain hamlet of Cooke City, Montana. Her husband was in another tent about forty feet away. But he'd been at the rum pretty hard that night and didn't hear a thing.

Yelling wasn't working, so Freele decided to play dead. The bear loosened its grip, only to snap down again on her lower arm, squeezing with its teeth and jaws and pushing, pushing down. She heard another snap. This time it was a bone.

She wondered: "Does it think it has me by the neck? This thing thinks it's killing me."

Pinned on her side, she couldn't reach the bear pepper spray beside her in the tent. She couldn't strike out. She decided to go limp, thinking that if the bear tried to roll her over she'd have a chance to grab the pepper spray.

For maybe a minute she suffered in near silence. She could see stars overhead, and she could hear the bear's heavy breath, with blood or saliva gurgling in its throat.

Then she heard sounds from the next campsite. Voices in a tent. Feet scurrying to a vehicle. Doors slamming and an engine starting. Headlights flashed across her husband's silent tent.

And the bear went away.

"It dropped me, and I didn't move an eyelash," Freele, fifty-eight, says months later from her home in London, Ontario. "I was afraid it would pounce on me."

The car from the neighboring campsite stopped, and a window opened. "We're getting help," somebody said. The car contained a family with young children. Too terrified to leave the car, they drove around the campsite's upper loop, honking the horn and trying to rouse somebody. Most people ignored them, suspecting drunks or hooligans, likely.

And Freele lay there alone, in the dark, her tent demolished, her arm shredded like a chicken wing, knowing not where that bear had gone. She took the safety off her bear spray and sat partway up. It would be twenty minutes before the neighbors came back with help.

Freele didn't know it at the time, but she wasn't the bear's first victim. A few minutes earlier, at about 2:00 a.m. and a couple of hundred yards upstream, the grizzly had attacked another tent. Though the tent contained two people and a dog, the bear moved it a few feet before biting through the fabric and sinking its teeth into the leg of Ronald Singer, a twenty-one-year-old former high school wrestler who came up swinging, while his girlfriend began to scream. The sharp blows and the racket helped the bear change its mind, and it didn't stick around. Neither did Singer. His girlfriend's parents drove him to Cooke City, looking for medical help. Freele saw them drive by her camp, but they didn't stop, probably didn't even know the bear had struck again.

After these two attacks, the grizzly—a scrawny animal supporting three yearling cubs—kept moving downstream until she hit the camp of Kevin Kammer, of Grand Rapids, Michigan. All but three of the Soda Butte Campground's twenty-seven sites contained campers that night, most of them in tents. Like Freele's site and Singer's, Kammer's site was a little isolated, with only one neighbor. And Kammer's site, No. 26, was one of the most isolated. The closest camp stood sixty yards away, it was very dark, and a nearby creek masked noises. Nobody saw or heard a thing.

And nobody found his body until a couple of hours later, after campers had raised the alarm and a Park County sheriff's deputy, with a spotlight and a loudspeaker, began rousting campers, ordering them to leave. He found a ghastly scene. The bear had pulled Kammer from his tent by the head and shoulders and he bled to death within four feet of the tent, investigators determined. Then she pulled his body another ten yards, and that's where the deputy found him, his torso partially consumed by mother and cubs.

By that time game wardens, deputies, people from the Forest Service and the National Park Service, most of them armed, had sent the groggy campers on their way, most of them leaving their gear on the ground for the night. Dawn dragged its heels that morning.

—◦—

"What made her cross that line that night will haunt me forever," Kevin Frey says of the attacking grizzly. He is a bear management specialist in the Yellowstone area for the Montana Department of Fish, Wildlife and Parks. That job keeps him increasingly busy as the region's bear population grows and the number of human visitors and residents continues to climb. He's a man who cares about grizzly bears and wild country.

In normal years he works with landowners to help bearproof their properties, and during hunting seasons he's the guy who has to crawl through dense brush, trying to find the grizzly bear a surprised hunter says he fired at but didn't track down. He doesn't much enjoy that part of his job. In 2010 when a late spring meant poor crops of natural food and far-ranging bears, he worked well over two months without a day off, trying to solve problems or avoid them.

He has investigated dozens of bear attacks over the years. He's trapped and handled scores of bears, tried to educate thousands of people about living safely in bear country.

And he says he's never seen an attack like this one.

Analyze most grizzly attacks, and you'll find some sort of explanation: a surprise encounter, a hunter bounces one out of a day bed, a photographer pushes his luck, a hapless hiker winds up between the bear and its cubs or between the bear and a carcass it is protecting, or somebody feeds the bear, teaching it to see humans as a source of food.

But none of that happened in this case. Frey's report, compiled in the weeks after the attack, pieced together what happened. But it couldn't tell us why.

"There is no clear explanation for the aggressive, predatory behavior," the report says.

It does rule out a number of factors. At 220 pounds the bear was small but not abnormally so. The cubs were undersized, too. But they were not starving. The mother carried an average load of parasites. She probably had lived near the campground all her life, at least ten years. She knew where it was, had seen it and smelled it and mostly shunned it.

She was not rabid. She was not in the habit of eating garbage or horse feed or birdseed or somebody's lunch. Relatively new technology means scientists can identify, through analysis of the isotopes in hair, the main ingredients of a bear's diet for the previous two years. She had lived almost exclusively on vegetation, unlike most of the Yellowstone area's meat-eating bears. Sometime in the previous couple of weeks, she'd been eating meat, though not much of it. She'd been a vegetarian, mostly.

Yellowstone's dwindling stock of whitebark pine trees hadn't produced much of a crop that year, but that explained nothing. This bear rarely ate pine nuts, the isotopes in her hair showed, and it was too early in the season for bears to be rooting out squirrel caches anyway.

None of the people attacked that night had any food or other attractants in their tents to tempt a bear's sensitive nose. Everybody in the campground had secured all their food and utensils in their vehicles or the bearproof boxes at each campsite.

The bear had never been trapped or tranquilized, and she had no history of aggression toward people. The only known encounter had come a few days earlier when a woman, jogging on the highway near the park entrance, surprised the bear family along the road. The startled mother offered a bluff charge, then backed off when the jogger stopped running and started yelling at her, which is typical behavior. She was being protective, not predatory.

If anybody in the Cooke City area had problems with grizzlies grabbing garbage or other food that summer, they didn't report it.

Rumors circulated that a local photographer had been feeding the bears, which could have taught them to associate humans with food. Investigators chased leads but could find no evidence of such bear baiting. And the hair analysis ruled out any significant amount of human or livestock food.

While it took a while to sort out these details, the evidence that Frey and Warden Captain Sam Sheppard found on the ground made for a clear case, one as unusual as it was grim: This grizzly bear was treating people like food, like prey. And for that she had to die. Anybody who pays any attention in grizzly country knows you should never, ever, give a bear a food reward. Don't do it on purpose. Don't let it happen accidentally. It just teaches them to look for more of the same. And this bear and her cubs had found a food reward in a person they killed.

—❦—

By 6:00 p.m. on July 28, about sixteen hours after Kammer's death, the bear had returned to his camp, where Frey had draped the rain fly from Kammer's tent over a culvert trap just six feet from where the father of four had died. She climbed into the steel tube, looking for more food, and the door slammed shut behind her. Within another twelve hours Frey had captured all three cubs, too.

While Frey's team already knew this had been a predatory attack, an effort to make a meal of people, they waited for definitive proof that they had the right bear. The next day some deft work by the crime lab in neighboring Wyoming made sure Frey and his crew had what they needed: DNA from hairs gathered at the attack matched DNA from the bear in the trap. Also, the snapped tooth in Freele's tent matched a broken canine on the mother bear. Frey and Sheppard had the right bear.

Less than two hours later, a plunger dropped on a big syringe, and the mother bear nodded into death. Her cubs were sent to a Billings, Montana, zoo, which ran into money problems and had to ship the cubs to another zoo.

Frey and Sheppard said they have no regrets about the decision to put the mother bear down. Bears who learn to rely on things like garbage and pet food cause problems enough. A bear that has killed and eaten a person cannot be tolerated.

—❦—

News of the attacks spread quickly around the world. Media in Europe, China, and Australia covered it. For some reason lots of people felt more sympathy for the bear than for the man she killed. Some grew livid. Hundreds of e-mails poured into FWP offices, enough to clog servers. Some blamed Kammer for being there. Others put on a stupefying display of ignorance and fantasy.

"The bear had been to the area before the campers were there and when she noticed a strange presence she immediately went into survival mode, doing what was necessary to ensure the protection of her cubs," wrote one woman, who then offered to lock herself in a room with the bear to prove "it won't purposely kill me."

"What a bunch of morons!!!!" a man wrote. "The mother bear and cubs were simply looking for food in their natural habitat."

"You will burn in hell for murdering God's beloved creations," wrote another.

Off in the blogosphere, things got worse. People even took shots at Kammer in the comments section of an online obituary.

Investigators saw it differently.

"That man deserves nothing but respect and sympathy," Sheppard said of Kammer.

Kammer, forty-eight, had taken a break from a career as a medical technologist to be a stay-at-home dad to his four kids, the youngest just nine and the oldest nineteen. Two of them attended a Christian school. News accounts and comments from friends provide at least a partial picture: Dedicated to his family, he was the kind of dad who showed up at school board meetings when a decision affected his kids. He was affable and friendly, and when coworkers had a bad day, they could count on him to elicit a laugh. He liked fishing and camping and kayaking, fixing up the house, and relaxing in the hot tub.

His camp at Soda Butte was clean. His food was properly stored. And contrary to the opinions of Internet cheap-shot artists, he wasn't in the wilderness: He was in a campground, a few feet from his car, a place with toilets and picnic tables and improved roads. Though surrounded by wild country, this place was built for people. He did nothing wrong.

Freele said she was in the ambulance on the way to a hospital in Cody, Wyoming, when she learned there had been more attacks, that a man had died. Until that point she'd been feeling she was the unlucky one. She knew she was in bear country and had done everything right. She never cooked on the fire pit, not wanting to leave any food residue in there. She kept her camp stove and food locked away. She poured her dishwater into the outhouse and even brushed her teeth there, to keep attractive odors out of her camp. She didn't use any lotions, and she changed her clothes before going to bed. She kept her bear spray handy all the time, and if she found fresh bear sign on her daily fishing trips, she went somewhere else. She followed all the rules, and somehow the bear chose her tent that night. She has no doubt it was trying to make a meal of her.

Anonymous commenters on the Internet attacked her, too.

"That bothered me," she says, but not as much as the knowledge that Kammer died nearby.

She wonders, now, if she couldn't have helped. She hopes he didn't suffer. She worries about his family. She wonders if she couldn't have tried harder to reach her bear spray, if she couldn't have maybe chased the grizzly away, into the woods, away from people.

"Survivor's guilt, I guess," is the way she sums it up.

✦

Somebody gets nailed in grizzly country every year. Almost always, they survive these attacks by animals that can take down a bull elk or an Angus steer, though the injuries can be gruesome. This, more than anything, refutes the myth that grizzlies are man hunters that lust for human flesh. If they wanted to kill us, they could do it in short order. But their power, their capacity for ferocity, is also what makes them so compelling.

Attacks like the ones at the Soda Butte Campground remain incredibly rare. The last time anything similar happened in greater Yellowstone was in 1984, when Britta Fredenhagen, of Basel, Switzerland, died in the park's remote Pelican Valley. Like Kammer she had kept a clean camp and obeyed the rules, but a bear dragged her from her tent and ate much of her body anyway.

"Bears very rarely exhibit that kind of behavior," Sheppard says. "But every one of them is capable of it."

And this bear had proven itself not just capable, but willing.

And that's why the official response at Soda Butte was swift and immediate. Bear managers don't want to give bears a chance to repeat that kind of thing. Cynics respond that fear of lawsuits drives such decisions. But the world is not that simple.

"There's a need to keep the community safe," Sheppard said. "We couldn't put a bear out there that we knew had cost somebody their life."

Not everybody buys that reasoning, as witnessed by the outpouring of invective over the death of the Soda Butte bear. Some people argue that killing an innocent man in a campground and attacking two other people should not warrant a death sentence for a bear.

But killing that bear might have saved other bears. Too often hunters and hikers lose their cool and start shooting at any bear that seems threatening. In 2010 people killed at least fifty grizzlies in and near Yellowstone. That's nearly a record number (the record occurred in 2008), and at least eighteen of those deaths remained "under investigation" by the end of the year. If the Soda Butte grizzly had been released, how many more bears would be killed by people convinced that every bear is the "Cooke City man-eater?" The argument gains weight when you consider the federal government had recently allowed people, in some circumstances, to start carrying guns in nearby Yellowstone.

Shortly after the attack conservative blogger Bryan Fischer, writing for the American Family Foundation, weighed in on the issue: "Of course there is a simple answer. Shoot these maneaters on sight," he wrote. "God makes it clear in scripture that deaths of people and livestock at the hands of savage beasts is a sign that the land is under a curse."

And the 2011 Montana legislature considered but did not pass a bill that would mandate a state policy to "use preemptive management to control grizzly bear distribution and prevent conflicts, including trapping and lethal measures."

Grizzly advocates have made great progress in recent years. Fewer people (Fischer is a notable exception, along with comedian Stephen Colbert) consider bears to be bloodthirsty killers, more people choose bear spray over firearms, and more of them take the sometimes bothersome steps necessary to keep bears safe: hanging food and game carcasses safely in trees when camping, stowing the bird feeders and barbecues at ranches and rural subdivisions, whooping and hollering on trails when they'd rather just be quiet and blend in. It's all part of living with the great bear. And partly as a result, the bear population in Yellowstone has nearly tripled since 1975, to at least six hundred grizzlies, despite all the deaths.

That's a good thing.

But when a grizzly attacks people who didn't do anything wrong, when she kills a man sleeping in a clean tent, then grizzly advocates deserve to feel uncomfortable. We have painted the bear as a magnificent symbol of wilderness, which it is. But symbols of wilderness matter only to people. The bear needs the real thing, and to keep the bear alive in a world of voracious human appetite, abstractions won't do the job. The bear's needs are deceptively simple: food and habitat and some protection. But to obtain that it needs people like Kevin Frey, who work the difficult and sometimes dangerous zone, who patrol the lines where humans and grizzlies intersect. And people like Frey don't need the scorn of self-appointed experts on the Internet.

An attack like the one at Soda Butte is unlikely to be repeated anytime soon. As Sheppard notes, every grizzly is capable of doing such damage. But they almost always choose not to.

But the reaction to the bear's death—enough nasty e-mails to clog a government computer server—seems sadly to epitomize our modern era: Misguided emotions and abstractions flood across a landscape, attempting to drown unpleasant realities, like the too-soon death of Kevin Kammer, the grief of his children.

As we move on with the seemingly interminable disputes over Endangered Species Act protections for grizzlies, as we argue over which places and under which conditions the growing population of grizzlies should roam, as we contemplate mathematical models and political theories and a raft of other abstractions, let's keep this in mind: Kevin Kammer was a real person with a real family. He's gone now. And we don't know why.

That's not an abstraction.

It's as real as it gets.

24

Epilogue: Mark of the Grizzly

GO TO THE GROUND WITH A GRIZZLY BEAR AND THE EXPERIENCE CHANGES life. Occasionally, sadly, it ends life, and that's not an easy way to go. Most people survive, but always the attack leaves a mark. Sometimes it's a brutal scar, a limb that doesn't work, or an eye that won't see. Sometimes it's only a scratch. Sometimes it's not even that. But always there is a mark on the inside of the person, one the world doesn't see but that makes you look at life in a different way. The focus depends on your perspective. For some, such as Ann Quarterman, life is richer and better for surviving the attack. She gained stability and balance from it, though it took a while to sort things out. Mark Matheny and Troy Hurtubise built life-consuming ventures around the grizzly's mark.

Bear attacks are not unique in this way. A car wreck, a violent crime, or even something as common as a cruel word from a loved one can etch an indelible mark, too. And these are all things we hope to avoid, like a bear attack. Nobody in this book wanted to be attacked. But none of the survivors I talked to harbors a consuming vengeance toward bears, which surprised me a little. I expected to find someone like that, and the guy may be out there, nursing wounds and grudges, aiming them at all bears, but through thousands of miles and dozens of interviews, I couldn't find him. Rather, most of them became or remained advocates of letting wild grizzlies be grizzlies. Some, such as Jim Cole, who survived two maulings, grew even more passionate for bears.

For some reason the people who call loudest for killing all the grizzlies have never felt their teeth or claws. Every mauling victim I talked to knows incredible fear, yet they remain tolerant. The grizzly haters only imagine that fear and grow livid.

"The only place in Idaho we should find dangerous predators who threaten human lives, property, and wildlife is right here, behind bars," Stan

Hawkins told a news conference at a zoo. He was a state senator in Idaho and wanted to enact laws that ban grizzlies, that make it illegal for a wolf to eat a deer in the winter. And people actually vote for a man like that.

There are more like him. They keep getting elected.

Holding a grudge against bears would be like holding a grudge against automobiles because one of them cracked your head open or broke your leg on an icy street. You would of course be more careful around them in the future, and you might be too scared to drive again. If the offending car had been altered or tampered with in some way to make it especially dangerous, you would want it off the street. But you wouldn't blame all cars or call for their removal. They can be dangerous if we grow careless, but if we handle them with respect and caution, they add much to our lives.

"In the night, imagining some fear, how easy is a bush supposed a bear," Shakespeare noted in *A Midsummer Night's Dream*. There hadn't been a wild bear in England for hundreds of years when he wrote that line, and I doubt that Shakespeare thought much about bears one way or another. They were for him a literary metaphor, yet he knew his largely illiterate audience would understand it. A bear in the bushes gets your heart going, even if it's just an idea. Even then, even in a place with no bears, they held such power. It is no accident that the earliest human religions centered around cave bears instead of deer or turtles.

Our challenge now is to make sure grizzly bears can continue to exist in the wild as well as in our metaphors, in a world where people like Stan Hawkins wield power. The bears are in trouble in many places, and future generations of people may be deprived of bears in all but the remotest of places. This doesn't mean grizzlies belong everywhere. We don't want them in our homes and neighborhoods. But people who live in rural areas are showing increasing tolerance of bears, doing what it takes to let grizzlies survive. That's a trend I admire, but I still fear that our technology and hunger, our increasing tendency to focus on computer screens instead of landscapes may swallow them up, send them to the zoos, eliminate them like the cave bear.

If a future Shakespeare arrives in another six hundred years, I'm sure he'll find that bears still provide a potent metaphor. But I hope they provide more than that. I hope they still live in the bushes and not just in the memory, that they still make us open our eyes and noses and minds when we go into their country. I don't like the world Stan Hawkins envisions, a world where the bears are behind bars, where the stories are all we have left.

Selected Bibliography

Brown, Gary. *The Great Bear Almanac.* New York: Lyons and Burford, 1993.

Brunner, Bernd. *Bears: A Brief History.* Translated by Lori Lantz. New Haven, CT: Yale, 2007.

Cole, Jim. *Lives of Grizzlies, Montana and Wyoming.* Helena, MT: Farcountry Press, 2004.

Cole, Jim, and Tim Vandehey. *Blindsided: Surviving a Grizzly Attack and Still Loving the Great Bear.* New York: St. Martin's Press, 2010.

Craighead, John J., Jay S. Sumner, and John A. Mitchell. *The Grizzly Bears of Yellowstone: Their Ecology in the Yellowstone Ecosystem, 1959–1992.* Washington, DC: Island Press, 2005.

Herrero, Stephen. *Bear Attacks: Their Causes and Avoidance.* Rev. ed. Guilford, CT: The Lyons Press, 2002.

Lapinski, Michael. *Death in the Grizzly Maze: The Timothy Treadwell Story.* Guilford, CT: Falcon, 2005.

Murphy, Bob. *Bears I Have Known: A Park Ranger's True Tales from Yellowstone and Glacier National Parks.* Helena, MT: Riverbend Publishing, 2006.

Neal, Chuck. *Grizzlies in the Mist.* Moose, WY: Homestead Publishing, 2003.

Olsen, Jack. *Night of the Grizzlies.* Moose, WY: Homestead Publishing, 1969 and 1996.

Peacock, Doug. *Grizzly Years: In Search of the American Wilderness.* New York: Henry Holt, 1990.

Peacock, Doug, and Andrea Peacock. *In the Presence of Grizzlies: The Ancient Bond between Men and Bears.* Guilford, CT: The Lyons Press, 2009.

Rockwell, David. *Giving Voice to Bear: North American Indian Myths, Rituals, and Images of the Bear.* Niwot, CO: Roberts Rinehart, 1991.

Rubbert, Tim. *Hiking With Grizzlies: Lessons Learned.* Helena, MT: Riverbend Publishing, 2006.

Schneider, Bill. *Bear Aware: The Quick Reference Bear Country Survival Guide.* Guilford, CT: Falcon, 1996.

Schneider, Bill. *Where the Grizzly Walks: The Future of the Great Bear.* Falcon, 2004.

Schullery, Paul. *The Bears of Yellowstone.* Worland, WY: High Plains, 1992.

Schullery, Paul. *Lewis and Clark among the Grizzlies: Legend and Legacy in the American West.* Falcon, 2002.

Shepard, Paul, and Barry Sanders. *The Sacred Paw: The Bear in Nature, Myth, and Literature.* New York: Viking, 1985.

Smith, Howard L. *In the Company of Wild Bears: A Celebration of Backcountry Grizzlies and Black Bears.* Guilford, CT: The Lyons Press, 2006.

Stevens, Montague. *Meet Mr. Grizzly: A Saga on the Passing of the Grizzly Bear.* San Lorenzo, NM: High-Lonesome Books, 1943 and 1990.

Treadwell, Timothy, and Jewel Palovak. *Among Grizzlies: Living with Wild Bears in Alaska.* New York: Ballantine Books, 1997.

Whittlesey, Lee H. *Death in Yellowstone: Accidents and Foolhardiness in the First National Park.* Boulder, CO: Roberts Rinehart, 1995.

INDEX

About the Author

After living in places as varied as New York City, South Korea, and Antarctica, Scott McMillion returned in 1988 to his native Montana, where his family has lived for four generations.

A journalist for more than 20 years, his writing has appeared in newspapers and magazines around the nation and has won many awards for investigative and environmental reporting. He is senior editor for the award-winning literary news journal *Montana Quarterly*. You can see more of his work at www.scottmcmillion.com.

He lives in Livingston, Montana, with his wife, Jennifer.